IN THE MIDDLE OF A MUDDLE

How **NOT** to Reinvent Government

IN THE MIDDLE
OF A MUDDLE

How NOT to Reinvent Government

Bruce A. Reinhart, Ph.D.

Manta Press

FIRST EDITION

Designed by Watson Scott Swail

Library of Congress Catalogue Card Number 99-93098.

Reinhart, Bruce, 1926-
    In the Middle of a Muddle: How NOT to Reinvent Government /
Bruce Reinhart. - 1st ed.

ISBN 0-9672850-0-3
1. Public Policy and Government. 2. Education. 3. Organizational Development. 4. Current Affairs.

This book is dedicated to

federal civil servants who are . . .

Rebuked,
Reclaimed,
Reorganized, and
Reinvented

. . . with every change of administration.

Contents

ACRONYMS

AFGE	The American Federation of Government Employees
BIG	Blacks in Government
CEP	The Compensatory Education Program
ED	The U. S. Department of Education
EEO	Equal Employment Opportunity
EMC	Executive Management Committee
ESEA	The Elementary and Secondary Education Act
FTE	Full-time equivalent (position)
GAO	The General Accounting Office
GPRA	The Government Performance and Results Act
HHS	The U. S. Department of Health and Human Services
HRSIG	The Human Resources System Innovation Group
IAP	The Impact Aid Program
IEP	The Indian Education Program
IRT	Integrated Review Team
Goals 2000	The Goals 2000 Program
LEA	Local Education Agency
LMPC	The Labor Management Partnership Council
MDP	The Management Development Program
MEP	The Migrant Education Program
NAACP	The National Association for the Advancement of Colored People
NPR	The National Performance Review
OCR	The Office of Civil Rights
OERI	The Office of Educational Research and Improvement
OESE	The Office of Elementary and Secondary Education
OIE	The Office of Indian Education
OM	The Office of Management
OME	The Office of Migrant Education
OPM	The U. S. Office of Personnel Management
OSD Model	The Organizational Systems Design Model
OVAE	The Office of Vocational and Adult Education
PDT	The Professional Development Team

PMC	The President's Management Council
PST	Program Service Team
RCC	The Reinvention Coordination Council
RIF	Reduction in force
RRT	The Regional Restructuring Team
RST	Regional Service Team
SDFSP	The Safe and Drug Free Schools Program
SDOE	State Department of Education
SEA	State Education Agency
SES	Senior Executive Service
SIP	The School Improvement Program
TDC	The Training and Development Center
USDA	The U. S. Department of Agriculture

Acknowledgments

I would like to begin this piece where many authors finish it, by saying that I take full responsibility for anything that is wrong with this book. Of course, no mass-produced product such as a book ever gets published without the hard work and good will of many other people. On the other hand, there is no mass-produced product in our society that is so personal as a book. Consequently, every book is an interdependent effort in which the author is the principle decision maker.

I had two major concerns with the substance of the book — accuracy and technical validity. Three people were especially helpful with the accuracy. I gave an early draft to Carroll Dexter, a colleague and current employee in the Department, to check its accuracy and my interpretations. Receiving his assurances, I proceeded with confidence based on the approach described in the *Introduction*. A later draft was submitted to Mark A. Rhodes, an external consultant to the restructuring effort, who also assured me that there were no major errors in those events of which he had knowledge. Finally, I submitted a near-final draft to Janice Jackson, who had the major responsibility for the reinvention effort in the Office of Elementary and Secondary Education (OESE), and served as Deputy Assistant Secretary and Acting Assistant Secretary of OESE. She also found no significant errors. However, Janice did remind me that I did not have all of the information that a person in her position had, and that her interpretations of events were not always the same as mine. She pointed out that had I known the parameters within which she worked I would have better understood her actions. This was a "two sides of the same coin" situation. We both had information that the other did not have.

A second concern was that of professional and technical validity. In the field of education the book was reviewed by Scott D. Thomson, former Executive Secretary, National Policy Board for Educational Administration; and Diane Ravitch, Senior Research Fellow, New York University and Nonresident Fellow, The Brookings Institution. Diane had served as an assistant secretary within the Department in a previous administration.

In the area of organizational management and change it was reviewed by Paul Gustavson, President, Organizational Planning & Design, Inc., and

Geoffrey M. Bellman, consultant and author of "*The Consultant's Calling, The Quest for Staff Leadership,*" and other works. Mark A. Rhodes also reviewed the manuscript for professional validity as well as accuracy.

Carlene Reinhart, President, CLR Associates, Inc., reviewed the manuscript from her expertise in organizational change, design and performance. Her forthcoming guidebook, *The PD&A* Process Guide (*Performance Definition and Assessment),* is a guide to help organizations identify their barriers to performance and to implement the means to improve it. Her consulting services to numerous federal agencies also provided a common set of insightful experiences with which to assess the events in the Department of Education.

Julie O'Mara, a leading authority in diversity issues in organizations, and co-author of *Managing Workforce 2000: Gaining the Diversity Advantage,* reviewed the manuscript from her distinctive expertise. As the story unfolds, the reader will understand why expertise in this area was very important to me.

It was comforting to me that these reviewers had no major problems with the account. Much of the assistance I received was in the form of directing my attention to supplementary and complimentary sources of information that would strengthen the story and its interpretation.

I am greatly indebted to Kathleen Brown, Harriet Lawrence, Bart Astor, and Watson Scott Swail who helped me edit and prepare the manuscript for publication. Kathleen Brown, in particular, gave numerous hours to editing.

I am also indebted to the Woodlands Group, a support group of organizational and human resource professionals, who helped me think through the approach to the subject, and to Ken O'Sullivan and Margaret Bedrosian for their advice and coaching.

Finally, I am indebted to Carlene Reinhart, with whom I share so much of my life, not only for her professional expertise, but her uncommon sense about writing a book that differs so much from what has been published about organizations.

Part I

Introduction

Writing from the Inside

In 1988, I became a "career" civil servant in the Department of Education (ED), with no intention of making a career of it. In 1996, I left the Federal Government for good. Part of me says I stayed too long. Another part of me insists that it was my destiny. If I had not stayed through those last few years, this story would never be told.

This book is about the "reinvention" years in the ED. There were overall Department efforts from the beginning to reduce personnel and program regulations. The Department also responded to the Administration's call for reform by urging its offices to reinvent themselves according to the principles of the National Performance Review (renamed the National Partnership for Reinventing Government in 1998), namely: (1) putting customers first, (2) cutting red tape, (3) empowering employees to get results, and (4) getting back to basics. Several of the offices within the Department responded. Many of them reorganized with a team structure and there was also some reengineering of work processes. None, however, attempted such dramatic changes as did the Office of Elementary and Secondary Education (OESE). Consequently, the quintessence of the Department's reinvention is most starkly revealed in this Office. This prominent Office administered such notable programs as Goals 2000, Safe and Drug Free Schools, and Title I of the Elementary and Secondary Education Act, with budget of $11 billion.

The reinvention years were a period of rapid change, frequent frustration among staff members and all those who had connection with the Office, and pain and growth. There was a radical restructuring of the OESE's organization, with little attention given to the alignment of key elements such as incentives and decision making. The whole Office was assigned to teams, yet there was very little empowerment allocated to them. Work assignments were made with little attention given to performance capabilities. Many staff members worked overtime on plans and reports that wound up being totally ignored. In other words, there were many useless hours of fruitless discussion and busywork. Most disturbing was the fact that a form of racism backlash permeated nearly every activity. (For example, and ironically, I found my name on a list of racists by one distraught group of African Americans, while being given a certificate of appreciation by another black group honoring my "wisdom.")

This is my story of the gut-wrenching experiences the staff of OESE endured when this Office was given an injunction to reinvent itself in the partisan political theater of Washington, D.C. It was under this political environment that OESE launched its response to the reinvention mandate with an internally conceived plan, and progressed down a slippery slope of ignorance, lack of understanding, and preparation for the difficult tasks we undertook without external expertise to help us. There were, certainly, numerous opportunities to make substantial improvements in the ill-conceived plan. A few people worked very hard to this end, only to be ignored. Once the train had left the station, there was no switching of tracks.

My purpose in writing this story is to provide a realistic, unadorned view of this reinvention effort, identify the lessons learned, and relate them to the overall federal reinvention effort. As I looked at the devil with a fascinated eye, I did not find it difficult to sculpt the failures in bold relief. By focusing attention on OESE, one can more clearly see the true institutional character of the Department—it was a pressure point of sudden, radical change. I hope this story will help others who are currently undergoing a reinvention effort in other federal agencies, or who soon will, accurately assess more subtle changes and cull it from the official hype. Only then can results be related to causes, and the road to reform be more clearly discerned.

I should say at the outset that I am neither a management consultant promoting my business nor an academician attempting to enhance my career. I write this account as a participant from the *inside* of a federal agency, and as one who is now a disengaged citizen enjoying my retirement. If the federal government must "work better and cost less," we must learn what works and what doesn't. This was an extremely difficult and debilitating experience for me and many other federal employees who were involved. I am a survivor: we cannot afford to risk that others may not be!

4

From Consultant to Bureaucrat

On several occasions before becoming a career employee, I provided consulting services to the U.S. Department of Education (ED), as well as other federal agencies, and had just responded to a consulting assignment in 1988 when ED decided that all persons providing temporary services of any kind should be terminated. To retain my services, my superiors created a career position for me as a policy analyst on the staff of the Director of the Impact Aid Program (IAP). The position was particularly interesting to me because it focused my attention on dealing with policy and procedural problems, rather than the day to day routines of operating the program. After there was a change in program directors, I was moved into the position of a branch chief. In the beginning, this was an interesting and challenging job, mostly because I continued to work on some of the problems of the branch. But I soon became bored as I became more and more a manager and bureaucrat. I realized then that I either had to find a different position within ED or get out.

In the spring of 1993, I was offered the opportunity to participate in a year-long Management Development Program (MDP)—a program for upwardly mobile supervisory personnel with good prospects for achieving higher management positions in the Department. At the time I was 67 years old and had more management experience than most of the mid-level and many of the top-level managers in the Department. Nevertheless, I decided to accept the offer—mostly to get away from my desk in the IAP and into some current management literature and discussions that would stimulate my otherwise dull existence in IAP.

"Getting its Head Screwed On"

At that time, Richard W. Riley, Secretary of Education, had been in his office for about nine months, and Deputy Secretary Madeleine Kunin had reported in shortly thereafter. Most people in OESE had heard about the National Performance Review (NPR). The Program Director for IAP, Charles (Chuck) E. Hansen, had been a member of the team that reviewed the operations of the Department of Agriculture to make it work better. But not much was happening at the program level at ED.

Each administration reorganizes, introduces its particular *modus operandi*, and sooner or later the latest fads of management theory get tried out in the federal agencies. The total quality management (TQM) program of Lamar Alexander and David Kearns, Secretary and Deputy Secretary of

5

Education respectively under President George Bush, was now off the screen. I will not soon forget Assistant Secretary of OESE, John (Jack) T. MacDonald's affirmation when he was about to leave with the close of President Bush's administration, that he and his political associates were only the "Christmas help." "TQM is here to stay," he affirmed, "It has been institutionalized in the Department, as in all the federal agencies. The Federal Quality Institute has been established to support the move- ment regardless of administrations."

Shortly thereafter the Federal Quality Institute was downsized and folded into the Office of Personnel Management (OPM), later terminated, and TQM became a rapidly fading memory. Now there was a new gang up- stairs. The present administration of the ED was in the process of "getting its head screwed on." Reinvention was now the new game.

Vice President Gore's zest to reinvent government was taking form at the apex of the Department. Two new management teams were set up under Deputy Secretary, Kunin: The Executive Management Committee (EMC) and the Reinvention Coordinating Council (RCC). Several teams were chartered to look into a variety of concerns, but membership in these teams involved only a fraction of one percent of the rank and file. As a result, the staff knew little about what was happening with reinvention. The Council retained the mission statement of the previous administra- tion, but trashed the vision statement and the mountains of work done by the Mission Team and the Institutional Excellence Team of former Secre- tary Lamar Alexander. They were determined not to build on the work of Republicans.

The "Partnership" Period
There was a lot of talk about "partnership" between the new administra- tion and the ED staff. The Secretary, Deputy Secretary, and their chiefs of staff were using the term regularly in their talks and written communica- tions. But there was little that could be identified as partnership in everyday activities. One colleague called it "well-intentioned patriarchy." I suspect that this was an apt description.

One memorable experience involved a small group of middle managers in the Management Development Program, of which I was a member. Middle management had often come in for a great deal of criticism for causing the failure of any change in governmental agencies. In fact, on

August 15, 1993, Vice President Al Gore spoke to the National Governors' Conference in Tulsa. In his speech he attempted to enlist the governors in an effort to support the "reinvent government movement." Texas Governor Ann Richards warned Gore, "The thing that will defeat you is cynicism . . . particularly among middle managers." We had heard this kind of criticism before, and we thought that we could dispel some of the cynicism by initiating a dialogue between middle and upper management about the reinvention of the Department and demonstrate our willingness to help.

We planned and announced a small workshop for November 4, 1993, to which we invited Deputy Secretary Kunin, who had been appointed to lead the reinvention effort, Billy Webster, the Secretary's Chief of Staff, and Rod McCowen, the Deputy Secretary's Chief of Staff. The announced goal of the workshop was "To form a partnership between middle and upper management to establish a shared vision that will improve the performance, enhance the culture, and elevate the morale of the Department." A few days before the event, we discovered that the small workshop we had planned would not be so small. Nearly everyone who perceived himself a middle manager intended to be there. We quickly made plans for a much larger group. We arranged for a large auditorium in the nearby Health and Human Services Department building, altered our agenda, and arranged for the transmission of the meeting to personnel in our regional offices. We were not the only ones surprised. Upper management was also caught off guard. Nobody was prepared for this. Because of the overwhelming response from middle managers our small workshop had become a conference!

It had now been about a year after the election and not much had filtered down except a lot of talk about partnership. So middle managers wanted to know what was going on, how they would be impacted, and what role they were expected to have in the reinvention effort. They asked questions and made comments and suggestions about how middle managers could work with upper management. Those who could not get to a microphone to speak in that large auditorium were asked to write out their concerns and comments and leave them on their seats before they left. After we collected and recorded all submissions, I analyzed and categorized them for suggestions to strengthen the partnership.

After completing the analysis, I asked for an appointment on behalf of our Management Development Program work group to discuss a partnership with the Deputy Secretary. I received a thank-you note from the Deputy Secretary for holding the meeting, but no response to my request for an appointment. I waited for several weeks thinking that an invitation would soon arrive, but none came. Finally, I sent another request to the Deputy Secretary and received a phone call from her Chief of Staff asking what we wanted to discuss. I explained the goal of the conference and our intent to discuss a partnership, and the meeting was set up. We eventually held a meeting with the Deputy Secretary and her Chief of Staff.

The Management Development Program work group presented to Deputy Secretary Kunin and to her Chief of Staff, Rod McCowan, a written report of the conference that analyzed the comments and suggestions about communication, dialogue, involvement, culture, morale, incentives, training, vision, downsizing, and other concerns. Unfortunately, the discussion stayed at the level of general communication matters that were focused entirely upon the dissemination of information downward in the organization. After some lengthy discussion, I pointed out that we ought to be thinking about *two-way* communication—upward as well as downward. Ms. Kunin stated that she had never thought about that, and that it was certainly true, we did need to think about two-way communication. As I left the meeting I began to wonder what type of reinvention effort we were in for when the person responsible had not given any thought to something as basic as two-way communication. I also went away from the meeting saying to myself, "So much for partnership." How could the Department be talking about partnership without even thinking about two-way dialogue? And soon after, middle management got hit hard. With no professional association or union to represent them, and the administration clearly intent on enlarging the span of control with the union's blessing, middle management positions were eliminated while the ever expanding upper management positions remained virtually untouched.

The Story

With that as background, it wasn't until October 1994 that the employees in OESE really became involved in the reinvention effort. And this is where this story really begins. I was extensively involved in the reinvention of OESE, and intensively committed to making it successful. Although I was concerned from the beginning about it's slim chances of success, I hoped that the mistakes in its conception and launching could be overcome. When I discussed the effort with my friends in the management consultant industry, some of them encouraged me to document the story in a book. At first I saw no purpose in contributing another volume to the burgeoning shelves of management books until Paul Gustavson, President, Organizational Planning & Design, Inc., said: "We have a lot of books written by academicians and consultants who are on the *outside*. We don't have any good books written by people on the *inside*. You could provide a whole different perspective. I think you ought to write the book." It suddenly made a lot of sense.

Inside Approach

I write this story as a participant observer, which may sound like an oxymoron. On one hand I actively participated in a spirited and often virulent environment of organizational change. At the same time, I did everything I could to remain objective. I leave it to you to judge the degree of my success.

I take three approaches to this story, (1) contextual, (2) documentary, and (3) behavioral. The contextual leg comes from my knowledge of organizational change. My doctoral studies were in the sociology of organizations and institutions and I have become infused with the literature of organizational change as a result of a persistent fascination with the subject. I have also been involved in leadership development programs and workshops on organizational change, both of which contributed to my search for knowledge in organizational leadership.

Without a valid contextual grounding, the story could have been critically biased. So I have tried to tie the restructuring concepts, the resulting events, and the human behaviors to the theoretical constructs of professional practice. For example, I looked at the decision to put structure first in the design of the OESE in the light of the Organizational Systems Design (OSD) Model and the need for the alignment of elements. I assessed the role of the team leader in light of the implicit power, authority, control, and status of the position. I also assessed training efforts in the context of a strategic systems model in which needs are identified, analyzed, and plans for employee performance improvement are made as an outgrowth of an organization's strategic objectives. Race-related behavior is analyzed in reference to data published by the Department of Education and the Washington Metropolitan Council of Governments, and by widely acknowledged authorities on the socio-economic characteristics of racial groups in the nation's work force.

The documentary approach took an intensive effort on my part to obtain published documents from private and government sources and the review of everyday working materials of the Department and OESE. Hard copies of reports that came across my desk, handouts at meetings, and electronic mail were all a part of the documentation. But most important were the notes I made, off the job, of the conversations and observations I had while on the job. Often these notes dealt with the interpersonal exchanges and reactions to current events, behaviors, and emotions. My intent was to put my fingers on the pulse of the participants as changes were taking place. I wanted to document not only the actions of the leaders, but also the response of the staff. I wanted to be able to understand the problems in relation to the causes. When I wrote up this story—and I knew even while living through it that it needed to be written—I would use these notes to bring my readers *inside* the experience.

Above all, it is human behavior that truly defines the situations described in this book. For it is what people *do* in organizations and not what they *theorize* that determines outcomes. Much of the time theory explains behavior. But often this is not true. Indeed, it was not always true in this story.

In social research we sometimes find that conventional wisdom, rationale, and even theory are wrong. For example, if we were to collect data that we knew were valid and reliable but did not support our theory, we would not throw away the data. We would question the theory. Or, as Paul Gustavson says, "Organizations are perfectly designed to get the results they get." In this account of the reinvention of OESE, outcomes are the litmus test. To get different results one needs different behavior. To get different behavior we need a different design. In other words, I looked at the results and the behaviors that produced them, to describe what was real.

Ethnic Bias

Observing the world from another person's perspective is certainly one of the most difficult things humans are called upon to do. Most of us have ethnic identifications that focus our attention and limit our awareness of the world about us. I certainly believe that individuals within an ethnic group are neither stereotypes nor clones of each other. Nevertheless, I also have observed that members of a particular ethnic group have shared social, cultural, economic, historical, and religious experiences, and, therefore, have shared perspectives. As a result, I believe there are sometimes distinctive collective characteristics and behaviors that are unique and observable about an ethnic group. Because of our distinctive differences, we are *ALL* biased to some extent. No one is really color blind. I acknowledge that I have reported this account through my own unique perspective.

There was one major watershed experience in my life that will always be imbedded in my perspective of racial conflict. Prior to the Watts riot in the 1960s, I served as pastor of a predominantly white conservative church in Los Angeles. When we in the church agreed to rent some of our residential property to minorities, it was the spark that ignited the volatile anger of racial prejudice within the congregation. The congregation divided into two hostile groups, and my family and I were the objects of angry threats for having supported the civil rights of African Americans. I even received telephone calls in the middle of the night only to hear heavy breathing on the phone.

White, conservative groups within the metropolitan area came to my office with statements that repudiated the policies of social ethics of the Presbyterian Church (USA) and the National Council of Churches of which I was affiliated, and demanded that I sign them. I refused. For a brief time, the strife within the church became a media event in Southern California. Never before had I experienced such anger within a Christian congregation. Never before had I experienced so much anger directed at me. The anger came from whites, not blacks. Unfortunately, the leadership of the Presbyterian Church in Southern California was in transition at this time, and their inept, waffling "support" left me entirely on my own. Shortly thereafter, I left the Christian ministry to begin a new career at the University of California at Los Angeles. For years, I would relive these events and awaken with horrible nightmares. The racial anger and fear I experienced during the reengineering of OESE brought these feelings to the surface again.

Overview

There are three distinct sections to this book. In *Part I - Introduction*, I describe the setting into which the radical changes were introduced, how I became involved in it, and the nature of the inside approach. *Part II - The Story,* is an autobiographical narrative of the radical organizational intervention as I experienced it. I am keenly aware that I did not know all that was going on from the macro perspective at the top levels of the Department. I am equally certain that those at the top did not know much of what was happening within the Department. In *Part III - A Call for Institutional Leadership,* I step back, and view this reinvention experience from a leadership perspective. After all is said and done, organizational change is the domain of an organization's leadership. I call for a different type of leadership. I define what I mean by "institutional leadership," and why it is necessary for organizational change in both private and public institutions. The reader will clearly discern that the major problems of reinvention in the Department of Education are not unique, but pervasive in organizational change, especially in federal agencies.

Finally, I sound an ethical note. Writing from within an organization gives a person a different perspective about what happens to the people on the inside when radical change is taking place, especially if the leadership is not competent enough to design and manage the change.

In his book, *Divided We Fall: Gambling with History in the Nineties,* Haynes Johnson, the perceptive author and commentator on contemporary events, wrote: "I believe President Bill Clinton is correct when he says it's 'make or break time' for America in the Nineties" (1993: 18). Although the President had more on his mind than the reinvention of federal agencies when he made this assessment on February 19, 1993, in Chillicothe, Ohio, there is little doubt that it was a key element in the political system he wanted to change. In this book we come to understand how complex and difficult reinvention is.

Part II

The Story

one 1

Putting Structure First

In the past 10 years, anger at the government and disgust
with politicians have increased, causing voters to veer in
different directions in 1992 and 1994. At the same time,
political leaders, pundits and academics have issued a flurry
of prescriptions to restore trust in government: Replace the
current crop of politicians, return civility to the political
debate in Washington, transfer power to the states or perhaps even balance the federal budget (Richard Morin &
Dan Balz, *The Washington Post,* January 28: 1996).

Collapse of Trust

This assessment of political disenchantment is based upon a series of polls
conducted by *The Washington Post*, the Henry Kaiser Family Foundation,
and Harvard University (*Why Don't Americans Trust The Government?*: 1996).
The polling also reported that two in every three Americans believe that
most people could not be trusted. Half of our citizens believe that most
people would cheat others if they had the chance. An equal number agree
that most people are looking out for themselves. Consequently, Morin

15

and Balz conclude that "the reason our politics is behaving badly is because the whole country is behaving badly."

In addition to the collapse of trust in personal relationships, the government also suffers from other concerns, including the fear of crime, economic insecurity, and pessimism about the lives of future generations. There is a perceived failure of government in dealing with these discontents. Hence the polls revealed that Americans repeatedly expressed far less confidence in the federal government, the military, the Supreme Court, Congress, and virtually every other institution in contemporary society.

In contrast, in 1964, three in every four Americans trusted the federal government compared to one in four today. Yet during this time federal employees have been forced to stand on the sidelines and watch the presidential candidates and legislative wannabes bash the federal government. During these years we have seen five different study commissions established to prescribe reforming, reorganizing, restructuring, and reinventing government. Yet the disenchantment with the federal establishment has continued to grow. Obviously, this hasn't helped to build a positive culture in the federal labor force.

Bashing Bureaucracy

President Clinton also ran a campaign against the federal government to help him get elected. After the election, President Clinton focused this disenchantment on the rule-bound apparatus of formal structures and complex procedures that Americans can identify with the pejorative label of "bureaucracy." The President expressed this shift from politics to bureaucracy when he announced the National Performance Review (NPR): "This performance review is not about politics. Programs passed by . . . both parties, and supported by the American people at the time, are being undermined by an inefficient and outdated bureaucracy." By this approach to organizational change in the federal government, the President not only identified with, but also responded to, the nation's disenchantment. At the same time he depersonalized it, at least for the time being, for the civil servants who staffed the federal establishment. In brief, he placed the blame on an unavoidable institutional phenomenon civil servants had experienced, and not on themselves.

Fast Start — Little Notice

The National Performance Review (NPR), the mechanism by which the Clinton/Gore administration would reinvent the federal bureaucracy, got off to a fast start. Sometimes called the "reinventing government initiative," the NPR takes much of its agenda, including its title, from David Osbourne and Ted Gaebler's best seller, *Reinventing Government* (1993). The NPR was delegated to Al Gore. The Vice President established a staff in the White House and traveled from coast to coast making impassioned "reinvention" speeches. He also went from agency to agency in the federal government with his message. He benefited from early media attention and praise and encouragement from academics, union leaders, and policy makers from both political parties.

The staff of the Office of Elementary and Secondary Education (OESE) were aware that the reinvention effort was coming its way, but few people thought much about it. The fact that one of its staff, Charles (Chuck) Hansen, Director of the Impact Aid Program (IAP), was detailed to the team that assessed the Department of Agriculture, brought it a little closer home, but they had been through reform initiatives before. The prevailing attitude among the rank and file was that this, too, would come and go, and they would continue to do their work with little change. At this early point it was out of sight and out of mind.

Recommendations Announced

On September 7, 1993, just six months after the NPR initiative was announced, the Clinton administration released the first report entitled *From Red Tape to Results: Creating a Government that Works Better and Costs Less*. The recommendations covered twenty-seven government agencies and fourteen "government systems," such as personnel procedures, budgeting, procurement, and technologies. It contained 384 major recommendations for streamlining the federal bureaucracy. The point was made that these recommendations came not from a presidential commission of people *outside* the federal government, but from leadership *within* the government itself. Some 200 federal employees were organized into reinvention teams that became the eyes, ears, hands and feet of the NPR. They gathered and analyzed data about the performance of federal agencies and systems, from which they prescribed their recommendations for the reinvention. Those enthusiastic about the NPR claimed that this difference gave the NPR a much better chance of success.

A team of six persons developed twelve recommendations for the Department of Education (*National Performance Review*: 1993). I tried for months after the announced release to get a copy of their report from the Department library as well as from other sources, and was repeatedly told that it was still in review and not available. I did eventually get a copy. But clearly there was no significant effort to announce it or discuss it with the rank and file in the Department. Without at least informing the staff, I got the distinct impression that the reinvention of the Department was considered to be the purview of the hierarchy, not the staff.

NPR and ED

If the recommendations did not get attention from the rank and file, there were two matters that did. Secretary Richard W. Riley was exceptionally successful in obtaining four important pieces of legislation upon which the programmatic reinvention of the Department would be based, and they made a significant impact upon the work of the Office of Elementary and Secondary Education. The staff had to change the way they did business and write new regulations that would accommodate them. Although the staff did not associate their new, heavy work load with the NPR, this legislation would be directly linked to the restructuring of OESE that came later.

Another matter that got our attention was the downsizing of the Department. Within weeks of the NPR's report, the Administration and the Congress found themselves dealing with reductions in costs. Candidate Clinton had promised to reduce the federal labor force by 100,000 persons. Later in the NPR review, this figure was increased to 252,000 government workers. Congress increased this to 272,900 positions by the end of fiscal year 1999. The fact that the attrition rates of federal workers had slowed considerably in recent years did not make the task any easier. To avoid a reduction in force (RIFs, according to the government jargon), the administration adopted a "buyout" plan to encourage retirements. The buyout was anything but a "golden parachute," but it did include a little extra money. I believe the buyout was focussed on mid-level management as a way to avoid alienating the federal unions and to facilitate an increase in the span of control. Many government workers ready for retirement did, in fact, hang in long enough to take advantage of the extra money. They added to the number of retirees, and helped make the buyout a success. While Con-

gress botched the Department's time schedule by delaying the legislation in the Senate, passage resulted in a significant and instant reduction
in the federal civil work force.

OESE Restructures

On August 12, 1994, the Assistant Secretary, Thomas W. Payzant, distributed two memos from Madeleine Kunin, Deputy Secretary,
concerning streamlining, restructuring, and protection of grade levels
while restructuring. The Assistant Secretary distributed the Kunin memos
with his own memo that stated: " I want to inform you that OESE is
beginning to consider fundamental changes in the way we operate and
carry out our responsibilities . . . At this time plans for restructuring and
streamlining OESE are at a preliminary stage. Although no final decisions have been made about structure, I want to assure you that as we
undertake reinvention, *we are committed to avoiding any disruptive action
that could result in RIFs or downgrades.*" [Italics supplied.]

I had assumed that the memos were distributed because of the anxiety
over recent buyout announcements. The downsizing of the federal
government was always important news to people in the Washington
metropolitan area, because so many people are government employees. So the press gave extensive coverage to it. There was considerable
concern among the rank and file in ED about a reduction in force
(RIF). Some staff were highly distrustful of management's true intent.
They asserted that "restructuring" was a disguise for getting rid of
people. There had been some deep cuts during the Reagan administration, not to mention an attempt to eliminate the Department, and
some speculated as to how deep the cuts would go this time. In fact,
this fear endured long into the restructuring effort.

Restructuring Announced. I was on vacation when the restructuring
of OESE was announced at an "All Hands" meeting on September 27,
1994. When I returned to my office the next week, I found the agenda
for the All Hands meeting in my mail. The agenda indicated that the
bulk of the meeting had been devoted to the restructuring of OESE. I
had known that something was in the works because my boss, Chuck
Hansen, who had concluded his work with the NPR and had since
returned to ED, had been turning over most of his work in the Impact
Aid Program to Cathy Schagh, his deputy. From time to time, Chuck
asked me questions that related to organizational change.

"Just Another Reorganization." I walked out of my office with a copy of the agenda of the meeting in my hand and buttonholed several colleagues. I was anxious to learn what was announced at the All Hands meeting. The first few people with whom I spoke had not gone to the meeting and did not seem to be interested in what occurred. Others I spoke with who had attended mirrored the response from Curt Van Horn, a field officer in the IAP. Curt asserted, "They said we are going to go through another reorganization. Every administration has to have a reorganization sooner or later. This administration has finally gotten around to announcing its reorganization."

With the exception of the downsizing, there was little interest in the subject of restructuring. Most of the old timers had seen reorganizations come and go and they believed that they could survive this one too.

Plan Unveiled. On October 18, 1994, I found a packet of information in my in-box with a covering memo (See Appendix) from Thomas Payzant, which provided some of the information I was seeking. The Assistant Secretary stated:

> The Elementary and Secondary Education Act (ESEA) has been passed by Congress and will be signed into law this week. It is now time for implementation [of the restructuring of OESE]. The challenges are great. We can meet each challenge by working together. The first attachment in this packet gives a detailed explanation of the plans presented at the All Hands meeting. The second outlines the next steps and gives a brief statement about each team's mission . . . The third attachment is a form to volunteer for a restructuring team
>
> . . . I encourage you to volunteer for a team. Janice Jackson, Deputy Assistant Secretary, will coordinate the restructuring process.

As I examined the packet, I said to myself, "So this is what Hansen's group has been forging." When I read the section on restructuring, I knew that Chuck's leadership was at the heart of it. Chuck was one of the few visionaries that I had met within the Department. This was not the first time that Chuck had entertained new ideas about the way to work. He had been gung-ho about TQM, and he had suggested a number of alternatives for conducting the work of the Impact Aid Program. Now he had been successful in introducing a fundamental change in the way the OESE would conduct its work.

The New Structure. In the packet of materials on OESE restructuring, the Senior Leadership Team (Assistant and Deputy Secretaries, program directors and selected others) explained that the new structure would "adopt several substantive modifications" of the present structure, but retain the basic work responsibilities required for the continuation of a programmatic base. It would use "generic" supervisors who would coordinate program and team operations. In addition, the program offices would be reconfigured into three components: (1) a program base, (2) regions comprised of cross-program teams, and (3) cross-cutting teams. The Senior Leadership Team acknowledged that the reconfiguration assumed at least three important kinds of expertise: (1) program expertise, (2) expertise about regions being served, and (3) managerial expertise. They described the structure as follows:

Program base. The OESE program components would retain the present structure and responsibility. So programs such as migrant education, Indian education, impact aid, school improvement, compensatory education, and the newly formed safe and drug free schools, would remain distinctive programs. Each office would retain individuals who would be responsible for program policy and administration as well as the professional development of teams. The GOALS 2000 Program was an exception. It would operate as a self-contained unit much as it had in the past.

Cross-program teams. Service to the field would be delivered through regional teams that would be responsible for a specific cluster of states. The teams, composed of staff from each program, would provide a combination of program services to the states and school districts in specified geographical regions. Each cross-program team would be physically located together.

Cross-cutting teams. The Senior Leadership Team also perceived that there would be a need to organize teams around functional areas or issues. These teams would also cut across program areas, but would not deal with programs per se. They identified professional development, healthy children, technology, integrated services, and joint monitoring as examples of such functional areas.

The Senior Leadership Team provided the following example of the new configuration: "The Program Director of the School Improvement Programs would have responsibility for all the program functions for the School Improvement Programs, the coordination and oversight for two regional teams, and coordination and oversight for an *ad hoc* team on joint monitoring." (Figures A-1 and A-2 on pages 276 and 277 in the Appendix illustrate the change in the structure. Figure A-3 on page 278 represents the overall perceptual model.)

Obviously, the new structure was more than modifications in the way OESE was conducting its business. This was a fundamental and radical change. It was also clear that structure came first in their thinking. Everything about the packet of information revealed that structure was driving the change. The packet was entitled the "OESE Restructuring Plan" and the subject of the covering memo was designated "OESE Restructuring." Putting structure first was a fundamental decision in the failure of the reinvention effort.

Mission and Vision Statements. The packet contained new mission and vision statements for OESE; some goals, objectives, and guiding principles; a statement about the anticipated new structure; and material about the restructuring team and its subgroups. The mission statement read:

> The mission of the Office of Elementary and Secondary Education (OESE) is to promote academic excellence, enhance educational opportunities and equity for all of America's children, youth, and families and to improve the quality of teaching and learning by providing leadership, technical assistance and financial support.

The vision statement proclaimed:

> The mission of the Office of Elementary and Secondary Education (OESE) is to advance systemic education reform by providing educational program direction, technical assistance, and financial support to promote excellence, improve teach-

ing and learning, and enhance educational opportunity and equity for America's children, youth, and families.

I assumed that the word "mission" in the vision statement was an error, but I was not certain. It read more like a mission statement than a vision statement.

Goals, Objectives, Guiding Principles and Parameters. Clearly, several people had spent a great deal of time specifying the goals, objectives, guiding principles, and parameters (listed in the Appendix). I assumed that they were initially constructed by Chuck Hansen's team and adopted by the Senior Leadership Team. This was confirmed later. When I revisited the goals and objectives after the restructuring had evolved, I realized that they were a point of departure that did not necessarily prescribe what would actually take place. Some were idealistic, such as "sustain and institutionalize systemic reform," and "holistic problem solving." Others were mandatory, such as "meet program statutory requirements." Additionally, others were intrinsic to the restructuring plan, such as "reduce the number of GS-13/15 supervisory and management positions." I found it interesting that there were no references to some of the features of the restructuring, such as the role of teams or their empowerment. The fact that these goals, objectives, principles, and parameters were never referred to again while I was in the Department, led me to conclude that they were not controlling the evolution of the restructuring.

From Concept to Reengineering

As I continued to read through the packet I thought to myself that "this was the type of product that Hansen was capable of producing." I could not help but wonder how many other people were contributing to it. By persistently asking questions, I found six people who claimed they were members of Hansen's team. Most members of Hansen's group conceded that their participation was intermittent, some a part of it in the beginning and others contributing at a later time.

One member of the Hansen team, William Wooten, Director of the Management and Policy Staff, reported that in the beginning they entertained an informal concept of establishing regional teams while retaining the six program areas of OESE. This point of departure became the basic idea for restructuring the office. The six programs would have to be kept intact because of legislative mandates for Indian Education, Migrant Education, and Title I, Elementary and Secondary Education (ESEA). One could not fiddle with these programs without getting Congress involved, and that was a headache nobody wanted. At that time, according to Wooten, nobody was thinking in terms of a reengineering effort, but a reorganization to improve the delivery of the OESE programs.

"When the thinking and plans for the restructuring were brought to the program directors for consideration they would be discussed," said Wooten, "and everybody would go along because this was what Tom [Thomas W. Payzant, Assistant Secretary] wanted. Rarely would anybody have anything to say. Yet there was no 'buy-in' then, nor is there any buy-in now." It appeared to me that the program directors were quite concerned about what was going to happen to their programs and would go to great lengths to protect their interests.

The packet of mission and vision statements had been formulated by a small in-house group, discussed and, I believe, reluctantly approved by the Senior Leadership Team. It was then announced at an All Hands meeting, and distributed to the staff. I would see this procedure occur again and again. I believed that they were now coopting the staff because they needed their participation.

I had to decide whether I would be a part of the restructuring process or leave the Department. While working in the IAP did not provide sufficient stimulation to keep me there, involvement in organizational change was something that did. I had a long-time fascination with organizational behavior. I now asked myself, "Why not hang in a little longer and see what happens in the crucible?"

Initial Observations

Fuzzy Thinking. As the restructuring continued, there seemed to be extensive confusion about what it was all about. Tom Payzant's memo of August 12th stated, "I want to inform you that OESE is beginning to consider fundamental changes in the way we operate and carry out our responsibilities." Two months later in the packet of materials distributed on October 18th, his cover memo stated: "We must emphasize changes in roles/relationships and behaviors rather than undertaking a fundamental reorganization." Was this fundamental change or merely some nonfundamental changes in roles and relationships? Guiding principle # 4 provides another clue to what some in management saw in the restructuring effort. As stated it read: "Use restructuring as a comprehensive strategy for holistic problem solving and achieving organizational change." This is how that principle was explained:

> Restructuring is only one way to influence the culture and behavior of an organization. Although we have not determined the detail of the new configuration, we have agreed on the cultural principles that must be nurtured and which are reflected in the Department's organizational values. Essentially we envision OESE as follows:
>
> • "Customer oriented" and responsive to the educational needs of the learners.
>
> • A learning organization that listens to and learns from its external customers and employees.
>
> • An organization where staff are unafraid to take risks and where mistakes and problems are viewed as opportunities for learning and growth.
>
> To achieve these values, we recognize the necessity for replacing our hierarchical pyramid with a flattened structure. The new structure would have as its core collaborative teams who use and respect the knowledge, skills and expertise of all employees, regardless of grade or position. To this end, we have begun to look at delayering the supervisory structure in a consistent way throughout OESE by modifying the branch/division structure. (The Restructuring Packet.)

Certainly, this was a principled conception of OESE—a "customer oriented, learning organization where staff are unafraid to take risks and make mistakes." And this was all going to be facilitated through tearing down the hierarchical pyramid of authority, power, control and status that had existed since the formation of the Department, and by establishing teams where work assignments are based on knowledge, skills and expertise, regardless of grade or position. In other words, the branch and division structure would be jettisoned along with the branch chiefs and division directors.

I could not imagine how OESE was going to make this radical change. I wondered if Janice Jackson had this kind of expertise. If not, how would OESE acquire the expertise it needed? It all sounded very idealistic and naive to me. Yet nobody seemed to be alarmed. I figured that the rank and file did not really know the import of what was coming down. And I sensed that under the best conditions the next few years were going to be one very rough ride.

I had never worked in an organization with so few risk takers. The public's perception of risking-taking in the federal government being an oxymoron was accurate. So was the term "learning organization" when applied to the federal government. I had never even heard or seen this term used in the Department before this time. I mulled over the terms "customer-oriented," "learning organization," and "risk takers" and thought to myself, "Evidently somebody had been reading organizational change literature from the private sector. They are at least getting the jargon down."

No Environmental Assessment. When questioned, some members of the Senior Leadership Team acknowledged that they had some problems with the cross-program concept when it came to the Office of Indian Education, the Office of Migrant Education, and the Impact Aid Program because they did not have clients in the same way as other programs. What the Senior Leadership Team acknowledged was soon to surface and persist as a major problem. During late January and February, discussion of the restructuring was getting very active and many things were being expressed throughout the Department that were not true and often based on rumor. To correct misperceptions and to allow people to vent, feedback sessions were scheduled by the Senior Leadership Team. The problem of the integration of programs was raised at each session. On February 1, 1995, Ross Byington, a staff member in the Office of Indian Education (OIE), sent an e-mail message to each of the restructuring team leaders, with a copy to Janice Jackson, which read in part:

> Prior to finalizing the extent of the OIE involvement in the
> reengineering/restructuring process, there should be an ef-

fort made to assess the needs of the American Indian community which we serve. Our legislation identifies our purpose [as meeting] the "special" educational and "culturally related" academic needs of the American Indians and Alaska Natives . . . If one of the objectives of the reengineering/restructuring process is improved service to our clients, then there should be some evaluation as to how Indian students will be better served through the regional teams concept, acknowledging that our program directly serves LEAs, Tribes, Indian organizations and BIA schools, while other OESE programs generally deal directly with SEAs . . .

When I read the e-mail message, I linked it to the fact that there had been no environmental scan completed prior to prescribing the new structure. For example, no systematic study and analysis of OESE's customers had been done. In contrast, before prescribing organizational design characteristics, consultants normally gather data from three sources—environmental scanning, technical analysis and social analysis (See Figure 1, page 29). So I responded to Ross and copied all those who were on Ross' distribution list, with the following message:

> I believe that your concerns about the program of OIE and the people who work there provide a good illustration of a point that I have been trying to make informally . . . It appears to me that the only reason we are restructuring around regions is that the Department has always been structured by regions. Why can't we use other criteria?

> Unfortunately, we have not done our work in studying our customers. If we were to study our customers from other points of view, such as need or characteristics, I believe that we could provide a better structure . . . For example, in addition to the school districts with high percentages of Native Americans, we have inner-city school districts, suburban school districts, rural school districts and school districts in Alaska spread over vast geographical areas. We do not have just one type of school district.

> I share your concerns and believe that because we haven't done our homework on our customers, we are going to lock

in again on geographical regions and be stuck there for another 10 to 20 years!

When Janice Jackson read my reply to Ross, she then replied with the following:

> Bruce, I just read your response to Ross Byington re: the use of regional team structure. I am somewhat taken aback by your comments. It is incorrect to say that we have not done our work with our customers and that we have selected a regional team design because of tradition. We have not formally surveyed all the customers. We have gotten tremendous feedback from customers in other ways—feedback sessions and discussions at conferences, interaction in our daily work, meetings with individuals and groups, written communication, etc. Our structure takes into consideration the concerns and issues that have been raised to us . . .
>
> *Janice*

When I received the above reaction from Janice, I felt she was merely legitimizing the decision to restructure around regional teams. She may have agreed with me, but she could not take any other position once the commitment to regional teams had been made. Consequently, I responded to Janice, pointing out that while she felt they had gotten tremendous feedback, there was no systematic study and no data gathered about what our customers wanted.

On February 9th, Janice and I had an opportunity to have a one-on-one chat about the e-mail exchange on the relationship between the customer and the regional restructuring of OESE. At that time, she stated that she could not ignore my e-mail response to Ross, since others were aware that I was knowledgeable about organizational design, and because management had made a firm commitment to having regional teams. She acknowledged to me that there had, indeed, been no systematic study of OESE customers and explained that she could not let people think that the Department had gone into regional teams blindly.

Figure 1. Data Gathering for Organizational Design

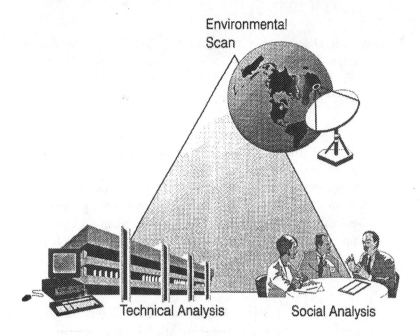

Environmental
Scan

Technical Analysis   Social Analysis

Source: Organization Planning and Design, 1994. Organizational Systems Design Guidebook, San Jose, CA:25.

Although I let the issue drop at that point, I continued to be a strong advocate for a systematic study of environmental factors. Later, when Mark Rhodes provided some consulting services, he recommended the conducting of an environmental scan, but none was ever done. The integration of OESE programs, especially Indian Education and Impact Aid, into the regional teams continued to be a persistent problem undermining the success of the restructuring.

Doubtful Assumptions. The Senior Leadership Team also assumed that as team members worked together there would be a major reduction in the numbers of people needed to serve the customers, because we would all be cross trained. This assumed, of course, that the OESE staff would have gained sufficient knowledge and skill to consult with the professional educators in the field about all OESE programs and be able to give technical advice about systemic reform and consolidated state plans. Needless to say, I and many of my colleagues had

29

serious doubts about these assumptions. Yet they were central to the new structure of OESE.

Anxiety over Delayering. On August 8, 1994, the Deputy Secretary Kunin, sent a memo to the Senior Leadership Team of OESE indicating that the pressure was on the Clinton administration to reduce the federal government. She began that memo by saying:

> At a recent meeting of the President's Management Council (PMC), the Vice President made it clear that agency streamlining plans are not big enough, not moving fast enough, and are not sufficiently on target to meet National Performance Review (NPR) goals. To meet these goals, he asked the PMC members to revise their plans to ensure compliance with Administrative guidelines . . . Revised plans must be submitted to the Office of Management and Budget within 60 days.

Push had now come to shove. Deputy Secretary Kunin's memo stated that in order to comply, the Department of Education must reduce the ratio of supervisors to other personnel from 1:6 to 1:12 by 1999. [Author's note: that would mean 342 supervisory positions in the Department would have to be eliminated.] In response to the NPR mandate, the configuration of OESE was designed to facilitate this reduction in supervisory staff by eliminating branch chiefs, and restructuring with team leaders of cross-program teams who would not be considered supervisors.

These two major issues relating to this reduction and change of role would preoccupy middle managers for the next several months. Since supervisors and managers in the Department of Education had no professional association or union to look after our interests and provide briefings the way the American Federation of Government Employees (AFGE) did for their members, we were all quite concerned and had many discussions about it.

After two or three months of mounting anxiety, Janice Jackson called a meeting of GS-14s and GS 15s, to which she invited Phyllis Barajas, Special Assistant to Rodney McCowan, who had recently become Director of the Office of Management (OM). Thomas Lambiase and Thomas

Johnston were also there from OM to take questions about Departmental requirements on reorganizations and personnel classification issues. Robert Morgan, representative of the AFGE, was also invited to attend although the union had no jurisdiction over middle managers.

Thomas Lambiase fielded the first question, which was directed at the strategy of restructuring with teams that appeared to do away with mid-level managers. His response was that adopting a work-group structure was a way of realizing a greater span of control quickly. He assured the audience that no staff person would lose his or her grade level in the transition and that ceiling levels at ED were not as restrictive as they were in some other agencies.

Concerning job classifications, Thomas Johnston acknowledged that there seemed to be inordinate anxiety and discomfort over adapting the classification system to the demands of the new work structure. He stated that OM was trying to be creative with the standard regulations for job classifications. This left some doubt in my mind about how much success had so far been achieved in working with these restrictive regulations. This was reinforced by Phyllis Barajas who made it clear that there would be no movement to higher grades simply as a result of the restructuring.

After a number of questions and answers that did not appear to alleviate the anxiety, Phyllis displayed a drawing on a flip chart containing three intersecting circles entitled "current state," "transition," and "future state." She described the transition as dealing with behaviors, norms, values and assumptions. One person, who acknowledged that he was only GS-13 and had come to the meeting out of a personal concern, spoke up, saying that Phyllis's diagram and comments "were much too vague to be helpful to anyone." He continued, " I want specifics. What can you tell me about the future of a GS-13 who wants to make a career of the federal service and is interested in his chances of upward mobility?" He was told that there would still be openings from time to time for which he could compete, but there would be no movement to a higher grade related to the restructuring of OESE. He was not reassured. Not long afterward, he left the Department of Education.

There were a number of questions about the political battles going on between the Congress and the Administration. One person wanted to know if there were any scenarios being studied for possible outcomes. Phyllis stated that "No scenarios were being studied. There were no good answers. We are politically in a flux. Nobody knows." Janice apparently felt the need to say that the Department leadership was "thinking about these things. They were thinking about all kinds of developments." These two different responses did not provide much confidence for those concerned about their vulnerability to political outcomes.

At the time I had been reading *Reinventing Government: Appraisal of the National Performance Review* by Donald Kettl (1994). I held the book in the air and said, "This book reports that the government's most significant layering problem occurs at the very top, not the middle." Since it appeared to me that the Department was targeting the mid-level managers only, I asked, admittedly with a slight tone of defensiveness, "What is being done about delayering the delayerers?" Phyllis Barajas replied that the reorganization of the whole Department was being studied. When I pressed about specific reductions in top level staff, she could only say that there would be some reductions.

Robert Morgan (AFGE representative) then stated that he was concerned that increasing the span of control would remove many good leaders. He also asked, "Is there any redlining [blocking out certain sections of ED that would not be affected] taking place?" Thomas Johnston responded that there was no redlining occurring, and Phyllis interjected that "The focus for future leadership would be in relation to the nature of the work to be done."

Numerous other questions were raised for which there were few definitive or comforting answers. As the hour came to a close, Phyllis Barajas, uncomfortable with the hostility she experienced, appeared anxious to terminate the meeting. For days afterward, those of us who attended the meeting were discussing our continued concerns. There was a consensus among us that the meeting provided very little new information, failed to give definitive answers to numerous questions, and did not reduce anxiety levels. With no professional association to represent middle managers or to provide a venue for unresolved concerns, our anxiety persisted.

Confusion over Roles and Functions. The roles and functions of employees in the new structure were confusing and difficult to define from the very beginning. First, the whole restructuring plan had to be approved by the Office of Management and American Federation of Government Employees. Satisfying the regulations of OM was, itself, an arduous, complicated and tedious problem-solving feat, although it could be accomplished by persistently working on the organizational details. Satisfying AFGE, on the other hand, meant dealing with highly emotional situations. It would be a frustrating pursuit that involved extensive negotiation and mediation. The middle-management roles had not been contemplated nor prescribed in any detail. They would have to be worked out as problems emerged through a succession of iterations. In addition, defining the roles of the group leaders and team leaders was especially troublesome and, in fact, changed repeatedly. The definitions developed through a succession of expanding iterations. Initially, they had to be defined in the reorganization plan that must be submitted to the Office of Management. Subsequently, they were also defined over and over again during the implementation of the restructuring and the operation of OESE.

Secondly, communicating the operational roles to the rank and file was difficult. In July, when it looked as if the AFGE would not approve the restructuring plan, the leadership attempted to communicate employee roles with hypothetical scenarios. One scenario describes Sally, a GS-12 employee, working as a policy and evaluation specialist on a program service team (PST):

> Sally is one of eight program service team members whose diverse functions range from secretarial/clerical to the senior executive service (SES) program director. As a policy and evaluation specialist, Sally reports to the GS-15 group leader, whose duties include supervisory responsibility for the activities of the Office of Migrant Education (OME) program service team.
>
> Sally's work assignments will normally come from the program service team group leader, who rates the quality of her work and who is responsible for her professional growth and development. As a member of this team, beyond her specific duties, Sally works in a team setting with the other member of the office. In this work atmosphere, in addition to the experience she brings to the team, Sally will acquire a broad

understanding of many program service team activities as well as those of the Regional Service Teams (RSTs), thus broadening the scope of her knowledge and experience.

Another scenario describes a person in a regional service team (RST):

This scenario features Walter, a GS-12 migrant education specialist who is a member of a regional service team attached to the Compensatory Education Program (CEP) office. Walter is one of fourteen members on a team whose service responsibility includes the three north central states of Illinois, Wisconsin and Minnesota. As one of the migrant education specialists on the RST, Walter's work deals with migrant activities for these states. He will acquire a broad understanding of OESE programs as he works on the cross-program team. This will broaden his knowledge and expertise as we work to foster comprehensive services . . .

Walter's rating and supervision are the responsibility of the migrant education group leader. Although the group leader works out of the Migrant Education Program office, s/he will be responsible for keeping Walter current regarding OME program regulations, policies and procedures, as well as other programmatic developments. S/he would be responsible for coordinating Walter's activities with migrant education colleagues serving on other teams and for Walter's professional growth and development.

As Walter's supervisor/rater, the group leader would rate Walter's programmatic performance, considering such areas as program knowledge, skills and growth. Walter's rater will review Walter's work along with the RST team leader. This review could include such things as written correspondence, reports written by Walter individually or with the team.

The scenarios did not appear to help very much. There had been many reorganizations in the Department before, but the staff never had to adjust to something as confusing as this new structure. It would take much more explanation than two scenarios.

Involving Staff

In the presentation of the new reconfiguration of OESE, the Senior Leadership Team addressed the staff with these words from the restructuring packet:

> The process of restructuring, in consideration of program arrangements, hierarchical staffing, and organizational culture, is indeed challenging and complex. There are many details to work out. This is just the beginning. Our response to the opportunities presented will significantly enhance the Department's responsiveness to its customers, both internal and external, and the needs of learners for a long time to come. We look forward to working with the OESE staff members as we proceed with restructuring and reengineering implementation teams.

Janice Jackson was in charge of the restructuring. It was up to her to make it all happen. She first put together a large restructuring team with six sub-groups (which were actually called teams from the beginning). Sixty staff members (approximately 25 percent of OESE) volunteered. They responded for a variety of reasons. Some were obviously enthusiastic about being a part of the change effort. Another large group knew that they should go with the flow if they wanted a future in the Department. Others were curious and later dropped out after two or three meetings. I doubted if anybody really understood the dimensions of the problems on which they would be working. Janice put them all to work in the six teams according to their preferences.

1. Originally the *"Area Offices Team"* would deal with both the program administration and the regional teams. But these functions were split into two separate teams—one known as the *"Program Administration/Policy Team"* and the other known as the *"Regional Team."* The Program Administration/Policy Team would deal with how each of the seven programs within OESE would administer their programs and relate their work to the regional teams. The Regional Team would make recommendations about the number of regions, the geographical areas served by the regions, the number and kinds of program staff for the regions, duties of team members, and the relationship to the program staff. They would also deal with the criteria and the processes for the reassignment of

staff, and the generic position descriptions of all staff. This team had a tiger by the tail.

2. The "*Internal Communications Team*" was a slow walk compared to the Regional Team. They were charged with developing internal and external communication systems about OESE restructuring and reengineering and for communicating program information with the regions. While this could have been a formidable task, their work was reduced by the members' limited understanding of the complete task.

3. The "*Professional Development Team*" would develop a professional development strategy to support restructuring and reengineering. The plan was to provide for the needs of four layers of organization: staff, team leaders, group leaders/coaches, and senior leadership. The team members were told that their plan could include such things as understanding the change process, chaos management, team leadership and facilitation skills, team building and working in teams, conflict resolution, program/customer services, and methods of joint monitoring and evaluation. Although this team worked hard at its task, by not starting with desired outcomes for OESE the task was reduced to developing a laundry list of training needs in a traditional fashion.

4. A "*Space Team*" already in existence had its work enlarged to include a transition plan for the co-location of reassigned staff in the restructured of OESE.

5. The "*Reengineering Team*" was charged with designing a strategy to be used for changing the way OESE did its work. It would spell out the steps to be taken by a program office or cross-cutting team to change core processes. I became a co-leader of this team, and was successful in getting the team charter enlarged to focus on the overall restructuring effort, not just the core business processes. This was accomplished by pointing out that the overall restructuring effort of OESE was a "fundamental rethinking" and a "radical redesign," and this was defined as reengineering by Hammer & Champy's *Reengineering the Corporation* (1993). This gave me the opportunity to focus the team's discussion on OESE's overall

change effort, which, I felt, was missing in the prescribed work of the restructuring teams.

6. Finally, the *"Dissemination Team"* would develop a plan to disseminate information to persons not a part of OESE. This information would deal with the revision of legislation and the restructured OESE.

Janice decided that she would accept all volunteers. I thought that this was an unusual way to go about implementation, rather than putting our most qualified people in responsible positions to make something successful. Unrestricted volunteerism was typical of Janice—she was a true believer in inclusive participation.

Lessons Learned

The restructuring of OESE was borne of distrust and discontent in American government. It was a discontent that expressed itself in the fervent politics of the presidential election of 1992 and the mid-term election of 1994, when Republicans wrested control of the Congress from the Democrats. President Clinton felt it necessary to bash the federal establishment to get elected and then demonstrate that he could reform it to keep his office. The NPR would define his goals and launch the reinvention machine. Later, when the Congress discussed eliminating the Department of Education, the pressure increased to speed the reform so as to justify keeping the agency intact. Some of the lessons we learn from this are as follows:

•   **Governmental agencies are living in a different kind of world.** There is now considerable external pressure upon federal agencies to make fundamental, radical changes in their organizations within a short period of time. Future leadership in governmental agencies will have to know how to effect such rapid, radical changes. It is not unusual to have to make fundamental change quickly in the private sector, because competition can put a private enterprise out of business when it can not respond rapidly. But it has not been common for federal agencies to have to make a radical change within a short time frame or face extinction. Yet this is what happened in the Department of Education.

Whether private or public, the failure rate of organizations increases dramatically with rapid radical change. States John Kotter in the *Harvard Business Review,* "The most general lesson to be learned from the more successful cases of organizational change is that the change process goes through a series of phases that, in total, usually require a considerable length of time. Skipping steps creates only the illusion of speed and never produces a satisfying result" (March/April: 1995). It is easy for professionals to make critical mistakes when they have plenty of time. In OESE, non-professionals were making fundamental changes under political pressure in a very short period of time. This was a high risk endeavor that, according to the tenets of John Kotter, would not yield a satisfying result.

- **Early decisions of organizational change often prescribe what can and cannot be done at a later time.** Consequently, decisions must be made with knowledge and care. One of the formative factors in OESE's change was putting structure first and restructuring the functions around the structure. OESE's leadership set up teams such as reengineering, communication, training and office space to implement the proposed structure. Professionals in organizational design go about it differently. They look at the functions and then construct a structure that accommodates the functions. Outside professionals could have helped OESE with the alignment of structure, technical systems, people systems, reward systems, decision making, and renewal systems. But the top management chose, instead, to start by reorganizing. This is common in government agencies, where, it seems, there is a reorganization every time there is a change in administration.

- **The locus of power, authority and control is of immense importance in determining what can and what cannot be changed in organizations.** A major factor in the ultimate outcome of OESE's restructuring effort was the locus of power, authority, and control in the Senior Leadership Team. The Senior Leadership Team was mostly composed of program directors. Of course, the Assistant Secretary wanted the restructuring, and the Deputy Assistant Secretary was responsible for leading the effort. But most decision making was passed through the program directors whose first priority was responsibility for their programs—not the success of the restructuring. The program directors manifested their power whenever possible, often circumventing the welfare of the overall effort to protect the welfare of their programs.

Organizational design professionals would have more likely advised that a steering committee be formed that had authority and control over the planning and implementation. Janice Jackson did establish a steering committee later in this effort. But it served primarily as a sounding board to obtain feedback to further her own interests. Professionals would have instead created a representative group of customers, stakeholders, influencers, government officials, and others to serve on the steering committee, and would have given them the major decision-making role. They also would have established a design team to pursue a variety of organizational elements that would have to be developed and kept in alignment. They would most certainly have done an environmental scan, and established some requisite outcomes before prescribing the structure. In contrast, the structure the OESE leaders designed was idealistically conceived without a foundation in reality.

- **Without a clear, viable vision, an attempt to make significant changes in an organization will fail.** From the very beginning there was an inordinate amount of fuzzy thinking in the organizational design revealed by the numerous conflicting statements in the official communication. For example, the staff was told that there would merely be "changes in roles/relationships and behaviors rather than undertaking a fundamental reorganization." At another place, the staff was told that "OESE is beginning to consider fundamental changes in the way we operate and carry out our responsibilities." The staff, whose job it would be to carry out the reorganization, was confused about whether a few roles would change or whether fundamental changes would completely alter their jobs.

While there were mission and vision statements, with their guiding principles, goals and objectives, for the most part they were drafted and soon forgotten. It was not until the two people who had launched the restructuring, Tom Payzant and Janice Jackson, had left, and the new Assistant Secretary arrived, that the mission and vision statements were even posted. Ironically, the mission statement he posted came from the previous administration. The fact was that after the restructuring was launched, it was the structure that got the attention, not the rationale or the functions. To make the kind of fundamental changes OESE was attempting, we needed a vision and empowerment of others to act on the vision. This did not happen.

To implement such a broad and radical change in OESE, the importance of credibility and commitment from the very beginning cannot be overstated. From the start, the restructuring did not have credibility with the leadership or the staff. Many staff felt that the program directors did not give the restructuring plan a wholehearted "buy-in." Rather, it was felt, they were responding to the political leadership. And it was clear to us that some of the Senior Leadership Team never felt comfortable about it. The program directors were also worried about their programs. The staff sensed some of the uncertainty of the OESE management. They also perceived the problems of incorporating the IEP and the IAP into the regional team activities. They saw problems with the roles and functions. Some knew that they did not have the numbers of staff or the expertise to deliver the anticipated services.

Nevertheless, the die was cast. From here on, everything was destined to take on a distinctive character from the way the restructuring was conceived and approached. The launching of the change shaped what followed. To a large extent, this is a story of how the distinctive character of OESE developed from what was done in the beginning.

two

Restructuring Deficit

Launching the Teams

On November 9, 1994, I entered the South Building of the Department of Agriculture (USDA). The building covers two square blocks on Independence Avenue and is surrounded on three sides with smaller USDA satellite buildings which contrast sharply with this giant pile of brick and stone. Every time I entered this maze of corridors, I sensed the magnitude of this federal agency. We were meeting in this facility of the Department of Agriculture because our Department of Education facility was being renovated and we were temporarily housed in an office building. Since I arrived early, I helped arrange furniture: chairs for the entire group, and tables for the break-out groups. This was the day that the new Deputy Assistant Secretary, Janice Jackson, would energize and turn loose the restructuring teams.

I watched the OESE staff flow into the meeting room. Only two program directors walked through the door—Alicia Cora, Director of the School Improvement Program, and my boss, Cathy Schagh, Director of Impact Aid. "Where were all the other program directors?" I asked myself. The other 58 people represented all categories from support staff to supervisors. Janice had invited all and had excluded nobody. Anyone who wanted to be a part of the effort was asked to submit a memo specifying a group interest and reasons for the choice. I had asked to be included in the reengineering group because of my leadership in reengineering the accounts receivable processes in the Impact Aid Program and in improving the timeliness of Impact Aid payments with another team. I also cited the work I did analyzing the effort to employ teams in the Office of Civil Rights. I was given the assignment I requested, as were most of the other volunteers. Now I was anxious to meet the members of my team and to see with whom I would be working.

Janice Jackson introduced herself as the Deputy Assistant Secretary. She said nothing more about herself, but her presence drew the attention of everyone in the room. There was no doubt that the restructuring of OESE was a challenge for her, but she had been in challenging positions before. She had extensive experience in the Milwaukee Public Schools in a variety of roles when the schools were undergoing court-ordered desegregation and decentralization. She had a varied career of participation and leadership in African American affairs. That included four years as Executive Director of the Office for Black Catholic Concerns for the Archdiocese of Milwaukee. She also served for a short time as a Superintendent Intern in the San Diego City Schools where her current boss was the Superintendent.

Few, if anyone in the room, knew of her past work experience. Nor did they know that she had two master's degrees in education and one in theology. They could see clearly that she had a commanding presence and an inclusive smile. They gave her their undivided attention as she described the planned restructuring of OESE.

Since I had not been at the All Hands meeting, this was the first time I had heard anyone officially describe what I had read in the packet. I posed a number of questions for Janice during the question and answer session, attempting to confirm what I had heard and read. I was stunned by the radical change in which I soon would be involved. This was going to be a major trauma for OESE. It did not seem to me that many people in the room were aware of the magnitude of the proposed effort. But everyone seemed to sense that something big was coming down and they were in on it.

This was the first of many meetings in which Janice would have to provide answers to the same questions. At this initial meeting, many people wanted to know what the staff of the regional teams would do. Others wanted to know about the relationship between the regional service teams and the program service teams. Many were interested in their own outcomes and asked questions about the reassignment of staff. There were questions about the roles and responsibilities of supervisors and managers. There were questions about what the organizational structure and the diagrams of the future structure, as displayed in the packet of information disseminated to all staff. And there were questions about the delayering of the organization and the desired supervisory ratio of 15:1. People asked nervously if this flattening of OESE was going to result in reductions in staff, grade and pay.

Janice assured everyone that there would be no reductions in grade or pay, and she did not anticipate any reductions in force, although she indicated there might be buyout opportunities. She clarified information when necessary, but to most questions she responded, "You will provide the answers to these questions. They will come from you and your teams."

Janice ended her talk with a few words about working teams and distributed a couple of handouts about them and some brief team assignments. She directed the teams to reassemble at designated tables, get acquainted, develop some ground rules, establish a schedule, and agree on what they believed their task to be.

Among the nine members assigned to the Reengineering Team, there were some folks who knew each other. I suggested that each person introduce him- or herself and state why he or she was interested in working on the Reengineering Team. I was encouraged to learn that two members of the team, David Jackson and Sheila Cooper, had recently completed week-long courses in business process reengineering at the Federal Quality Institute. They could be of great help. I also sensed that one member of the team, Michelle Padilla, was very good at focusing on and clarifying issues. I felt she would be useful in keeping our discussions clear and the work focused.

While the teams were meeting, Janice was moving from table to table answering questions. When she came to our table, I quizzed her about how she perceived the magnitude of the change required and what she perceived to be the nature and significance of reengineering. I wanted to clarify the fuzzy thinking in the restructuring packet. I used the key terms from Hammer and Champy's (1993) definition of reengineering: "Do you consider this a *fundamental* rethinking of how we work? Is it a *radical redesign* rather than a modification? Is it *dramatic* change rather than incremental change?" To each of these questions she answered in the affirmative. I responded, "Then, this really is reengineering we are all talking about!" I was excited!

As I left the meeting, Janice approached me and said, "I hope you will stay with us in the restructuring effort. We need people like you." I had already taken the bait, and now the hook was set. I decided to hang in with OESE for a while longer and see what developed.

On Their Own

The restructuring teams were now on their own. During the early meetings of the Reengineering Team, there was some natural floundering. The team needed answers to four questions:

1. What is the team supposed to be doing? We had not been given a charter.

2. What are supposed to be the outcomes of this reengineering? (How is OESE to serve its clientele differently?)

3. What is reengineering? Members of the team had different perceptions or no perceptions at all.

4. Where can the team turn for help? The team needed professional help.

No team had received a charter for its work. At the second meeting, the team designated me to get a charter from Janice, but none was forthcoming. Each team had only been given a few sentences of description about their subject area. Since none of the teams was given a charter or boundaries, no one knew how far the teams were empowered to go. Nor did we know what assumptions and decisions we could make. This lack of information and direction was to cause some major problems. Like the other teams, the Reengineering Team was left to develop its own charter and determine its own boundaries.

"One Face to the Customer"

I knew that Chuck Hansen had been the key person in the conception of the restructuring plan. Consequently, I suggested that the team go straight to the originator of the plan and request a meeting with him. Chuck had left OESE to become Deputy Assistant Secretary for the Office of Educational Research and Information (OERI), but he welcomed the opportunity to meet with the Reengineering Team. In our meeting, he explained that he had envisioned regional teams that would present "one face to the customer" with members of regional teams representing all programs of OESE, not just the one in which they currently worked. He acknowledged that this service would not be possible in the beginning. It would require considerable cross training and working together across programs. But this was the expectation.

Chuck also talked about the decentralized matrix structure proposed for OESE. He said that it would reduce the number of supervisors and facilitate the type of customer service he had dreamed about. Chuck's dream would cut staff. There could be coordinated field reviews with fewer staff. People could cover for each other after they had been cross trained, and a single person could work with a superintendent or other administrator to help solve problems, and attain one's goals with OESE's combined resources.

As I sized up the task that a member of a regional team was expected to perform, I wondered how many people in OESE could handle it. What specific performance outcomes would be required of regional team members? There had been no job assessments or job models, and no restructuring team had been assigned to address them. I knew that the IAP had staff that could not be sent out to the field to represent their own program because they didn't have sufficient knowledge. How could they possibly represent six or seven different programs?

When Chuck had been the director of the IAP, he expressed a desire to correct this shortcoming, but he wasn't there long enough to make it happen. In fact, the plan to set up the OESE staff to provide "one face to the customer" was an escalation of what Chuck had wanted to do in IAP on a smaller scale. This was the thing that concerned me most. I felt that this goal was unrealistic when applied to all of OESE programs and staff. I also recognized that this was a fundamental premise of the restructuring, but I was not yet ready to challenge it.

Reengineering More than Processes

One of the most troubling concepts for the Reengineering Team was the concept of reengineering itself. I came to the team's second meeting with copies of a number of printed resources I thought would be helpful for all the members. Among those I shared with the team were selected passages from *Reengineering the Corporation* (Hammer & Champy, 1993); "A Reengineering Primer" (Theodore B. Kinni, January 1994); "How to Make Reengineering Really Work" (Gene Hall, Jim Rosenthal, & Judy Wade, 1993); "Reengineering the Hot New Managing Tool" (T. A. Stewart, 1993); "The Core Competence of the Corporation" (C. K. Prahalad & Gary Hamel, 1990); and a few additional papers and lighter magazine articles. I recommended that the members all buy *Reengineering the Corporation.* I told them that I had attempted to get the workbook for the course on business process reengineering from the Federal Quality Institute, but they would not give me a copy without taking the course. I later got a copy from David Jackson, who had taken the course, and made copies for all members.

For the two members who had taken the course on business process reengineering from the Federal Quality Institute, reengineering was limited to core business processes. While I acknowledged that this was an indispensable component of reengineering, I believed that one could not focus only on the business processes without concern for the total institutional environment in which the process changes would be made. Both Hammer and Champy, who had recently defined and popularized the concept, never limited it to work processes alone. And when they both followed up *Reengineering the Corporation* with their separate books, *Reengineering Management* (James Champy: 1995) and *The Reengineering Revolution* (Michael Hammer & Steven A. Stanton: 1994), they laid the reasons for failure on many other aspects of organizational change. I was familiar with a number of models for organizational design and had an academic background in the sociology of organizations and institutions. For me, organizational change involved the integration of many types of behaviors within a supporting culture. I felt that ignoring the institutional environment and focusing only on work processes, at a time when OESE was fundamentally rethinking and radically redesigning the way it conducted business within a brief time period, would guarantee failure. To me it seemed that OESE was not merely trying to restructure their organization—it was trying to reengineer!

The frustrating part of the proposed restructuring was that the OESE leadership did not view OESE as a social institution of integrated values and behaviors. What I did not yet understand was that this holistic perception was not a part of the original, idealistic concept of the new OESE. Consequently, the launching of the restructuring was not complete. So I naively pushed to bring the larger picture into focus.

In fact, I was surprised that none of the restructuring teams had the assignment to look at the overall picture. I also noted that there was no steering committee or other group with specific responsibility for the development and integration of the change process. Rather, the power and decision making was left in the hands of the Senior Leadership Team, which consisted of the Assistant and Deputy Secretaries, the program directors and a few administrative staff. For me, this was a problem. Little did I realize how formidable a problem it would be.

Expanding the Team Charter

What I did perceive was a role for the Reengineering Team in pursuing the big picture. So I expressed this need from the beginning in the team's discussions. It was not long before I received sufficient support from members of the team to go to Janice and request the responsibility of pursuing the larger picture, which I did. But the issue of expanding the work of the team was never resolved with all of its members.

It did not help that one member of our team, David Jackson, one of those who had taken the course on business process reengineering from the Federal Quality Institute, didn't comprehend the big picture. David had been working with some of the staff of the Human Resources System Innovation Group (HRSIG) that had been set up in OM to work with others involved in reinvention of the Department. David looked to them to backup his understanding of reengineering, and the team had given him permission to bring in some of their staff for a discussion of reengineering. On February 13, 1995, Joe Fucello and David Murray of HRSIG attended the team meeting for a discussion. I introduced the Organizational Systems Design (OSD) Model (Organization Planning & Design, Inc., 1994) as my way of talking about the larger picture. (See Figure 2.) They had never seen or heard of this model or anything like it. I saw no evidence of understanding an organization as a social institution. And, although they perceived reengineering as limited to work processes, they did not understand

Figure 2. Organizational Systems Design (OSD) Model

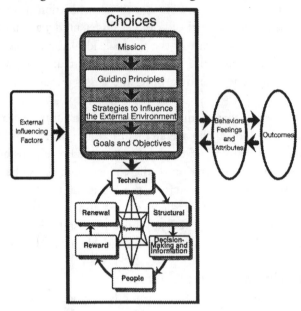

Source. Organziational Planning and Design, 1994. *Organizational Systems Design Guidebook*, San Jose, CA: 3.

my distinction between enabling and core work processes. A few days later, I dropped by their offices and gave them a copy of the *Organizational Systems Design Guidebook*, (Organizational Planning & Design, Inc.,1994) and said that I would like to talk with them about it after they had time to examine it. Joe responded, "I need a little time to digest what was discussed at the meeting." When I did not hear from Joe in a couple of weeks, I phoned his office and left a message asking to get together for the discussion. Joe never returned my call. This was my first experience with the HRSIG, but it would not be my last. They all ended in disappointments.

Getting the Big Picture
After a few team discussions about reengineering, I sensed that our differing concepts of reengineering, and my aggressive leadership, were causing rifts within the team, especially with David Jackson, who now felt that he had a position to defend. I also sensed the need for backup, but I didn't feel I could go to the HRSIG. I would go outside the Department. At the November 9th meeting, there had been a question about the use of consultants to assist the restructuring teams in their work. Janice had indicated

that outside experts could be hired, despite the fact that resources were limited, and she gave us permission to seek one.

Steve Jacobs, a partner in the Organizational Systems Design Alliance, Inc., a consulting firm that had been one of the pioneers in the areas of strategic architecture, organizational reengineering, and large-scale leadership agreed to work with us. He agreed to work with the team by means of teleconferencing. In preparation for the teleconference, I mailed Steve information about the restructuring of OESE. In turn, he sent me some case study material about the establishing of American Transtech after the divestiture of AT&T in 1884. The team was fascinated with Steve's account of this case study. He presented an all-encompassing picture of large-scale organizational change. Among the materials Steve had sent to the team was a diagram of the OSD Model. When Steve related the OSD Model to the development of American Transtech, he made a breakthrough with the team. Now the team was getting a grip on the big picture. The two-hour teleconference moved swiftly, and it ramped up the members' excitement about their change. Steve had driven home the importance of working with all facets of an organization. Unfortunately, not all members of the Reengineering Team had been present, but there would not be any question about the importance of the big picture among those who were.

At the next meeting of the team, I brought copies of Paul Gustavson's *"Organizational Systems Design Guidebook"* (1994) for everyone. The "Guidebook" was a further amplification of Steve's teleconference, with a wealth of explanation and detail on design choices. The OSD Model became a keystone in the thinking and the work of the Reengineering Team. It eventually gained some important other advocates, including Janice Jackson. Unfortunately, this framework for analyzing OESE and its functions would never be implemented.

Getting Help

Now the Reengineering Team had experienced a mind-stretching experience of looking at the whole picture with the OSD Model and a resource guide. The team felt a need for more knowledge and more help. Since Steve Jacobs was unavailable, I drew up a list of 15 small firms from which the team selected Mark Rhodes, a former colleague of Steve Jacobs at Harvard, and a participant in the American Transtech reengineering. He had done organizational design work with National

Semiconductor, AT&T Capital Corp., American Express, Fres-co System USA, Hill's Pet Nutrition, and others. I got Janice to agree to one day of consulting as long as the meeting was open to the leadership of the other restructuring teams. All other team leaders were invited to the meeting with Mark.

Meeting with a consultant. On January 6, 1995, the members of the Reengineering Team met with Mark. No leaders from other teams were present, but two teams sent representatives. From our team, Michelle Padilla and two other members could not attend. And David Jackson attended only part of the meeting. Most disconcerting to me was the fact that Janice Jackson did not attend as a result of a fluke in communication.

I had given Mark a briefing over the phone on what OESE was attempting to do and how we were going about it, told him about the teleconference with Steve Jacobs, and mailed him what I considered to be the most important handouts about the OESE restructuring. At the beginning of the meeting, Mark asked the group how he could most help them. Since the Reengineering Team had to provide the Leadership Team with a progress report on January 17th, and a final report by February 15th, we requested help in developing our report. "The report," the leadership team had said, "should provide a road map to designing and implementing the overall reengineering effort and to reengineering the core work processes." So most of the day was spent focusing on the key concepts and activities of a plan. Mark worked from the OSD Model in a way that fit hand-in-glove with what Steve Jacobs had presented. Toward the end of the day, we understood what we would have to deal with in developing our own plan, and we laid out our report writing task. Mark offered to meet with the team without charge to go over their plan on the morning of January 18th, because he had to come to Washington for another client.

It had been a very productive session, but those of us in attendance were disappointed that so few people were there. Sadly, this was par for the restructuring teams. I estimated that between 25 to 33 percent of the volunteers on these teams dropped out after a few sessions. The most capable people were also in high demand by their programs, and the program directors were demanding their services.

50

The team left the session with Mark knowing that the Senior Leadership Team would have to get the big picture if there would be any chance of success. They wanted the Senior Leadership Team to have a minimum of two days with Mark, preferably more. It took me less than 24 hours to learn that this was out of the question. "The Senior Leadership Team," I was told, "would not have the time to devote two or more days of training with Mark."

Mark returned as planned for a half-day of consulting on January 18th. He knew in advance that the hopes and dreams of the Reengineering Team had been battered because the Senior Leadership Team would not devote the time necessary for training. He returned anyway to help the team salvage something and decide on how to move from this early setback. This time the experience showed more promise. There was no significant representation from the other restructuring teams, but members of the Reengineering Team that missed the first session were there. Most important, Janice was present, and she became caught up in the discussion. The meeting dealt with the concerns of the team about organizational change, which Mark helped the members better understand. Mark refocused the discussion on the steps that could be taken to move the restructuring forward. On January 21, 1995, Janice sent me the following e-mail:

> Bruce, as you know, I was extremely impressed with Mark Rhodes. I would like to involve him in our work. Please give me a phone number so that I can give him a call.
>
> Thank you for getting him involved.
>
> *Janice*

Request for a proposal. Janice did get in contact with Mark and asked him to put together a modest proposal to assist OESE. In brief, his proposal included the following five elements and their rationale:

1. **Organizational Training.** To insure the success of the OESE organizational redesign efforts, we must ensure that all members receive sufficient training and development in areas of technical, interpersonal and business competencies. These training efforts will cover a long period of time and must be carefully planned and orchestrated.

Selection of training vendors, as well as internal resources, will be a key to the overall success of the new OESE design.

2. **Consulting to "Micro Design Teams."** The OESE organizational design plans have been specified at the "macro" level. To ensure effectiveness of the implementation of this design, we will need to further streamline various work processes to reengineer the OESE into a highly effective customer focused organization.

3. **Consulting on the Selection of Team Leaders.** Leadership will be an important component of OESE's ongoing change process. The skills and background required to manage and lead in a traditional manner are often quite different from those competencies necessary for leading a modern, innovative and customer focused organization.

4. **Leadership Development.** Leadership will be an important component of the OESE's ongoing change processes. It will be important to provide leaders with sufficient training and development resources so that they may lead the OESE's critical change effort.

5. **Consulting Support to Organizational Communication, Planning & Implementation.** The success of OESE's recent redesign process will depend a great deal upon the effectiveness of communication to all members of the organization about the upcoming change process. Communication efforts should allow members of the organization an opportunity to air their feelings and participate in decision making.

Mark's plan also included activities and time requirements. He would later be asked to amplify his proposal, which he did with much more specificity including the scheduling of more detailed time requirements.

Team Leader Partnership
When the Reengineering Team first got together, we did not wish to select a team leader. The members expressed a mutual feeling that we ought to meet for awhile and get to know each other better before we chose a leader. In place of a specified leader, the team rotated the team leader and the recorder positions at each meeting. This system did not work. Often, the responsible person did not attend, or did not function well in the designated role.

In this leadership vacuum, Michelle and I would normally provide the leadership. My contributions usually resulted from my knowledge of organizational behavior, the preparation work I did between meetings, and the resources I brought to the team meetings. For example, I took on the task of identifying, contacting, and acquiring information about potential consultants. I always sought a consensus or direction from the team. And when I did get it, I ran with it and came to the next meeting with the needed information and guidance.

Michelle played a very different role. Although she did not have the background in organizational behavior, she was very effective in clarifying problems and issues and very good at moderating differences of opinion. The end result of the nomination process was that Michelle and I became co-leaders. This partnership worked out well, especially when there needed to be a division of labor between the business process reengineering and the overall reengineering of OESE.

Writing and Presenting Reports

A schedule of dates had been given to the teams on November 9th, when the teams met for the first time, that included:

First meeting of the restructuring teams	11/9/94
Interim report to the Senior Leadership Team	1/17/95
Team leaders report to OESE "All Hands" meeting	1/24/95
Final reports from the teams	2/15/95
Decision by the Senior Leadership Team	2/21/95

In addition, the Senior Leadership Team planned to schedule presentations by each of the teams at their weekly meetings. The Reengineering Team would lead off, because they were focusing a part of their work on overall reengineering.

Shortly after Michelle and I were selected to share the leadership of the team, the work on the team's report began in earnest. In the division of labor, those interested in working on the overall reengineering worked with me and those interested in business processes worked with Michelle.

Interim report. When it came time to present a one-page interim report, I drafted the wording and the team adopted it with minor changes. A portion of the report read as follows:

At the present time, this is our understanding of reengineering:

1. We know the concept well.

2. We are certain that it is a high-risk endeavor.

3. We understand the importance of organizational design.

4. We have begun an in-depth study of reengineering's essential components.

5. We are beginning to comprehend the processes of reengineering.

6. We know that without an in-depth knowledge and commitment by management to reengineering it is severely endangered.

7. We are beginning to apply our knowledge to the reengineering of OESE.

In addition, the team had been requested to include a few initial recommendations in the interim report. Three of the recommendations were that:

- The Assistant Secretary make public at every available opportunity his commitment to reengineering as his top priority and give at least 25 percent of his time to it.

- The Senior Leadership Team and other top managers of OESE be trained in the basic essentials of reengineering (or example, organizational design, essential components, processes, etc.) ASAP.

- A full-time reengineering team be established with a knowledgeable staff, under the leadership of the Deputy Assistant Secretary, to assist in the overall effort.

The interim report was probably the first clue others had as to what the Reengineering Team was thinking. There was no response from the Senior Leadership Team. Since the Reengineering Team did not receive any feedback, we assumed our work was acceptable.

Presentation to staff. A week later, each of the restructuring teams were asked to make a brief presentation to the entire OESE staff. In anticipation of their presentations, Janice Jackson called the team leaders to a meeting to brief them on what she expected of them. I requested that the Reengineering Team be granted time for two presentations— one for the business processes and another for the overall effort. Each presentation was to take from three to five minutes. I was scheduled first to present the overview. I had three objectives in mind. I wanted to (1) impress upon everyone the magnitude of the change we were undertaking, (2) convey the fact that it was a total systems change, and (3) make a few early recommendations. Feeling frustrated by the short time I had been given for the presentation, I decided that once I got the floor I would take from seven to eight minutes. I developed a set of overhead slides and practiced my presentation until I had it limited to my time goal.

In order to convey the magnitude of change, I made a distinction between "restructuring" and "reengineering." "The restructuring of OESE," I said, "was more than a reorganization of boxes on an organization chart." I asserted that what we were really reengineering. I used Hammer and Champy's definition of reengineering emphasizing the wording "fundamental rethinking," "radial redesign" and "dramatic improvements." I made a distinction between incremental change over a long period of time and radical change in a short period of time. I said it was a "high risk" effort. I quoted Thomas A. Stewart as saying, "The most important lesson from business' experience with reengineering: don't do it if you don't have to." I quoted Thomas H. Davenport's warning, "This hammer is incredibly powerful, but you can't use it on everything" (1993). "The point," I said, "was that this reengineering effort would take total commitment, dedication and hard work from everyone."

Using the metaphor of building a home with plumbing systems, electrical systems, heating systems, etc., I declared that organization building also has its systems. With a diagram of the OSD Model, I talked about organizational architecture as having technical, structural, decision making, information, people, and reward systems that must be integrated. I also pointed out that the strategic, coordinating, and the operating systems must be integrated. Finally, I presented the initial recommendations that the team included in their interim report.

I felt satisfied with the presentation; I knew that I had captured everyone's attention, including the members of the Senior Leadership Team. In the days following the presentation, numerous people approached me to talk about my presentation and the reengineering of OESE.

Michelle Padilla made the presentation on business process reengineering later in the meeting. She had been very busy in the Safe and Drug Free Schools Program, and her group had not yet done much work on their report. Nevertheless, she defined a core process, gave a couple examples, and made a few brief statements about the activities of business process reengineering. It was a good presentation, brief and to the point.

I felt that interest in the reengineering of OESE had been given a big boost at the All Hands meeting. The presentations of the restructuring teams revealed to the uninvolved staff that their peers were working actively on the reengineering. They saw them talk enthusiastically about the change of OESE. There was a lot of discussion among the staff and speculation about outcomes. It also raised many questions, especially about where staff would find their role in the restructuring.

Presentations to Senior Leadership Team. The next step was meeting with the Senior Leadership Team, which we knew was of vital importance. These were, after all, the people who were calling the shots. If they could not be convinced that the reinvention they were involved in was more that restructuring there was little chance of success.

By this time, the character of the restructuring teams had been formed. They might have more accurately been called "committees" or "work groups." About one-half of the members dropped out or attended so infrequently as to contribute very little. Work on their programs, including travel, made it difficult for many of the restructuring team members to participate. Most of the work done between meetings was done by very few people. The Reengineering Team was no exception.

Each of the restructuring teams was given up to 30 minutes with the Leadership Team. They were scheduled weekly until all had reported. Again, I led the series of presentations, because Janice thought it appropriate to start with the overview.

On January 31, 1995, our team met with the Senior Leadership Team. After introducing the team members, I launched into my presentation with an overhead projector and a set of transparencies. I began my presentation making a distinction between incremental change over a lengthy period of time, versus making major, fundamental change over a short period of time. I projected Hammer & Champy's definition of reengineering on the screen, which read:

> Reengineering is the fundamental rethinking and radical redesign of business processes to achieve dramatic improvements in critical, contemporary measures of performance, such as cost, quality, service, and speed.

I then dealt with the key words individually—"fundamental rethinking," "radical redesign," "dramatic improvements," and "business processes"—and related them to the restructuring plan of OESE. I declared that "This would be a short-term, gut-wrenching, shock treatment that would be difficult to accomplish successfully."

As in my presentation at the All Hands meeting, I emphasized the risk involved in reengineering. In addition to repeating the same quotations from that meeting, I informed the Senior Leadership Team that James Champy had just published another book that examined the reasons for the high failure rate in reengineering, and concluded that the key problem is management. I reported that Champy declares that "radical change is impossible unless managers know how to, in his words, 'organize, inspire, employ, enable, measure, and reward value-added operation work' " (1995: 3).

As I surveyed the faces of those in attendance, I found myself looking into a group of poker-faced, expressionless people. I wondered why such strong words had not evoked some response. Later, reflecting upon this experience, I realized that the members of the Senior Leadership Team had never really thought about the dynamics of organizational change beyond the common manipulation which they had labeled "restructuring." The interpersonal consequences of shifting organizational structures was not really appreciated.

I moved on to organizational system design. I projected a diagram of the OSD Model from the *Organizational System Design Guidebook*. I introduced the OSD Model by talking about organizational architecture. I explained: "If we were to build a house, we would construct a foundation, erect the walls, build a roof, and frame in the rooms. But, before closing in the interior framework with wallboard, we would install the systems. Initially, the plumbing would be installed because that is the least flexible. Then the heating and air conditioning system would be installed because it takes a lot of space. Next the electrical system is installed along with other flexible systems such as telephone lines, television cables, stereo wiring, etc."

I said that one can compare the overall framework of the house to the design choices, such as mission, goals and objectives, and the strategic plan. I explained: "We may liken the systems in the house to the systems of an organization displayed in the OSD Model labeled as technical, structure, decision making and information, people, reward, and renewal." I advised that an important objective is to keep the systems aligned and in balance. I further said, "Right now we are sitting on something like a three-legged stool with differing leg lengths. For example, we now have a long leg for structure, but short legs for people, and incentive systems. Because of the primary emphasis on structure," I declared, "we have a reengineering situation that is unaligned and anxiety is growing rapidly." I said that it is the recommendation of the Reengineering Team that the OSD Model be used as the overall guide for reengineering OESE.

I then commented upon the design choices of the OSD Model. I had more time to talk about the design choices than at the All Hands meeting, but still not enough time to explain them fully. I stated that there had not been a systematic study of the OESE environment of customers, stakeholders, and others, and stated that this should have been done prior to prescribing the structure. I acknowledged the existence of a mission statement, guiding principles, goals and objectives. I stated that the goals and objectives ought to be revisited with reference to the criteria of being specific, measurable, achievable, related to the mission, and oriented to time commitments. I then talked briefly about technical systems structure, decision-making, people systems, reward systems, and renewal.

At this point in the presentation there were a number of questions. In general, the Senior Leadership Team wanted more information about technical systems, people systems, and the nature of an organizational scan. I attempted to give them explanations and examples, but I was sensing that time was running out, and at the first chance I moved on with an explanation that these elements deserved more time than we could give them in the time provided.

As I continued talking I described three types of work—operating, strategic, and coordinating. I stated that these types of work would go through a change and adjustment in the new structure. Setting strategic direction would continue to be directed by the leadership of OESE. The operational work would be implemented differently, especially in the regional teams. "The big challenge," I said, "will be the coordination of strategic and operational core work. Working out the roles of regional teams and program service teams is going to be the big challenge."

Next, I projected the target-shaped OESE structural model as displayed in the restructuring packet (See Figure A-4 in the Appendix), and contrasted it with a target-shaped diagram envisaged by the Reengineering Team. I pointed out that the OESE structural model had the Office of the Assistant Secretary in the center, but the Reengineering Team diagram had the customer in the center. I stated that the team believes that we have to get beyond the top-down, hierarchical thinking in the restructuring effort that places the Assistant Secretary at the center of the effort, and master the concept of placing the customer in the center of our thinking.

I also talked briefly about a six-phased program to manage OESE's organizational change which had been prescribed by Paul Gustavson in the "Organizational Systems Design Workbook" (1994). I identified the phases as (1) launching, (2) analysis, (3) design, (4) development, (5) implementation, and (6) evaluation. I warned that OESE had skipped over some important tasks and had no plans for some of the others. "This is risky," I warned.

Finally, I came to the initial recommendations. After reading the first recommendation, "The Assistant Secretary make public at every available opportunity his commitment to reengineering as his top priority and give at least 25 percent of his time to it," I looked straight at the Assistant Secretary, waiting for a response. Tom responded, "If we only had more than 24 hours in a day, I might be able to do that." Although Tom did show up for a few of the meetings of restructuring teams after that, and usually had some supporting words for the restructuring effort, he essentially left the restructuring to Janice Jackson.

The other initial recommendations included training for the Senior Leadership Team, the establishment of a reengineering unit of at least four people to work under the direction of Janice, and the development of a plan for consulting services. In brief, the recommendations all had to do with leadership and management. I reasoned that these were the messages the Senior Leadership Team ought to hear.

In the Q&A that followed, some of the questions appeared to be honest inquiries from members who really wanted a fuller explanation, and some questions were pejorative in intent. There were also numerous questions about the OSD Model. They were especially interested in the reengineering of core business processes, and wanted more information than could be provided in the time available. I promised that they would get time to discuss work process reengineering when Michelle presented the other part of the Reengineering Team's report in a few weeks.

As in previous settings, I felt I was plowing virgin soil. After all, this material was new to the Reengineering Team when Mark Rhodes and Steve Jacobs presented it. It was new to the staff at the All Hands meeting when I presented it there. It was even new to Janice when it was first presented to her. I sensed that I had been talking about things that the members of the Senior Leadership Team had never thought about previously.

As I gathered up my transparencies, my projector, and my left-over handouts, I knew that I had come on strong with material that was largely foreign to the members of the Senior Leadership Team. I knew that our written report would present the materials again and consultants would talk about many of the same things in the future. I hoped that the Senior Leadership Team would realize they were in a new type of ball game, and that they would acknowledge the need to look at organizational change differently.

Short Shrift For Business Processes

The Business Process Subgroup, led by Michelle Padilla, had their report postponed several times and did not make their presentation until February 21, 1995. I was on leave at the time and could not attend. When I returned, I met Sheila Cooper, one of the team members, and stopped her long enough in the hall to get her view on how the report was received. She was depressed about the whole experience.

Sheila told me that when the Reengineering Team Subgroup walked into the meeting room some members of the Senior Leadership Team who had arrived early asked them why they were there. They responded that they were there at the request of the Senior Leadership Team to discuss business process reengineering as addressed in the report of the Reengineering Team. They soon discovered that the Senior Leadership Team had a full agenda, and they had been given very little time to present and discuss the subject. By this time, the Reengineering Team had submitted their written report. Sheila told me that it was evident that "the program directors had not read the report and they did not know anything about the recommendations in it." She asserted that they asked very basic questions, as if they knew nothing about reengineering. The thing that angered her most was that the work she had put in had been of no interest to them. Later, when the Reengineering Team came together to consider the implementation of some business process reengineering, Sheila no longer wanted to be part of the team.

Final Report

About a week before our final report was due, we received word that the Senior Leadership Team wanted it submitted by February 13th, two days early. This request made it impossible for the whole team to discuss both subgroup's reports prior to submission. The team made the decision that the overview would become Part A of the report, and the report on business processes would be Part B. Part A was distributed to the team on Friday, February 10th, for final review and discussion Monday morning, February 13th, at their team meeting. Part B was attached to Part A on Tuesday, February 14th, without review. Consequently, there were redundancies in the combined report. Late on Tuesday, a last-minute direction was sent to all team leaders that the recommendations should be organized in terms of who should make the decisions: the Assistant Secretary, Deputy Assistant Secretary, Senior Leadership Team, or others. So another last hurry-up effort was made to comply with this latest request.

In general, the Reengineering Team made recommendations for leadership and management of the reengineering effort, design efforts to implement the OSD Model, and procedures for identifying and improving core business processes.

Outcomes of the Reengineering Team

The Reengineering Team and the other restructuring teams had just been through the staff involvement phase of OESE's change process. Many of us saw this as the phase when all the staff of OESE were invited to advise the leadership on how the restructuring should be carried out. Some did not see it this way. For example, David Jackson and Bob Palone were just two of the influential people who took the position that restructuring was the administration's way of downsizing and getting rid of people. Others were asserting that this was merely an attempt to co-opt the staff. They asserted that if the staff had been involved in the design decisions, the goals and processes of restructuring would have been different—the administration had to involve the staff or they would not succeed with the restructuring.

It had yet to be seen what the leadership would do with the recommendations of the staff involvement phase. Ted Parker, a member of Janice's staff, was assigned the task of getting the recommendations arrayed for consideration by the Senior Leadership Team. On March 6, 1995, *OESE Today*, the OESE weekly newsletter, published a summary of the "decisions required to move OESE's restructuring to the next phase." It was something of an encouragement for the Reengineering Team to read:

> The decisions for consideration are grouped in six categories, based on the Organizational Systems Design Model used by the Reengineering Team. The categories or systems are [as follows]: technical, structural, decision making and information, reward, and renewal. Each system contributes

to an organizational model that reflects a variety of influences, such as the Department's mission, our legislation, public expectations, improved customer service, and systemic reform . . . The OSD systems . . . complement the OESE structure.

The Reengineering Team members were also pleased to see eight of our recommendations listed under the category of "technical systems," although the rationale for listing them as technical systems was puzzling. (The technical systems deal with the way products and services are produced and the methods and systems needed to do it. This includes the organization's business processes, technologies and facilities.) They were:

1. Train managers in the basic essentials of reengineering.

2. Develop a plan for consulting services and retain a managing consultant.

3. Include AFGE in the planning and training.

4. Conduct an audit of our culture and bring it into alignment with the plan.

5. Revise the OESE mission statement, and make the goals specific, measurable, achievable, and related to our mission.

6. Identify core competencies and identify those that are needed for the future.

7. Make an environmental review of the important groups in our environment and specify desired outcomes in relation to design choices.

8. Develop a work team development model with specific outcomes and expectations, and plan the training and support needed to reach desired outcomes.

Even if the OSD Model was not totally understood, the Reengineering Team was pleased to see that it was used to give the whole OESE restructuring effort an overall perspective. Janice accepted its validity and referred to it frequently. Phyllis Barajas, who had been transferred from OM to OESE , posted a diagram of it on her wall and referred to it even when she did not really understand it. In brief, it became a meaningful reference for some of the key people, even though it never became a controlling influence upon the reengineering effort.

The first two recommendations were acted upon: the AFGE was involved to the fullest extent in all deliberations and did become a controlling influence (although I doubted the AFGE was brought into the deliberations because of our recommendation. The OESE and the AFGE had a *Collective Bargaining Agreement,* which made their involvement mandatory.) And there was some, though a limited amount, of training in the basic essentials of reengineering for managers. (The Senior Leadership Team did have an introduction to the OSD Model as a part of their brief training with Mark Rhodes. The team leaders and group leaders also had an introduction to it from Mark, as a component in one of their training sessions.)

Nothing was ever done about the other six recommendations.

The Reengineering Team also discovered three of our recommendations under the category of "decision making and information." (Again, there was little understanding of the OSD Model. Decision-making systems deal with what decisions are made, where they are made, how they are made, who should make them, and the information needed to make them.) The three recommendations stated:

1. That OESE establish a permanent Reengineering unit of four or more staff to assist management in the reengineering process.

2. That the OESE acquire the expertise of an external consultant with reengineering experience.

3. That ongoing staff and team training for reengineering be undertaken.

None of the other recommendations were acted upon. Although a permanent reengineering unit of four or more staff was not established, a special assistant for restructuring was appointed in the reassignment phase. He had no particular knowledge about his role. Phyllis Barajas, who first came to OESE when OM was downsizing, was later made a Special Assistant to the Assistant Secretary, and helped Janice Jackson. And although Mark Rhodes was used for a very limited amount of consulting, he was never contracted to implement his proposed plan.

At the end of the article in *OESE Today* the newsletter stated: "All of the above [recommendations] are under consideration by the Senior Staff, who welcome your comments and suggestions." The newsletter had nothing to say about a number of other recommendations by the Reengineering Team. Presumably, they were not under consideration.

Months later I inquired of Ted Parker, who attended most of the meetings of the Senior Leadership Team as a staff member assigned to Janice, what they had done about the team reports. Ted responded, "There never was a response of any kind from the Senior Leadership Team about the work of the restructuring teams. Those reports and their recommendations went into the 'black box.'" I turned this information over in my mind. Six teams, sixty staff, 25 percent of OESE, worked on this restructuring for fifteen weeks. There was no report other than the coverage given by *OESE Today,* saying that the Senior Leadership Team had some of their recommendations under consideration. The people who volunteered for this work were their greatest asset in the restructuring effort. If we figure that each team member gave four hours of work a week (and I know that some gave much more and some gave much less), 21,600 person hours of work had gone unacknowledged and mostly disregarded!

A number of other outcomes, though limited, could also be credited to the Reengineering Team:

- The Assistant Secretary showed up at one of the team meetings I attended, presumably to indicate his interest in the restructuring work of the team. Whether he attended any other meetings I do not know. He did speak on behalf of the restructuring at some of the All Hands meetings. How much of his time he devoted to the restructuring of OESE is also unknown. From my perspective, there was very little visible evidence of his personal involvement for the rank and file to witness.

- Mark Rhodes was asked to present a plan and later asked to put it into a proposal. His proposal laid out his plan in the form of a Gannt chart (a chart which displays a project's task and time allocations). It was discussed on three scheduled meetings (February 2, 1995; March 14, 1995; and April 13, 1995) but never implemented. Mark's capabilities were never used in the types of work in which he was most effective and which OESE so desperately needed.

- Craig Polite, another consultant, was used on a few occasions. He was also used in a fairly superficial way. He did not have the depth of knowledge or the experience that Mark had.

- Core process reengineering was explored with the Human Resource Systems Innovation Group, and later with Mark Rhodes, but it was never implemented. Joseph Colantuoni, Director of HRSE, and Joseph Fucello of his staff, met with Janice and the Reengineering Team on several occasions to negotiate assistance with business process reengineering. The HRSE presented a proposal in August 1995, that was considered non-responsive and no assistance was requested. In addition, a team was assembled to reengineer the travel planning and reimbursement system, but that was abandoned when it was discovered that the Department had awarded a contract to greatly modify it.

Lessons Learned

By the end of the planning phase with the volunteer restructuring teams, a number of problems had become evident, and some important lessons were being driven home. The lessons would be reinforced as the restructuring of OESE evolved. The problems were (1) attempting organizational change with inadequate leadership, (2) not utilizing professional experts when in-house expertise was inadequate, (3) attempting to accomplish radical change with a bottom-up approach, and (4) not providing the restructuring teams with specific charters and boundaries.

- **Organizational change, especially a fundamental rethinking and radical departure from the past, requires knowledgeable and skilled leadership.** The formation and implementation of the Reengineering Team, and other restructuring teams, revealed as much about the leadership of OESE's restructuring as it did about the teams. Measured against professional standards, Tom Payzant was not providing sufficient time to the restructuring effort, Janice Jackson was in over her head and overloaded, and the Senior Leadership Team did not see the big picture and were making decisions that supported their programs to the detriment of the restructuring process. These leadership deficits would take their toll over the course of the restructuring. Consider the following:

First, Tom formally supported the restructuring effort, but did not devote a large amount of time to the effort. He presided over the meetings of the Senior Leadership Team, where the restructuring effort was one of many agenda considerations, but this was not visible to most of the staff. He made formal statements at the All Hands meetings supporting the restructuring, which was visible to the rank and file. But it appeared that the restructuring was only one of a number of concerns that he addressed. His response to me at the time of my oral report indicated that he was not willing to give any more time to it. In a paper by Hall, Rosenthal, & Wade on "How to Make Reengineering Really Work" (1993), the authors state that the chief executive should give 20 to 50 percent of his time to a reengineering project. It did not appear that the Assistant Secretary was giving this level of effort to the reengineering of his Office.

Second, Tom had delegated the restructuring to Janice, the Deputy Assistant Secretary. She had an unreasonable work load. It soon became known that she was spending many long days and her weekends trying to keep up with the work of restructuring. Because of this, the Reengineering Team had recommended that a staff of up to four persons be provided to help her do her job. The one person helping her, Ted Parker, was reassigned to the IAP during the reassignment of staff. And later two more staff were provided to give Janice assistance: Frank Robinson, who had no special knowledge of organizational change, was assigned because of the absence of any appropriate criteria in the reassignment process. And Phyllis Barajas was brought to OESE from OM. Their depth of knowledge in restructuring proved to be insufficient.

A third leadership problem was the fact that the Senior Leadership Team never really bought into the big picture. The restructuring of OESE remained a reorganization, not a reengineering issue. It never became an issue of institutional change with technical and social systems that had to be kept in alignment. The Reengineering Team attempted to get at this limited vision with the OSD Model, but we were not successful. There was a superficial recognition of its validity and a superficial understanding of it, but it was never given serious consideration in practice. In addition, the Reengineering Team attempted to redefine the restructuring effort in terms of reengineering, driving home the fact that it was a fundamental rethinking and a radical departure from the past, taking place in a short period of time.

A fourth problem was the embodiment of decision making within the Senior Leadership Team, consisting of the Assistant and Deputy Assistant Secretaries, the program directors and a few administrative staff. The program directors were a formidable body of decision-makers, both as members of the Senior Leadership Team and as independent managers of their programs. But program responsibilities came before team responsibilities. And program directors would not weaken their programs for a restructuring effort for which they were not held personally accountable.

Lastly, there was no steering committee or other body to make decisions and guide the reengineering. If a broad-based steering committee with authority and power had been established in the beginning, there would have been a broader perspective and a different entity to lead the change effort. Perhaps the myopic viewpoints of the Senior Leadership Team would not have prevailed.

- **With inadequate "in-house" expertise, it is necessary to obtain expertise from the outside.** A major problem for this in-house project was the fact that they did not have the expertise to pull it off. Most of the leadership had been involved in reorganizations, and some of them had training in facilitating small groups. Although Janice Jackson had been involved in reorganization projects prior to coming to ED, they were nothing like the OESE "restructuring." Phyllis Barajas had some training in organizational change at the Kennedy Center and demonstrated knowledge of small group facilitation techniques, but this degree of organizational change seemed beyond her. The most critical knowledge deficiency for the situation in which OESE found itself was that of organizational design. As Paul Gustavson says, "Organizations are perfectly designed to get the results they get" (*Organizational Systems Design Guidebook* 1993: 1). Nobody in-house had the knowledge to design an organization that would obtain the results they desired, and nobody in-house understood the cause and effect relationships between what they were doing and what they were getting.

Furthermore, by not having the knowledge to conceptualize a reasonable design and expedite work on it, they did not know that they needed help. They were reorganizing, not reengineering. Janice and a few others were exceptions. She did seek a proposal and an elaboration of it for possible outside assistance from Mark Rhodes, but it was never implemented.

- **"Attempting to reengineer from the bottom (or middle) up is one of the common causes of failure."** So states Theodore B. Kinni, in his paper entitled "A Reengineering Primer" (1994). And, Hall, Rosenthal and Wade (1993), writing about why reengineering projects fail, assert that assigning average performers is one of the particularly damaging practices. OESE did not know any better.

When one considers the roles of the restructuring teams, such as the Reengineering Team, it is evident that the leadership had decided to use a bottom-up approach rather than a top-down approach. Any person could volunteer for one of the teams, and no volunteers were refused membership. Few volunteers had any significant knowledge or experience for the teams to which they were assigned, and no training as team members. I saw very little in the reports of the other teams that indicated any special knowledge. I knew that much of what was recommended would not be implemented. I assume that this was a major reason why the reports were ignored by the Senior Leadership Team.

Not only were the teams weak in expertise, but they were also not given support. The better team members were at the mercy of their program bosses when it came to priorities. They were constantly being siphoned off for program work, which came first. Others left the teams for a variety of reasons and nobody really showed any concern about the problem. In the end, work fell to a few of the self-motivated, and conscientious staff who were willing to contribute an extra effort.

- **When teams are constituted they must have a clear charter and a clear focus on outcomes.** The restructuring teams could not tell from the few sentences describing their work where it started and ended. There were no boundaries for decision making, and there were no specific limits to their empowerment. For example, the Reengineering Team requested a more specific charter, but never received it. Later, we wanted an endorsement to look at the big picture and even persuaded Janice to let us have a go at it. But some teams never asked if what they were doing was acceptable. They made assumptions, adopted expectations, and acted upon them, whether they were acceptable or not. Like the Reengineering Team, several of the other teams attempted to get their message across to the Senior Leadership Team. All but one of the teams' reports were ignored.

In addition, the restructuring teams were working with vague and varied notions about performance outcomes. Chuck Hansen and his team were thinking "outside the box" when they proposed the restructuring of OESE. Theirs was a fundamental rethinking and radical redesign of OESE. Putting aside the questions of whether giving "one face to the customer" was realistic, the OESE leadership had not determined what a person working in a regional team had to know or be able to do to make this proposed structure work. For example, nobody had done any job analyses or any job models of what a regional team member would do, and no team perceived that this was needed. Without working with desired outcomes, specific objectives, and job performance models, the work of the restructuring teams resulted in futile, unfocused busywork.

Both of these mistakes—the lack of a charter and the lack of a clear focus on outcomes—had their impact in other phases of the restructuring. Later I discuss the impact of no charter in other types of teams and how a lack of focus on desired outcomes wasted much of the effort put into training.

Although they did not realize it, the leadership of OESE was moving into the *Middle of a Muddle*. They did not have in-house expertise to implement fundamental, radical changes in conducting their business, and they did not perceive a need to acquire it. Add to this the extensive work of the restructuring teams without clear charters or boundaries, composed of volunteers with little expertise, and they did not have much of a foundation on which to build. In spite of their desire to delay the implementation, Deputy Secretary Madeleine Kunin was insisting that we move ahead on schedule. They now had a stack of team reports. What were they going to do with this stuff? Most of it would be ignored. It would get worse!

three

Reassignment Debacle

Mary Jean LeTendre, Program Director for the Compensatory Education Program (CEP), that is, Title 1, ESEA, acknowledged on August 24, 1995 that she was very concerned about getting the work of her program done under the new OESE structure. She did so at a meeting of program directors, group leaders, and team leaders that had been called to discuss the problems and issues of implementing the restructuring. After she posed a number of questions related to her concern I remarked, "I can give you another half-dozen questions that relate to the same problem of getting work done, and getting it done right. The day we reassign everyone to his or her position in the new structure is the day we'll see a marked drop in productivity!" My statement obviously startled the participants. When Joe Colantouni, the facilitator, asked what I meant by that statement, I explained "I thought many people would be assigned jobs they could not perform well or at all, that the expertise we have well organized and focused now will be in disarray. We'll have to develop the expertise in other people or make other arrangements with the people who already have the expertise." Joe announced that it was time for a break and the room began to buzz.

Mary Jean turned to me and wanted to talk. I saw that she was worried and emotionally involved with this problem. She was concerned about the competence of the staff that would be assigned to her. She asked, "How can I get the work done when longevity is more important than quality in the assignment of staff?" She was referring to the fact that an employee with more longevity in the federal government would be given preference in the reassignment process over persons more qualified. I reminded her that in the reassignment process program directors have the last word; they would be able to make adjustments in the assignments needed to make their programs work. She didn't think so. In her mind, making such adjustments could be a major task and expressed doubt that she would be allowed to do it.

"But you are accountable for your program and as a manager, you can't allow incapable staff to be assigned to you," I said. "Yes," she replied, "I am accountable, but I don't know what I'll be allowed to do."

Reassignment by Staff Preference

The Regional Restructuring Team (RRT) had been given the responsibility for prescribing the criteria and the processes that would be used in the reassignment of staff. When they began their work they assumed that they would complete and submit it on the same schedule as the other restructuring teams. At the time of its submission Harris Taylor, speaking for the team said, "If they don't like our recommendations, let them change them. They are the managers. It is their job to make decisions." But Janice Jackson (Deputy Assistant Secretary) would not let them off the hook. This was a highly emotional issue, and she wanted to be able to say that she was implementing the recommendations of the RRT. Consequently, she kept the RRT in the fray for many months.

Most members of the RRT were African Americans and felt that they were the victims of discrimination. They did not trust management to be fair in the reassignments. An organization called Blacks in Government (BIG) was also making its influence felt. And during this period of negotiation, the charge of racism had boiled over in anger and bitterness. Deputy Secretary Janice Jackson did not want it to appear that management was forcing the reassignment process down the throats of the staff, but, rather, that the recommendations came from the RRT. Whenever she discussed the reassignment process, she kept reiterating that it must be perceived as fair or it would not be accepted.

Amos Goodfox, the leader of the RRT, had a difficult time with his team. Like the other restructuring teams, the RRT had been given no charter and hardly any boundaries. So they developed their ideas as they saw fit. Amos invited me to attend his team meetings to observe what was happening and to provide any help I could.

Amos' team was pursuing a wide open reassignment process in which staff from any program could move to any other program, and could apply for any position in that program within their own grade classification and level. (The administration had affirmed that there would be no grade or salary mobility in the reassignment process, in other words, only lateral moves.) A portion of the Office of Educational Research and Information (OERI) had implemented a similar approach to personnel assignments, and over a period of a few years they had been fairly successful in giving most staff the assignments they desired. However, they did not attempt to accommodate all requests in a single year—they spread it over a three-year period. A spokesperson from OERI had briefed the Senior Leadership Team on their experience and had given their reassignment process a positive spin. Although the program directors had a great deal of anxiety about it, they went along with it.

On April 7, 1995, I attended my first meeting of the RRT. My interest was high and I was anxious to see what was occurring. I had no intention of entering into any debates. I knew that I had my own set of biases and did not want to introduce them at this time. This was their team and I was an outside observer.

I did not have to wait long. Shortly after the meeting started, Dorothea Perkins stated emphatically that the team members intended to design a process that would not allow management to pick and choose the people it wanted and to place them wherever it pleased. She asserted that staff members should have the right to select the programs, teams, and positions they wanted. She argued that this would give the staff the opportunity to move out of undesirable positions and into a "new career" within OESE.

From the emotional tone of Dorothea's remarks, and the remarks of other minority members on the team, I sensed that this was, at least partially, a racially motivated intervention through which minority

75

staff could overturn the personnel decisions of management. Nobody in the room took exception with Dorothea's remark. Everyone appeared to support a wide open reassignment process and evidently saw a benefit in it for themselves. This became increasingly apparent as the reassignment process was designed and implemented.

Staffing for Program Needs

Staffing by staff preference and staffing to meet program needs were conflicting goals heading for a collision. Months before the reassignment process had been determined, program directors had been asked to plan the personnel needs of their programs with the regional service teams and the program service teams in mind. Cathy Schagh, Program Director of the Impact Aid Program (IAP), called Carroll Dexter, Arnett Smith and me into a meeting to think through the personnel needs for the various teams. At this point in time, none of us had a very realistic perception of how the reassignments would be made and assumed more influence than any of us would have. We were concerned, but not as concerned as we would have been had we realized how little influence we would have on the reassignments.

The four of us thought through how many and which IAP staff would be needed for each regional team. Most of the staff were specialists, not generalists. Some had little experience in the field, some had considerable experience. Consequently, we knew that we would have to pair experienced staff with inexperienced staff plus take into consideration special knowledge and skills. Finally, there was the likely problem of losing some whose loss would be a severe hardship for the program. We all feared what this would do.

At the same time we had to consider the personnel needs of the Program Service Team. These people would deal with the policy, administration, and basic functions of the IAP, rather than with daily customer services. At least, that was the rationale. It was assumed that most of the people in these jobs would want to stay in these positions, although if they were not protected, they could be bumped by someone with greater seniority. There were also a couple of positions that needed to be phased out or combined with other positions. Cathy had been waiting for the reassignment of staff to make those adjustments.

Janice scheduled meetings with each of the program directors to try to understand their personnel needs and concerns prior to the reassignment. Cathy brought three of her "lieutenants"—Carroll Dexter, Arnett Smith, and me—together to think through the personnel reassignment problems and discuss them with Janice. The four of us met prior to the meeting with Janice and discussed a few of the problems. When we discussed the probable loss of valuable staff, Cathy said, "Nobody should be held back from what he or she wanted, if possible."

When Janice arrived, Cathy distributed a list of IAP staff and asked Carroll, Arnett and I to describe the staff that we supervised and their importance to the Program. Cathy started with her immediate staff. Skill and personality issues of various staff members were discussed in terms of how they performed their jobs and the ease by which they could be transferred to other programs. I had never been in a meeting in which personnel were discussed with such frankness. The frankness was prompted by the seriousness of the reassignment process. The character of the staff could make or break a program.

Janice then turned the discussion to the overall problems and concerns of reengineering and wanted to know how the IAP would be effected. The following issues were discussed:

- **Loss of Community.** While the staff of the IAP now occupied one large suite of offices, many would soon be dispersed throughout two floors of the building. We all believed that the anticipated withering sense of community would be a significant loss.

- **Security of Files.** We were all concerned about the security and availability of the "official files," since our centralized filing system would now be decentralized. Control and availability of files, we thought, would be a major problem.

- **Complexity of the IAP.** The complexity of the IAP and its application to school districts and states required a relatively long apprenticeship. It was not realistic for others in the regional teams and new people to the Program to learn it quickly. It was also going to be difficult for staff in the IAP to learn parts of the program with which they had never dealt.

- **Preparing for Change.** The shift to the new organizational structure would not be easy, especially considering the scale of the change. Getting the staff ready for it was going to be a problem.

- **Choice.** There would be problems in giving staff an opportunity to change jobs while still meeting the needs of the customers. Many of the staff would not have the skill levels to meet customer needs until trained in their jobs. There would be a period of incapacity until this could be accomplished.

As we concluded the meeting I felt that Janice must have a much better understanding of the problems our Program was facing. But I really wondered if she had changed any of her thinking about integrating the IAP with other programs. Did she still think that IAP could be part of a "one face to the customer" approach? I also wondered what other program leaders were telling Janice about their programs.

By the end of March 1995, each of the program directors in OESE had gone through a similar process to plan for their personnel needs. The key leaders in each program had discussed their internal program needs, and they had communicated to Janice some of their concerns and personnel assessments. The process accentuated the contrast between the conflicting personnel goals of the directors and staff expectations for open reassignment. Anxiety about the reassignment was building. On one side, the RRT and other groups were pushing toward a major overhaul of the staffing configuration from their own perspectives. On the management side, the concern for program delivery without the requisite personnel was growing.

Minimizing the Work Force

In the years that I spent in the Department, first as a consultant who worked intermittently and later as a career employee, I observed a significant change in the qualifications of the work force. When I first worked in the Department, most of the professional grade employees had graduate degrees and professional experience in education, often in administrative and other leadership positions.

Over the years, I witnessed a reduction in the level of formal education and experience in education. Gradually, the education and experience criteria were dropped from the position descriptions, or other criteria could be substituted. This made it possible for more and more people without careers in education or collegiate degrees of any kind, to hold professional jobs. In contrast, when I first worked in IAP, the program was staffed with numerous employees who had been former superintendents, principals, financial officers, and other types of school officials. Because of the vast amount of experience they had in the field, these folks knew how school systems were administered, how schools managed their financial systems, and how the local districts interacted with the state departments of education. They could understand financial reports and knew how school systems disguised their financial statements to obtain larger entitlements from the IAP. Most importantly, they could tell when a school system was in a bind and really hurting. In those days there was a unique camaraderie and respect between educators in the field and educators in the Department.

One of the best examples of the reduction of expertise is the GS-1720 series. This classification of positions is also known as the "Education Program Series." It was established by the U. S. Office of Personnel Management specifically for the employment of professional personnel in the Department of Education. It covers grades five through 14. (See the general schedule grades for the Washington-Baltimore area in Table 1.) It had a point system applied to the criteria which resulted in the determination of an employee's grade qualification, that is, whether the person could be employed in this series at some level from GS-5 to GS-14. The general description of the series states:

> This series covers professional education positions responsible for promoting, coordinating, improving educational policies, program, standards, activities, and opportunities in accordance with national policies and objectives. Positions in this series primarily involve the performance, supervision, or formulation and implementation of policy concerning education problems and issues. These positions require a professional knowledge of educational theories, prin-

Table 1
1998 General Schedule Locality Rates for Washington-Baltimore

Grade	Annual Rates for Steps (in dollars)									
	1	2	3	4	5	6	7	8	9	10
1	13,902	14,366	14,828	15,288	15,753	16,024	16,479	16,939	16,958	17,393
2	15,630	16,003	16,521	16,958	17,147	17,651	18,155	18,660	19,164	19,668
3	17,055	17,623	18,192	18,760	19,329	19,898	20,466	21,035	21,603	22,172
4	19,146	19,784	20,422	21,060	21,699	22,337	22,975	23,613	24,252	24,890
5	21,421	22,135	22,850	23,564	24,278	24,993	25,707	26,422	27,136	27,851
6	23,876	24,672	25,468	26,264	27,060	27,856	28,652	29,448	30,244	31,040
7	26,532	27,416	28,300	29,184	30,068	30,952	31,836	32,719	33,603	34,487
8	29,384	30,364	31,343	32,323	33,302	34,281	35,261	36,240	37,219	38,199
9	32,457	33,539	34,621	35,704	36,786	37,868	38,951	40,033	41,116	42,198
10	35,742	36,934	38,126	39,318	40,509	41,701	42,893	44,085	45,277	46,468
11	39,270	40,579	41,888	43,197	44,505	45,814	47,123	48,431	49,740	51,049
12	47,066	48,635	50,205	51,774	53,343	54,913	56,482	58,051	59,621	61,190
13	55,969	57,835	59,700	61,565	63,431	65,296	67,162	69,027	70,893	72,758
14	66,138	68,343	70,547	72,752	74,956	77,160	79,365	81,569	83,774	85,978
15	77,798	80,391	82,985	85,579	88,173	90,767	93,360	95,954	98,548	101,142

Source: U.S. Office of Personnel Management.

ciples, processes, and practices at early childhood, elementary, secondary, or post-secondary levels, or in adult and continuing education . . . (U.S. Office of Personnel Management: 1982.)

At one time the 1720 series had a minimum requirement of a university degree that included at least 24 semester hours in a field related to the position in which at least 9 hours must have been in educational courses. As one ascended through GS-7 to GS-14, graduate study was required which included a master's and eventually a doctor's degree, or equivalents. Today there are no educational requirements or any experience requirements in schooling for these jobs.

When OESE decided to restructure, a powerful vehicle for minimizing work force qualifications came into being—a vehicle known as the "generic position description." The generic position descriptions developed for OESE were brief descriptions that fit a variety of jobs. The specificity was lost and prior criteria eliminated. For example, the description and criteria for the GS-1720 series was 61 pages long (admittedly an overkill). A generic position description used in the restructuring of OESE is two and one-half pages long. In fairness, it should be pointed out that the current GS-1720-14 position description does specify some general knowledge requirements, but there are no criteria for selection.

Without specifying professional standards or specific qualifications, administrators could place a wide range of "qualified" people in a position. Employees could also claim that they had the credentials for a much larger number of positions. With the reorganizing of OESE into regional teams, generic position descriptions provided the flexibility management needed to ease the reassignment problems. The trend toward fewer experienced educators in the Department expanded.

Today there are few barriers to keep minimally qualified people from obtaining professional positions in OESE. People making employment decisions now have a variety of other reasons to place individuals in jobs. And with the loss of the professional educator, the culture has drastically changed. A key question for OESE now is, "How is the minimizing of the personnel requirements affecting the delivery of services in the restructured OESE?"

Program Protection

The belief was widespread that the program directors were manipulating the reassignment process as best they could to preserve the capability of their programs to deliver services. Although the criteria and the processes for the reassignment of personnel were not finalized, the program directors knew enough to feel very uneasy. It wouldn't be unreasonable to predict that under this situation, the program directors would do anything they could to protect their ability to deliver on the programs for which they were accountable. So most, if not all program directors, were trying to keep as many good people in the program's service teams as possible. At the same time, they were trying to influence as many people as possible to remain with the whole program.

At this point, none of us knew who would have the final say in selecting the members of the "core" teams (i.e., program service teams). On April 17, 1995, I decided to attend another meeting of the RRT to see how the reassignment discussions were progressing. One member quoted Tom Payzant as saying, "The program directors will *not* have the final say in this selection . . . The RRT will come up with the criteria for the selection of core team members." Another team member pulled money out of his pocket and put it on the table: "I say that the program directors will be making those selections regardless of what Tom or Janice say. Does anybody want to take me on?" Nobody did.

Early one morning when I arrived for work, Harris Taylor was bringing some of his colleagues up-to-date with the reassignment discussion and presenting his views to a small group of staff just outside of my office. Harris, an influential member of the RRT and a persuasive person among his peers, was eagerly talking about the team meeting that had taken place the day before. He was uninhibited about discussing what was going on, and eager to predict what was going to take place. I thought that Harris's point of view was typical of the general attitude. Harris said: "The core teams are too big. The IAP is going to have 17 staff and CEP is going to have 16 staff. The directors will have the first pick of the people for their immediate staffs. There won't be much that any individual will be able to do about this." He continued, "This isn't in keeping with the purpose of the regional teams. They should have the strongest people because that is where the real action is."

Harris knew that the program directors had been asked to provide Janice with numbers, types and grades of people that would be assigned to each of the ten regional teams. He told me that he thought that in the end individuals would have little say about their assignments. He said that he partially based this statement on the fact that the RRT had proposed a committee made up of 50 percent grade 14s and above, and 50 percent grade 13s and below to determine assignments, but the idea was rejected. He implied that the program directors would not have any control over the reassignment process. I had not previously known of this proposal, or any of the arguments for or against it by the leadership, but I assumed that Harris was correct. I doubted if it had ever been given much consideration.

Harris was also concerned about the interpersonal dynamics of the assignment process. He asserted that it would be hard for a person who wanted a career in the Department to go against the wishes of a program director when that program director wanted a staff person in a particular slot. They had the most power over an employee's future.

In fact, I had heard several reliable reports that program directors were talking to staff in order to persuade them to request assignments that the program directors wanted them to take. I knew that most of the people with positions on the proposed IAP program service team did not want to move, but some were afraid they might be bumped. Janice became very defensive about these rumors. She frequently assured individuals and groups with which she met that they were not true. "The reassignments are not cast in stone!" she said.

Factoring in Buyout Reductions

On March 31, 1995, the Department gave buyouts to 382 staff. Thirty-seven of these came from OESE. The timing of the Department's buyouts, coming right in the middle of the reassignment of staff, added to the confusion. The IAP, in which I worked, lost 10 people. Fortunately, they were not all leaving at one time, but the loss of senior staff became a constant topic of discussion. How would such a significant loss be factored into the reassignments? How should one attempt to position oneself if he or she wanted to move into an upcoming vacancy?

This was one of four buyouts. The first buyout in the Department of Education was offered from April 29 to May 3, 1994, and 388 retirements were approved. The second buyout was from November 28 to December 30, 1994, and 28 were approved. The third buyout was offered between January 27 and February 3, 1995, and 15 were approved. The fourth round was offered between March 10 to March 31, 1995, making a total of 811 employees. Three hundred and thirty-two of these employees continued to work on a deferred basis, but all were gone by December 1996.

The significance of the buyouts was discussed from many perspectives, depending upon how a person saw it impacting upon his or her personal well-being. Those concerned about the delivery of programs were concerned about the loss of expertise, because most of the staff leaving were experienced. Those anxious to advance in their careers looked forward to opportunities these staff left behind. They often attempted to position themselves for selection.

Those who were leaving also reacted differently. Some were happy about the timing, because they would not have to go through the changes. Others, even if they had delayed their departure, decided that they would step out of their roles of responsibility in the reassignment process, because they could still keep their grade and salary. Most continued in their current roles until the day of departure came.

The Clinton administration officials could not be more upbeat about the downsizing of the federal work force. The civilian work force was down to 2.02 million after the two-year reduction at the end of 1995. By 1999, they expected to be down to 1.88 million, a 13% reduction. "Nothing has helped our credibility more on [reinventing government] than the fact that government is smaller," said Elaine Kamarch, who headed Vice President Gore's National Performance Review (*"Government Executive"* May: 1995).

Two National Performance Review (NPR) activities, the buyouts and the reengineering of OESE, occurred simultaneously. There were advantages and disadvantages of doing this. One advantage was cost. Although the buyout incentive cost up to $25,000 per person, a reduction in force (RIF) would have cost more. If "RIFed," the government would have to pay the laid-off employee severance pay, unemployment benefits, and the costs of out-placement services. Also, by targeting buyout offers, the Administration met the NPR goals of reducing the numbers of supervisors, managers and overhead employees. In the Department of Education, buyouts made the reduction in the span of control less contentious, because a large number of supervisors and managers would take the buyout and leave.

On the other hand, the loss of many supervisors and managers really hurt OESE in the loss of knowledge and skill. Thirty-one of the 37 people taking buyouts in OESE (84 percent) were in grades 13 through 15. Indeed, in a previous buyout, the loss of key people in the construction program within IAP had been devastating. When Cathy learned that I had applied for the buyout she was alarmed and wanted to talk with me about delaying it. After listening to my justification, she concurred that I was making a wise decision. Although most of the people took deferred buyouts, there is little doubt that they cost OESE in knowledge and skill when they did occur. It was not a planned reduction in the labor force related to specific roles. Although the Department originally placed certain limitations on the buyouts, in the end they decided to accommodate any employee who requested the buyout. OESE had to make adjustments in their labor force the best way they could.

Union Resistance

During the early phase of the reengineering of OESE, a modified collective bargaining agreement between the Department of Education and the American Federation of Government Employees was negotiated and became effective February 23, 1995. Because the management of OESE knew that it was essential to have the union involved in the restructuring, most meetings of the Senior Leadership Team were open to union representatives. The union also had a voice in the Labor-Management Partnership Council (LMPC) and through it shared in the decision making. The union had misgivings about the whole restructuring plan from the beginning, and the reassignment of staff was an especially difficult hurdle for them.

On May 11, 1995, I attended a three and one-half hour meeting of the so-called "Steering Committee" that was quite argumentative and, I think, illustrated many of the problems involved in the resolution of the reassignment process. Two union members were there to present their points of view. Debbie Kalnasy was also invited because of her expertise in personnel matters. Everyone sensed that this was a critical time in the resolution of the reassignment issues. I had made a special effort to get to this meeting.

The event that prompted the meeting was the lack of consensus between the RRT and management concerning the reassignment issues. There had been a previous discordant four-hour meeting between the RRT and management in which Janice Jackson had assumed agreement had been reached about the reassignment. However, a presentation by Daisey Greenfield of the RRT at the recent All Hands meeting revealed that this was not true. It appeared to me that Janice wanted to get a consensus from the Steering Committee to use as leverage to resolve the differences. She came to the meeting with two lists as handouts: a list of 20 restructuring steps (events) that the RRT had set forth, with some notes about management's differences, and a list of nine "Points of Consideration" for the reassignment activities that also cited her differences with the RRT.

The two union representatives at the meeting made it known that the union would have to approve the process used by OESE before it could be adopted. One of the union representatives, Carolyn Johnson, also pointed out that their presence at the meeting could not be construed as approval of any consensus they might reach but that people higher in the union would be making the decisions. This comment surely had to have dashed Janice's hopes of reaching a consensus with the union.

Two specific issues were on the top of the list of problems for the union representatives. They first wanted to know what the definition of "equally qualified" criterion meant. They claimed that there was no working definition of this criterion, so there was no way that it could be used. The second issue was the problem of incumbency. The union insisted that all incumbents have a right to their current position unless the position is altered by the restructuring plan. Many in the meeting did not agree with the union on this issue. For example, it was a new issue for Debbie Kalnasy, who worked in the "front office," and she was greatly disturbed. She exclaimed, "You mean that I will now have to fight to retain my position?" And although Janice tried to get the Committee to come to a consensus on the issue, she was unsuccessful.

Many people were also concerned about the openness of the process. Some felt that management could not be trusted with the reassignment process and that either the staff needed to share in the process or a neutral committee outside of OESE be delegated the responsibility. Some asserted that the only time that management should get into the process was at the end, and any changes made must be justified.

There was also disagreement about the openness of the preference forms submitted by the employees—the union wanted them open to all, others did not—and about what part the union would play in the decision-making process. Except for its role in the LMPC, management was limiting the union's role to observation only. Carolyn stated that two union representatives should be available at all times when personnel decisions were made. Janice, whose patience had begun to wear thin, responded, "I don't think so."

As time went on, it was clear to me that Janice was near the end of her rope and could not take much more controversy. She came to this meeting with the hope of getting a consensus on these divisive issues. Not only was she not successful, but she was also experiencing some new issues. People were staking out positions she could not accept. In these situations she kept saying, "I hear you. I hear you. Your point of view will be communicated." She kept calling, "Time" and moving on in frustration to other issues.

The meeting terminated long after my work day had ended, and I was tired. I gathered up my notes and handouts, took the elevator down to my office, secured my files, and walked three blocks to the Metro train for a ride home. I found a seat at the back of one of the cars, and tried to make some sense of the meeting in which I had just participated.

As I thought about the work of the RST, I was convinced that it had been a mistake to give them no parameters in prescribing the reassignment process. They had a complete lack of trust in management, and they had members who could take it to extremes. They could also take their points of view and carry the day with the union, LMPC, BIG, and others. They were like a team of horses that got the bit in their teeth and were running wild.

I also thought about the straight jacket that management was facing. The federal government was so bound up by the partnership agreement with the union and federal personnel regulations that it had become paralyzed. It was so difficult to fire and discipline employees that managers avoided these options at all cost. Consequently, the Department of Education had ended up with a labor force inadequate for the job. Because of this, management was forced to make decisions about their limited options for persons they placed in positions of responsibility and leadership. Of course, this led to management decisions that did not go over well with those who were passed over, which, in turn, created distrust, charges of discrimination, an acrimonious work force, and low morale.

The long established practice of "bumping" (taking another person's job because of seniority) had always been a problem for me. It was also used when there was a RIF. The intent was to bring some fairness for the employees in downsizing, but it was seldom helpful to the programs. The criteria for bumping were based on seniority, not competencies. And I knew that the reassignment effort was not going to be competency related either. I thought to myself, "So many systems in the federal government work against it."

All of this seemed to be feeding on itself like a self-generating explosion, and I was depressed. I asked myself, "How can we break this vicious cycle for the benefit of the people involved and the school children of the nation?" When I got to the end of the Metro line in Vienna, Virginia, I took the escalator to the ground level, walked to my car, drove home, and had a stiff drink.

On May 24th, there was another quarrelsome meeting of the Steering Committee to which Janice had invited two members from OERI. A similar open reassignment of staff had been carried out in OERI over a three-year period for a portion of the Office. Thomas Johnston, from the Human Resources Group, OM, was also in attendance as an expert in personnel regulations and procedures. Four union issues were made the focus of the meeting:

1. **Incumbency.** The union insisted that all incumbents have a right to their current position whenever the position was not changed in the restructuring. OESE leadership wanted every position to be open for possible change.

2. **Public reassignment processes.** Many staff wanted their preference forms available only to those few persons who are going to manage the assignments. The union wanted the preference forms open to all parties to view.

3. **Parties to the assignment process.** The union wanted to be a part of the reassignment process, not serve merely as an advisory observer. The management maintained that the Partnership Agreement with the union did not give them the right to place individuals in their jobs.

4. **Qualifications.** The union insisted that there was no working definition of "equally qualified," so there was no way that criterion could be applied. The management believed that a consensus could be reached on this issue when it occurred.

Janice was obviously upset about the union demands. After laying out the four issues, she proclaimed: "The union has been invited to all meetings and nothing has been discussed without them present. But somehow, the officials of the union were not listening to their own representatives. Now they come up with these objections. They want a role way beyond that of advisory." She also asserted that most of the staff are not in concurrence with the union officials in these matters. She warned: "If this can't be negotiated at the Office level through our own Partnership Council, we will have to go to the Department level . . . This delay means that we can not put any dates down yet for the reassignment."

The two persons from OERI said that they were having similar problems with the union. Carolyn Johnson, the union representative, confirmed that she had been communicating regularly with the union's Department officials and appeared sympathetic to Janice's concerns. But she reminded everyone, "I have been saying all along that I am not the person who makes the decisions."

Janice received support for most of her positions. Thomas Johnston said, "I see all kinds of grievances over the incumbency issue . . . How can we say 'openness,' but not certain positions?" I added, "I am not only opposed to the union participating in the reassignment of individuals, but I am also opposed to the Labor/Union Partnership Council having to approve the selections!" However, I also stated, "I don't see how the definition of 'equally qualified' can be applied without establishing criteria and there are no specific criteria in the position descriptions . . . There will certainly be problems getting consensus on that."

As I left the meeting, I wondered about the mounting confrontation with the union. I also knew that what was said at this meeting would likely be used in any confrontation that materialized.

For several weeks Janice negotiated with the RRT and the union, using the Steering Committee as a sounding board and as a means of developing consensus among the leaders of the restructuring teams. The whole process was taking its toll on Janice. She seemed to be carrying the whole responsibility for the restructuring on her shoulders. She went from meeting to meeting, listening to what people were saying, and trying to negotiate viable resolutions to the critical issues. The reengineering of OESE had never been set up with a steering committee that had the power to make decisions. There was nobody to whom Janice could turn. She was carrying the whole load. I was convinced that this was just another one of the costs of not getting this restructuring process off on the right foot in the beginning.

I also heard from Carroll Dexter, a colleague in IAP, who represented management on the LMPC, that it was likely the union would not go along with the whole restructuring process. The LMPC had been scheduling two-hour meetings that would take between four to six hours, ending long after the OESE staff had gone home for the day. Early one morning, after one of these extended meetings, I asked Carroll how the confrontation between the union and management was working out. Carroll closed the door to my office and sat down. Eager to express his frustrations he said: "Those of us representing management on the Council are placed in an impossible position. Management expects the Council to meet and make recommendations that would be either accepted or rejected . . . yet we can not anticipate and speak for management without a dialogue with them. How can we speak for management when we do not know where they stand? I'm afraid of what might happen if management should turn down some of the key recommendations of the Council."

I was sympathetic. I thought, "How can you have a labor/management partnership council without management decision makers on the Council?" I knew that Janice would sometimes attend the LMPC meetings, but much of the time it was a Council made up of delegated middle managers. The management representation on the LMPC was no different than the union representation. Neither group was empowered to make decisions for those they represented. The LMPC was where the battles were being fought, but both the union and management had distanced themselves from the negotiations.

Lessons Learned

With one exception described later, the major factors of the reassignment debacle had now been established. First, prior to the restructuring of OESE there had been a significant reduction in staff competency, which placed a premium on those persons with the requisite knowledge and experience. Second, there was a lack of boundaries for the work groups. Third, the factions battled for their own self-interests, especially those who would be held accountable. Fourth, the absence of any top-level decision-making body for the restructuring effort allowed the battles to intensify. And fifth, issues of racial disaffection had not been resolved and were manifesting themselves in a variety of forms.

More specifically, here are some of the lessons learned:

- **Personnel policies that determine the character of the labor force will eventually determine the character of the organization.** In hindsight, it was a mistake to allow the knowledge and expertise of the labor force to deteriorate. Not only did it accentuate the concern of management, especially the concern of program directors for the delivery of program services, but it undercut the capacity of OESE to deliver quality cross-program services as initially conceived. The move to generic position descriptions, which further diminished the education and experience criteria for employment and upward mobility, created an additional depreciation of expertise. Neither the level of education completed nor experience in schools were required. It was now possible to assign most anyone to a professional position which previously required a high level of expertise.

  Ironically, education did not become one of these criteria in this Office of the Department of Education. It is also ironic that experience in schooling did not become a requirement in an agency established to provide leadership for the nation's schools. Allowing a minimization of these criteria, over the years preceding the restructuring, contributed significantly to the concerns about the reassignment of staff who could provide program services. Hiring staff who did not have these characteristics contributed significantly to the point of view of many staff that it did not matter. Clearly, the leadership of the Department of Education had an option to develop a higher quality of work force, but they elected not to do it.

The buyout program accentuated the problem, because it resulted in a loss of the more experienced, higher-grade employees who played important roles in the delivery of services. Furthermore, it was not a planned downsizing. Anybody who qualified could accept the buyout offer. Some programs would be hurt more than others. It all depended upon who decided to leave. Some portions of the federal government placed program and organizational limits on the buyouts. In fact, OESE originally set a limit on the number of persons and the criteria for their selection, but later decided to let everyone go who applied.

- **The lack of boundaries for empowered work groups will often result in contentious disagreements over critical decision making, especially when a participatory environment has not been established.** The RRT, like other restructuring teams, was established without a specific charter and without boundaries. In fact, the work that ended up in the RRT was a small portion of the work that was initially perceived to be the responsibility of Area Program Offices Team (APOT), before these responsibilities were divided up and re-delegated. The APOT was just one of the numerous failures of adequate planning when the restructuring teams were originally established.

The lack of a clear charter and specific parameters for the RRT allowed aggressive and vocal team members to press for an open, staff-driven approach to the reassignments. The failure to specify a clear charter with parameters for the restructuring teams led to wide ranging assumptions, expectations, disappointments, and inevitable problems. There was the option to set up the restructuring teams differently in the beginning, and the option to learn that lesson from the RRT.

When the RRT was established, the criteria for the reassignment could also have been specified. This would have required management to decide what it would take to obtain competence in the reassigned positions. Unfortunately, competence was not a major concern of the RRT. In addition, a less aggressive goal could have been set for the employee selection of preferred assignments. It was the experience of OERI that it took them three years with a much smaller group of employees. Hence, both the decisions and the lack of decisions had ramifications for what followed.

- **When the performance of an organization is threatened, those held accountable for it will employ every means available to protect their self-interest.** At the same time that the RRT was prescribing the process and the criteria that would be used for the wide open reassignment of staff, the program directors were planning how the staff could be reassigned to regional service teams and program service teams and still deliver program services. They knew that the reassignment of staff according to individual preference presented them with the formidable problem of not being able to deliver their programs.

The program directors realized that many of their critical staff were well positioned to survive the reassignment process and end up in the program service teams doing essentially the same jobs they were doing. Consequently, the program service teams were kept as large as possible. Most program directors informally attempted to influence their staff to stay with their programs and current jobs. And, most important, most staff felt uncomfortable about going against the desires of their program directors if they saw their careers jeopardized.

If the RRT had a clear charter that gave program directors some assurance that they could have the essential personnel to deliver their programs, it would have alleviated the anxiety of the program directors and, perhaps, curtailed their furtive efforts to influence the process.

- **The absence of a top-level decision-making body for the restructuring allows alternative power centers to emerge and to promote their own self- interests.** The RRT, AFGE, and BIG all staked out strong positions advocating a wide open assignment of staff. Program directors and others concerned with the delivery of programs wanted more selectivity in assignments. The LMPC consisted of delegates from both the union and management. As such, it became one of the major battlegrounds where problems emerged and issues were defined. In representing staff in the lower grades, the union took the position of wide open staff selection with the exception of incumbency, a traditional union position. It also wanted to participate directly in the reassignment decision making, not merely as an observer. In contrast, those in management were sympathetic to the concerns related to program delivery.

But both the union and the management representatives on the LMPC were "delegates" rather than decision-makers. The union members did not always know what their higher level officials would support and occasionally had their positions overturned. Likewise, management representatives did not have sufficient direction from their decision-makers to know just how to represent them. Consequently, there were times in which higher officials of both groups were required to determine critical issues.

The "ring master" in this circus was Deputy Assistant Secretary Janice Jackson, who had the principal responsibility for the restructuring of OESE. This patient woman could be seen going from meeting to meeting, reporting on developments, clarifying problems and issues, responding to questions, dealing with rumors, listening to staff, and trying to read the pulse of each emerging anxiety. She used her "Steering Committee" as a sounding board and had one-on-one discussions with individuals, often trying to get a consensus. She negotiated her way through the problems to work out the most viable resolution of differences she could. Then she would take her plans and problems to the Assistant Secretary and the Senior Leadership Team and get the best deal she could.

OESE was fortunate to have a person such as Janice to perform this role. But good people cannot overcome poor organization. Janice should never have had all this stacked on her shoulders.

Professionals in organizational change would have advised that a steering committee be formed with the dominant authority and control over the planning and implementation of the restructuring. They would have established a representative group of customers, stakeholders, influencers, and participants as a steering committee, and given them the major decision-making role. A more democratic, representative body would have made decisions more fairly. They would have been the trump card. Power blocks would have been ameliorated. Union members and management representatives of the LMPC would have had specific decisions and directions to implement. Instead of the Deputy Assistant Secretary trying to negotiate between the factions and dealing with the Senior Leadership Team to get the best deal possible, she could have been putting her efforts toward more constructive pursuits.

- **The deployment of staff into different environments weakens the bonds of the primary communities of practice.** The assignment of staff to regional teams, consisting of members with allegiances to different work units, weakened the communities of practice which had developed within each of the individual OESE programs. The Impact Aid Program is a good example of what happened throughout OESE. The IAP staff were located within a suite of open-landscaped office facilities. If a person needed to communicate with a colleague concerning a work matter, discussing the issue was very convenient. And staff would often share personal experiences and social events with one another. In this environment many personal friendships developed. These friendships enriched and facilitated communication through the development of trust and interpersonal relationships. This combination of social community and working community developed into a productive community of practice.

However, when the IAP staff were assigned to regional teams and spread out over two floors of their office building it was much more difficult to communicate with their IAP colleagues. Their personal contacts became less frequent. So did their work-related communication. Other work tasks and relationships with different colleagues began to spawn other interests and loyalties. In brief, the IAP community of practice began to weaken. This lack of community could be seen in the quantity and quality of the work.

- Finally, when issues of racial disaffection are not dealt with when they occur, they will manifest themselves in a variety of accentuated forms. Racial tension was evident everywhere. Everyone in OESE knew it, saw it, and felt it. And while it was present in other offices of the Department of Education, it was more evident in OESE. Yet little or nothing was done about it. And when an organization keeps sweeping problems under the rug, sooner or later it will stumble over one of the lumps.

Space for Race

Although Uncle Sam was one of the first employers to officially eliminate racial and gender criteria for employment, agencies carefully track
and record race, sex and ethnic data. Federal workers are asked (but
not required) to fill out a "Race and National Origin Identification"
form. Most do, and for the few who do not, supervisors provide the
data. The Office of Personnel Management's (OPM) diversity office
collects the information and reports annually to Congress, as required
by the Civil Service Reform Act of 1978. Mike Causey, columnist for
the *Washington Post,* calls it the "don't-ask-but-do-tell system" (June
15: 1997).

OESE vs. Civilian Labor Force
The OPM monitors the diversity of the federal labor force and com-
pares it to the civilian labor force. If the federal labor force has a lower
percentage in a category than the civilian labor force, the federal labor
force is considered underrepresented. There were 4,621 employees in
the Department of Education, and 233 employees in OESE, according to the 1995 EEO data.

Table 2: Percent of Employees in the National and Department of
Education Labor Forces

	National	Department of Education	OESE
Women	46.3	60.7	68.7
African American	10.5	36.7	48.9
Hispanics	10.5	3.9	3.4
Native Americans	.8	.7	6.0
Asian & Pacific Islanders	3.4	3.0	1.7

Source: Office of Management, U.S. Office of Education, 1996.

The reasons for this particular pattern of diversity within OESE is
open for interpretation, although common knowledge supports some
likely hypotheses. For example, there are one and one-half times more
women in OESE than in the civilian labor force because women have
traditionally gone into the education profession. There are undoubtedly 7.5 times more Native Americans in the OESE labor force because
of the Indian Education Program whose authorizing legislation requires Native American staff. And there are almost five times more
African Americans in OESE than in the civilian labor force because of
the large, available pool of African Americans in the Washington metropolitan area. For example, consider the 1990 census data displayed
in Table 3 concerning Caucasians and African Americans.

Table 3: Percent of Caucasian and African American Groups

	Caucasian	African American
United States	74.0	11.8
Metropolitan Washington	65.8	26.6
District of Columbia	29.6	65.9
Department of Education	55.8	36.7
Office of Elementary & Secondary Education	39.9	48.9

Sources: The Metropolitan Council of Governments and the Office of Equal Employment
Opportunity in the Department of Education.

Educational Diversity. There is also a major difference in the educational backgrounds of the diverse groups in the Department of Education. Overall, the percentage of employees with a bachelor or higher degree in the Department is 61.6 percent. Among Caucasians, 77.2 percent have a bachelor or higher degree. Among African Americans the percentage is 35.4 percent, less than half that of the Caucasians. In the District, 63.7 percent of Caucasians have a bachelor or higher degree, compared with only 12.3 percent of African Americans, one-fifth the percentage of the Caucasians. Consequently, many African Americans are employed by the Department with less education and in lower grades than Caucasians.

The discrepancy in educational level prompts many Caucasians to argue that African Americans cannot expect to attain the same professional levels in the civil service. The expectation of entering the federal government at a clerical level and retiring at the professional level is a possibility for a few, but not realistic for the majority. Some Caucasians asserted that the reason the educational criterion was never used in the reassignment process was because African Americans would not qualify for the positions they wanted.

Expressions of African American Culture. Signithia Fordham, in her studies of black high school students in Washington, D. C., found that there was a significant difference in attitudes toward academic and career success between the generation of blacks that came of age during the civil rights struggle and their children (*Harvard Educational Review*, February 1988:54-84). For black parents who came of age in the 50s and 60s, the success of any one black person in any field was perceived also as a vicarious victory for the whole black community because the individual was opening doors that had been closed to blacks. So the black community rejoiced when Thurgood Marshall became a Supreme Court justice, when Ralph Bunche became undersecretary-general of the United Nations and a winner of the Nobel Prize, when Arthur Ashe became Wimbeldon and U.S. Open tennis champion, and others became lawyers, doctors, university professors and leading administrators.

But, Malcolm X had a much different view. In his autobiography he speaks sardonically of what he calls these "firsts"—black people who were hailed as the first to occupy any position that had previously been denied blacks. He said that very often it was these people, even more than whites, who would vociferously condemn other blacks like himself who did not buy into the notion of having to act white in order to advance themselves and their community. Perhaps the event that displayed the most distinctive difference in the African American culture of today and that of the civil rights era was the Million Man March of the Nation of Islam leader, Louis Farrakhan. Black men in the District of Columbia walked en masse out of the streets of the District and onto the mall where the rally took place. Many black men working for the Department of Education did not show up for work that day.

Fordham found that young black people now, following Malcolm X's lead, see things quite differently. What they see is that the success of the pioneers did not breed widespread success. A few more blacks made it into the professions but nowhere near the numbers necessary to lift up the whole community. Fordham reports that young black people see the strategy of using individual success to lead to community success as flawed. They have replaced it with a powerfully cohesive strategy that is based on the premise that the only way that the black community as a whole will advance is if all its members stick together and advance together. This way they can keep their ethnic identity intact (i.e., not having to "act white," as Malcolm X referred to the successful blacks of his era.)

In many ways, this aggressive, self-help agenda of Malcolm X and Louis Farrakhan is in stark contrast to the integrated society ideology of the NAACP. Throughout its history, the NAACP has insisted that African Americans be integrated into the nation's mainstream. In the civil rights era the NAACP was immensely successful in getting a raft of antidiscrimination laws on the books. But in the post-civil rights period, many blacks have become disenchanted with the progress of integration and prefer to live in black communities, improve the black schools, instill black pride, and collectively fight for their own stake in the economic world. Today in Washington, D.C., you can find African Americans who support the integration approach, others who prefer the Louis Farrakhan approach, and others who speak for both. Although it would be inaccurate to describe all African Americans in the Department as subscribing to a culture of aggressive, self-help fervor for economic improvement, the portion that does is vocal, active and sometimes angry. They can not be ignored.

Socio-economic Groups and the Labor Force. The African Americans in the Washington metropolitan area also have distinctive economic groups. For example, there is a large group of unskilled workers who are part of what social historians have called the "underclass," that is, those who are permanently unemployed because their unskilled labor is no longer required. A second, smaller group, are black middle-class professionals who administer the many public assistance programs designed to assist the underclass. Michael Brown and Steven Erie speak of this trend as "welfare colonialism," where blacks were called upon to administer their own state of dependence (1981:305). There is also an affluent and growing middle class whose public influence has partially deflected the attention of the swelling underclass.

Writes Jeremy Rifkin: "It is possible that the country might have taken greater notice of the impact that automation was having on black America in the 1960s and 1970s, had not a significant number of African Americans been absorbed into the public sector jobs" (1995:77).

As early as 1970, Sociologist Sidney Willhelm observed: "As the government becomes the foremost employer for the working force in general during the transition into automation, it becomes even more so for the black worker. Indeed, if it were not for the government, Negroes who lost their jobs in the business world would swell the unemployment ratio to fantastic heights" (1970:156-157). The Department of Education and other federal agencies have provided for their employment in the public sector.

The conflict. The conflict that erupted in OESE was primarily between the African Americans and the Caucasians, and, largely due to its distinct diversity profile. The large number of African Americans, who were primarily in the lower-level OESE jobs, brought a distinct culture with them from living in the Washington metropolitan area, and related it to their work environment in the Department of Education. If the group had been Mexican American or Asian, they would have brought a distinctively different culture with them, and there would have been an entirely different story to tell.

The Caucasians in OESE also had a distinct culture. But it was coupled with a different status in the OESE work force—though underrepresented in EEO/OPM data, whites held a larger percentage of the higher grades. When confronted with aggressive behavior from the African Americans, they went into "polite" mode, listened, and went off to discuss among themselves the events and the behavior of the blacks. If the African Americans had gone up against Mexican Americans, as they have occasionally in California, it would have been a different story. Or, if the capital of the United States had been Miami, the federal labor force would have looked much different. Some people think of diversity problems in the generic sense, but they never come that way.

Indeed, the diversity of the labor force in the Department had led to problems from the time of the Department's creation in 1980. For example, on one occasion two "diversity consultants" had been employed by the Department to conduct a two-day workshop in the Management Development Program (MDP). The workshop ended with participants shouting, accusing each other of prejudice, and agreeing only that they could not agree on very much. There were sincere attempts to follow up on what had broken down, but most of the participants simply wanted to avoid any further conflict and refused to participate in further "diversity" discussions.

Another disturbing incident took place one day in early February 1995. A white colleague stepped into the hall just ahead of me. I could tell that she was upset. Her complexion was pale. She appeared confused, not knowing what she wanted to do—not knowing which way to go down the hall. I stopped to ask her what was wrong. She explained that she had just been in a horrible staff meeting ended in shouting, anger, and ill will. One of the persons resigned following the meeting. My friend had just overheard an African American say, "Well, we just got rid of another honky."

Over the years there were numerous grievances filed in which race was either an overt or a covert factor. But for the most part, the tension between the races was suppressed. Despite that, I feel strongly that everyone knew that it was there. It was like a volcano getting ready to erupt.

"Quality for Diversity, or Diversity for Quality"

An All Hands meeting was held on June 15th devoted to progress reports on what was taking place in the restructuring of OESE. This was followed by a question and answer period to respond to staff queries. Assistant Secretary Tom Payzant and Deputy Assistant Secretary Janice Jackson were sharing the leadership. During the question and answer portion of the program, a "bomb" went off that overshadowed all other concerns in OESE and made the reengineering effort, especially the reassignment of personnel, much more difficult. Ricardo Sanchez, an Hispanic, stood up in the meeting and confronted Tom Payzant. He declared: "When you first came to OESE, you promised that you would support diversity. You recently had an opportunity to demonstrate your commitment to diversity with the vacancy of two program directors. Why did you fill these two positions with two white women?" (Ricardo was referring to the recent appointments of Cathy Schagh as Director of the Impact Aid Program, and Bayla White as the Director of the Office of Migrant Education.)

Tom's response to Ricardo's question produced a loud, spontaneous rumble of discontent throughout the auditorium. What many people heard Tom say was, "I will not sacrifice quality for diversity." What Tom insists he said was, "I will not sacrifice quality for diversity or diversity for quality." Regardless of what Tom said or what he meant to convey, the room was a buzz of conversation. Tom made an attempt to clarify what he said, and to speak of his commitment to racial diversity prior to coming to Washington, but the damage had been done. A few additional questions were asked, but few people were paying much attention. They wanted to get out of the meeting and talk.

Walking back to our offices, I noticed Cathy Schagh, whose appointment was the focus of the confrontation. She was noticeably upset. I asked her how she was feeling. She replied, "Right now, I would just as soon give up my job to anyone who wants it." I thought a minute and then said, awkwardly, "The people who are making all the noise don't know how difficult your job is or how well you do it." Then, to make her feel better, I told her that she had done a neat thing the previous week when she had brought in refreshments and had a celebration honoring the persons who had done a good job with a cross-training program. I complimented her for giving out $150 spot awards for the good work. Cathy seemed to feel a bit better, but I knew that she was really upset, and this would not be the end of it for her.

Back at the office, everyone was talking about Tom's response to Ricardo. One colleague said, "When Tom responded, 'He would not sacrifice quality for diversity' he made a big mistake. This made everybody mad! . . . I'm sure Tom would like to call this statement back, but it's too late now." Another colleague told me he had just heard one of IAP's marginal black employees claiming that she could do Cathy's job. He said, "That is the most ridiculous remark I've heard in a long time. She has no idea what that job requires."

The Offense Expressed. On the following day, all OESE staff received a copy of the following e-mail addressed to Tom Payzant from Carrolyn Andrews:

> As President of the Education Department's Chapter of Blacks in Government, and on behalf of all people of color in OESE, I am offended by your response to the concerns expressed in the OESE All Hands staff meeting on June 15th. With regard to the selection of senior management positions in Migrant Education and Impact Aid, you stated, "I will not sacrifice quality for diversity . . ." Your response implied that there are no minorities qualified in OESE who possess the qualities you alluded to, and it clearly demonstrates your lack of sensitivity and commitment to the mission of the Department to ensure diversity within the workplace. We take issue with your position and demand an immediate apology in this regard.
>
> *Carrolyn Andrews*

On June 20th, Tom sent the following reply to Carrolyn, with copies to all OESE staff and Secretary Riley.

> Carrolyn, I have received your June 16, 1995, e-mail message. I am deeply concerned that my comments were taken out of context. I wish to set the record straight. I [first] actually said, "I will not sacrifice quality for diversity or

diversity for quality." Each of these is important in personnel decisions.

Secondly, OESE is a diverse organization. As an educator, I am committed to achieving high educational outcomes for all children. In order to accomplish this, I am committed to fully motivating and engaging each member of OESE. Therefore, I consider managing our diverse work force well as critical to our mission.

I would like to meet with you and discuss the questions raised with regard to diversity. It is my hope that we can jointly explore actions we can take to create a more inclusive and respectful work environment. I will arrange a time in the next two weeks to discuss the concerns you've raised. I take these matters very seriously.

Tom Payzant

The next couple of weeks were dominated by rumors, as e-mail messages flew back and forth. As a white supervisor, I did not receive all the e-mail that was exchanged among minorities. But according to Harris Taylor, a black colleague, it was prolific and the situation was getting worse. I did hear about the following:

- People were talking about the qualifications of both Cathy and Bayla for their jobs and the qualifications of other people who might have been selected.

- The union held a meeting with Tom at which BIG was also represented.

- The situation was discussed by the Senior Leadership Team. Tom stated that there would be no apology for what he had said about diversity at the All Hands meeting.

- Investigations were being conducted by staff about Tom's superintendency in San Diego prior to his appointment as Assistant Secretary of OESE.

- There had been an inquiry from the Office of the Deputy Secretary about what was happening in OESE.

I could not confirm any of these rumors, but none would have surprised me. I thought it was a mistake on Tom's part not to act more quickly on the follow-up because emotions were growing more out of control each day.

Tom did eventually confirm by e-mail that he had heard from Carrolyn Andrews, and said she wanted him to set up a meeting that anyone could attend. A large-scale confrontation was in the making. Finally, Tom announced that he had booked a large room for a meeting on July 5th, in the nearby L'Enfant Plaza Hotel.

The Confrontation. July 5th came and the room was packed. Those who came late had to stand. Some who came were angry and planned to make their feelings known. Others were there because they sensed a momentous event in the making, and it was going to change their work environment. Tom, Janice, and Carrolyn were seated together at the head table. Tom opened the meeting with a chronology of events that led up to this meeting: Carrolyn's e-mail, his e-mail, the request for the expansion of the meeting to all staff, and the unfortunate but necessary delay in holding the meeting because of the need for a large room.

Carrolyn confirmed the chronology of events and stated that this meeting was necessary because Tom's response was not clear.

Tom then tried to clarify his response. He repeated what he had said in his e-mail, "I will not sacrifice quality for diversity or diversity for quality." He continued, "Quality and diversity are two important criteria in making personnel decisions. They must be considered in relation to a number of other factors, such as experience, knowledge, skill, and others. It is an unfortunate situation when one had to make a decision in which quality and diversity are the only criteria."

He also stated that he was disappointed by the reaction of some people to what he said. They had only heard half of his statement. He reported that he had participated in hundreds of appointments, and that he was only being judged on two of them. "If people would only look at the entire picture," he argued, "they would know that I support diversity."

Janice spoke up to say that OESE had "a long and troubled history with the problems of diversity," implying that it would not be easy to deal with such a long-standing problem. She also stated with some indignation that she was "insulted" when people interpreted some of her remarks at the All Hands meeting as protecting Tom.

The arguments of the meeting, which continued for over an hour, could be grouped into two general categories. First, much of argument appeared to be a hostile attack on Tom, in order to make him defend his two appointments of white women to program directorships. The second type of argument sounded like statements about the perceived general unfairness to minorities in OESE.

Following the opening remarks, Carrolyn said that Tom had still not explained why he had appointed Bayla White and Cathy Schagh to program director positions. Obviously frustrated, Tom explained that there were different reasons for each appointment, and went into more detail. He said that Bayla White came from the Office of Management and Budget (OMB), that he and others in the Department were impressed with Bayla's skills, and he felt that she would make an excellent addition to the leadership of OESE.

Cathy's appointment in IAP, Tom said, differed from Bayla's position in IMP, because when the previous director transferred out his Senior Executive Service position transferred with him. Since a director for IAP could not be recruited at this level, Tom said he decided to move the Deputy Director of IAP, Cathy Schagh, into the vacant position. He couldn't place a person in the deputy position, because he had no full-time equivalent position to replace her. "This situation," he said, "was not ideal."

These explanations were not satisfactory to many of the minorities at the meeting. Some argued that Tom had not answered the diversity question. Others claimed that there were people right in OESE who were qualified. One person stated that the directorships were not just any positions, they were symbols for everyone to see. Another argued that these two appointments were so grievous that they could not be ignored, a fundamental failure and a revelation of non-commitment to diversity. And finally, it was pointed out that all but one program [Office of Indian Education] had a white director, and that many were looking to him to correct the long-standing abuse of racial diversity within OESE.

As these and other complaints were expressed, often with emotion and anger, Tom responded, "I know that some people will disagree with the selections I made and that I could not convince you otherwise. But I should not be judged on these two selections alone . . . Don't say that Tom is not honoring the diversity criterion based on only two appointments."

As the discussion was turned to a broader perspective, it began to degenerate: there were complaints about general unfairness, the lack of using education as a criterion, the need to recruit from black universities, etc. The arguments became more and more personal, with specific charges made about specific individuals.

Finally, Tom interrupted one person's vindictive diatribe to say: "This is a public meeting. It's no place to put people down. We have to protect the rights of individuals from this sort of abusive comment. We are here to discuss issues, not individuals . . . " He added that there were other appropriate places to discuss individuals if there was a need for it.

Tom's comments about personal abuse in a public meeting stopped the flow of angry statements. After a brief pause, while everyone reflected upon the nature of the comments, Carrolyn asked, "Where do we go from here?" Tom suggested that three things might be done: (1) a task force could be set up to work with him and follow up this meeting, (2) follow-up activities in each of the programs might be started to focus on the problems related to diversity, and (3) he invited staff to e-mail further suggestions to him.

The Diversity Task Force. The next day, Carrolyn sent out an e-mail message inviting volunteers to join the Diversity Task Force. She received a large response. The program offices also began to move on approaches of their own.

One week later, there was another All Hands meeting which was largely devoted to the diversity issue. Tom opened the meeting by acknowledging that the July 5th meeting had been very frank and highly emotional. He reported that two days later there had been a meeting of 15 people, including Janice and Phyllis Barajas, in which his recommendation to establish a task force was acted on, and they already had 24 volunteers. He also reported that he had taken considerable time in two different meetings with the program directors discussing the diversity issue, and the program directors were each following up on it. He listed these planned actions:

Front Office	Will hold meetings to deal with diversity in this office.
CEP	Entire staff will meet to address the issues.
SDFS	A committee has been established.
OIE	Focus on the diversity issue of support staff.
Goals 2000	Staff with diversity concerns invited to attend peer reviews.
IAP	Office-wide meeting planned.
OME	Portions of staff meetings will address diversity issues, especially hiring.

Tom then turned the meeting over to Carrolyn Andrews and Dorothea Perkins, to talk about the Diversity Task Force. Carrolyn stated that the Task Force would be made up of volunteers. But other than stating that they wanted a broad representation and more support personnel, she didn't mention how volunteers would be selected. Dorothea said they would like to have two persons from each program area to work as liaison persons with the Task Force. She described an "OESE Diversity Issue Form" that would soon be distributed to all staff. The issue form would contain the following four sections:

1. Identify Issue (Personnel, Program, Morale, Etc.)

2. Describe Circumstances Around the Issue (Briefly give the particulars.)

3. Suggest Solutions to the Issue Identified (Specific actions steps.)

4. Comments (Suggestions, Opinions on Diversity or Other Related Comments.)

Each issue should include the names of the people involved and the dates of any events. Although the name of the person submitting the issue would be optional, including the name would help the Task Force follow up on the issue.

Over the course of the next several months, a list of complaints was drafted by the Task Force that was full of personal, vindictive statements and recommendations. Each incident or comment was an indictment of supervision and management that described either an action or a failure to act. The list was duplicated and distributed throughout the Office. According to a reliable source, when the list was taken to Janice, she would not accept it in its current form because it was personal and vindictive.

So the Task Force turned to the task of modifying the language. A second list was presented to Janice and this time I was astonished to find my name on the list as a "perpetrator of a prejudicial act." I had refused to raise an employee's grade who was in a career ladder position. I had asserted that the employee could not perform her job, in spite of the training she had received. Although I was later vindicated by a committee made up of both black and white staff, anyone who read only the account on the Task Force's list would have read a very incomplete and biased account.

On the second list there were a total of 88 specific complaints and two comments. They could be categorized as:

Promotions	30
Personnel Practices	27

Morale	12
Performance Appraisals	10
Employment Opportunities	9
Comments	2

Except for the outcome of the charge directed at me, I never heard of any other outcome. Shortly before my retirement about eighteen months later, I asked William Wooten, Director of Management, Policy and Budget for OESE, what had become of the list. Bill told me that he thought the departure of Tom Payzant and the subsequent appointment of Art Cole, an African American, to a position of program director had largely diffused the animosity.

IAP and Diversity. Following the July 5th meeting, Dorothea Perkins, an aggressive and articulate African American on the staff of IAP, immediately pushed Cathy to convene a staff meeting to address the racial diversity issue. She suggested not only agenda items, but also how the meeting should be conducted. Cathy did devote a major portion of her regular staff meeting on July 25th to the diversity issue and, included Dorothea's agenda suggestions, but not her procedural suggestions. The agenda went out on e-mail in advance of the meeting.

Because the diversity issue was on the agenda, all of the IAP staff made a special effort to attend. A number of the African Americans in IAP had felt that they had not been treated fairly because of their race. They came to the meeting to speak their minds, and it became a very heated meeting. When Cathy opened up the meeting she handed out a page of data which I had obtained from the EEO. Among other things, the data indicated that two-thirds of the IAP staff were African American, about a quarter white and less than five percent Asian. It also revealed that IAP was 65 percent female and 35 percent male and that grades 13-15 were evenly split between African Americans and whites, and between male and female.

In contrast, the OESE staff was half African American, 41 percent white, and 1.5 percent Asian. But in the highest grades, 13-15,over half were white and just one-third were African American (the males and females were about evenly split). So IAP had significantly more

African American staff, more female staff, and more African America staff in the upper three grades than did OESE, of which it was a part. The data indicated that IAP had hired more African Americans, more females, and were promoting more African Americans than any other program in OESE.

By handing out the data, Cathy was obviously attempting to get a discussion going that showed evidence favorable to the treatment of African Americans in IAP. But it was emotions, not data, that would motivate the discussion. One of the African American members spoke for her peers by dismissing the data as having nothing to do with diversity. What she said was that she and her friends wanted to talk about hiring, promotions, and morale.

A couple of the secretaries complained that there were few career ladder positions in IAP for secretaries to move to higher grades. Several people indicated that they should have been promoted to jobs which others had received, and could do just as well as those selected. And a couple of staff asserted that there was no hope for African Americans in this work environment.

Cathy calmly stated that she was in favor of career ladder development positions—and, in fact, established two the next year when she received an increase in staff allotments. She pointed out that there was a cap on hiring at that time, and the reassignment process did not allow advancement in grade. She did acknowledge, however, that there were a few highly specialized vacancies in OESE for which career ladder positions were not applicable.

I mentioned the difficulty of providing for upward mobility in the present situation. I pointed out that the downsizing and restructuring of the federal government, as currently taking place in OESE, was increasing the span of control and reducing the number of opportunities for people to move into middle management positions.

When Cathy moved on to the topic of morale, an African American woman began to go through her prepared list of gripes and suggestions, most of which had nothing to do with morale. Growing increasingly impatient, I broke into her laundry list by pointing out that her comments had little to do with morale. Everyone agreed and the woman stopped talking. Needless to say she was irritated with me for putting her down in front of everyone, but she took it without saying a word when everyone else agreed with me.

I continued, stating that in my judgment, morale had been a pervasive problem in the Department as long as I had been there. I alluded to a number of staff surveys and GAO reports that confirmed this conclusion. And I said that I felt "morale is a personal issue that is related to how we as individuals feel about our self-image and our role in the work environment now and in the future."

Cathy had kept a smile on her face for most of the meeting. But I knew that it must have been difficult for her. She was one of the two program directors who had to endure the brunt of the diversity attack. Dorothea, one of the more aggressive and impassioned spokespersons for the African Americans, was a member of Cathy's staff, and was especially effective when on the attack. Sometimes my stomach would knot up when I heard my colleagues speak with such anger and bitterness. Like many of my colleagues, my emotions were often close to the surface, and it was difficult for me to know when to speak up or what to say. I admired Cathy's ability to keep cool and keep smiling in a confrontation. I also felt she was doing a good job monitoring her comments so as not to escalate emotions.

A Forum of Anger. The diversity issue would have a long and lasting impact on the reengineering of OESE. I decided to attend one of several open forums sponsored by the LMPC in March 1996. Out of approximately 45 people, most were African American and only four were Caucasians—one union official, two others I didn't know who stayed for only a portion of the meeting, and me. Phyllis Barajas, an Hispanic political appointee from the Office of the Assistant Secretary, attended the meeting and played the role of responding to charges made against management as best she could.

It was a long and vitriolic meeting, and not all of the complaints expressed by the participants were specifically related to diversity issues. There were voices raised about the lack of communication with team leaders, the neglect of management to work with the LMPC on personnel changes, and the filing of an unfair practices complaint.

Most of the complaints were from African Americans about their mis-treatment by management. There was a report of a physical confrontation that had to be broken up the day before, calls for the removal of specific management officials, a complaint about the transfer of an African American employee with 33 years of federal service and a complaint about staff having to work in an unhealthy room environment.

At one point, Dorothea Perkins stated that it didn't matter what the problem was, there was a "pattern of management attitudes and a lack of trust." She complained, "They keep doing things to us, and we are always in a reactive mode."

Another woman began her livid speech saying, "I think that management wants the fighting to continue." She ended it saying, "We have to fight our own battles. Nobody is going to fight them for us." At that point Tyese Brooks, a member of the LMPC, reassured her: "The LMPC is fighting the battle for the blacks." To me, this was an open admission that the LMPC was seen by blacks as an instrument of black power fighting for black causes—not labor/management issues.

A few days later, I discussed this experience at the forum with Carroll Dexter who hadn't been able to attend the meeting, even though he was a member of the LMPC representing management. I told Carroll that it was the anger and bitterness that really got to me. I was sure that such anger and bitterness was not only destroying the reengineering of OESE, but also destroying the people who carried such anger. I acknowledged that when I left the meeting I had a sick feeling in my stomach. I recalled having that same feeling back in the 1960s when, as a pastor of a Presbyterian church in Los Angeles, my white parishioners had become embroiled in a vicious battle over the civil rights of African Americans. "The only difference," I said, "was that then it was the whites who were overcome by racial anger, now it is blacks!"

First Reassignments

The time for reassignment of personnel moved ahead, even though the union had not yet come forward with their decision about the restructuring of OESE. On August 2-3, 1995, the Senior Leadership Team met to make their decision about the group leaders and a special assistant to the Assistant Secretary, who would work with the Deputy

Assistant Secretary in the reengineering of OESE. I wanted the position of Special Assistant so that I might be involved full-time in the reengineering action.

I did not get the position because of what I considered to be an absurd procedure in the reassignment process: seniority, not person's knowledge, experience, educational level, and skill. According to the procedure, if more than one person applied for a position it would go to the person with the highest grade. If there was more than one person with that grade it would go the person who had been in the federal government the longest. I had the grade, but was passed over because of my shorter time in the civil service. Instead, I got my second choice: one of fourteen group leader positions.

The RRT had prescribed these criteria for the entire reassignment process because they were considered *objective*. There could be no argument about a person's grade, and there could be no argument about the date a person entered the civil service. Therefore, these criteria were considered objective. The RRT argued that they could not trust management to be fair and unprejudiced, so they had to have objective criteria. I argued that educational attainment could also be considered an objective criterion. One could document diplomas, degrees and years of education. And, after all, this was the Department of Education! Didn't we believe in education? Why were we working here? Where were our priorities? I got nowhere with the argument. I assumed that the reason why it was not acceptable was because African Americans could not often win on the education criterion.

Selecting Team Leaders

With the selection of the group leaders by the Senior Leadership Team, the first entity within the restructured OESE came into being. The fourteen group leaders, who seldom interacted with each other in the previous organization because of their distinctly different jobs, were now brought together for the highly important task of selecting the team leaders for the new structure.

On August 8, 1995, we had our first meeting with Frank Robinson, the new Special Assistant for Restructuring, Carolyn Johnson the union representative, and two facilitators, Janice Jackson and Phyllis Barajas. I knew a few from working with them on some OESE team or committee. Some I knew by sight only. And there were those I did not know at all. I had no idea what to expect. I wondered what thoughts they were harboring behind those faces. I figured that the others in the group were probably wondering about the same things.

The one major question in my mind was, "How would the highly charged diversity issue come into play in this group?" I knew it was present, but I did not know how it would show itself.

The facilitators distributed an agenda, statement of purpose, outcomes they had constructed for the meeting, a list of functions of the regional service teams, and a general list of competencies for both team and group leaders. Since many in the room didn't know each other very well, the participants spent some time introducing themselves and getting better acquainted by sharing some information unrelated to the job at hand.

Janice explained that the information on the applicants would not be distributed until after some procedures were decided, to avoid bias in creating procedures. She also emphasized that the team leaders had a *role* and not a *position*. She stated that in the future, team leaders would be selected by their teams, which would be self-directed. "But," she hedged, "we do not know how the new structure will work out with the teams."

Refining the Process. The group leaders spent several hours refining the selection process and ground rules. The RRT had prescribed the basic procedure and identified the criteria, but they did not provide procedures for all contingencies. For example, if the group limited their consideration of team leaders to their first choice, did that mean that those who requested a group leader position first but did not get it, would not be considered in the first round for a team leader position? If a person with a grade 14 made "team leader" a second choice, would a grade 13 get priority over the grade 14 because that person made "team leader" a first choice? In other words, how would we deal with the "best fit" criterion? Janice insisted that these and other questions would have to be settled before the applicants could even be considered. Since the ground rules specified that we reach consensus, Janice also said that the group would have to agree that we could live with a decision, even if we did not unanimously agree on it.

Since I was not pleased with the reassignment process in general, I had a difficult time accepting some of it. For example, one issue for discussion was whether we would select people by their choice of team, without consideration of others who might make better team leaders. After specifying a number of options, the majority of the members decided the answer to this question was "Yes." A few of us voted "No." When they asked those who had voted "No" if they could live with it, I was the only one who said I could not live with this method.

When asked why, I responded: "I think there will be situations in which people who aren't well qualified will end up selecting a particular team for their first choice, and we'll be bound to select from only those people when there are more qualified people who want the position . . . We have a lot at stake starting out with regional teams, and we need the best available people we can get into these team leader positions . . . We need to decide upon the *best fit* for these positions."

At this point, Janice asked me what it would take to get me to go along with the uncompromising procedure. I thought for a moment and said, "We would have to find some way to avoid the undesirable consequence."

After some discussion, Janice reminded the group that they would have to examine the overall selection of team leaders for *balance* prior to finalizing it. This introduced a discussion about balance. Everyone knew that the balance criterion was really the diversity criterion. Janice asked if I could live with the strict procedure if the best fit criterion was included in the balance. I responded, "I believe that I can trust my colleagues to implement this [including the best fit criterion as a part of balance]: I guess I could live with it." If I had known what was to come, I probably would not have agreed.

Race and Reassignment. With this bottleneck out of the way, Janice distributed the names of the applicants, by their preferences and by their regional team selections. I was surprised to see that there were only three grade 14s listed, and two of them had made team leader a second or third choice. All the rest were grade 13s, and two of them had made team leader a second and a third choice. I wondered whether grade 14s were uncomfortable with vagueness of the team leader role after being supervisors or managers. Did they anticipate difficulties in making the regional teams a cohesive working group when they had no authority? Was this resistance to downsizing?

In spite of the fact that most grade 14s had no interest in a team leader role, it did not take long to see that the selection of team leaders was considered a high stakes game by the group leaders. The process was long and contentious, and it took two 11-hour days to select ten team leaders.

The selection process began with one person reading the submission of the applicant. The applicants had been asked to respond to six criteria for a team leader in no more than a single page.

1. Dedication to the team approach

2. Coaching/mentoring skills

3. Sensitivity to diversity

4. Leadership ability

5. Goals/task completion

6. Ability to work with people in a collaborative style

Then the people who knew the applicant were asked to add their appraisal of the individual from their personal experience.

Without doubt, the major problem was the race issue. The problems that had boiled over after the Tom Payzant fiasco had obviously permeated the reassignment process. There was a concerted effort by African Americans to get as many blacks as possible selected as team leaders. I knew only about 35 percent of the applicants personally, but I quickly knew if they were African American or Caucasian, merely by the advocates who spoke for the candidates. Most of the arguments by African Americans on behalf of African Americans were straightforward. But I was especially intrigued by the approach of Arthur Cole, which was very effective. When Art saw an adjustment in the balance tending toward the selection of a white person, he would present a different option, and sometimes more than one, that always favored an African American. He would go back and bring someone into consideration who had previously been rejected, thereby making possible the selection of an African American.

This is not to say that African Americans did not vote for Caucasians and vice versa. Strong candidates from both races got votes across the racial divide. But aside from these few individuals, there was an ongoing battle for racial representation. I felt that some Caucasians became angry and acted defensively, although not overtly. We were simply doing what we could to maintain a balance. We did not speak up to challenge the race card directly. I considered it, but knew that I would have been targeted as a racist from then on if I had. I knew that other whites were responding the same way.

The Hispanic Deficiency. Late in the afternoon of the second day when the group leaders were working with the balance criterion and everyone was tired, Ramon Ruiz brought up the fact that no Hispanic had been selected to be a team leader. Ricardo Sanchez, the person who had brought up the awkward question for Tom Payzant about his choice of two women for program directors, was the only Hispanic who had applied for a team leader position. Ricardo had been considered, but not selected earlier. The fact that there were very few Hispanics in OESE, and two had been selected for group leaders, was not considered an acceptable excuse by Ramon for having no Hispanic team leader. Of course, to make room for one Hispanic, either a black or white person would have to be sacrificed. The problem was acerbated by the fact that Ricardo had requested the leadership of a specific team and had said "No" to other team leader positions. (The group leaders had tried to contact him to see if he would accept leadership of a different team, but were unable because he was out of town.) The group leaders spent about three hours on this issue. At one point, Ramon angrily got up from his seat and walked out on the process. Phyllis Barajas ran after him and brought him back into the room and the discussion.

When I saw the battle shaping up again between taking a black or a white off the list to accommodate an Hispanic, I saw an opportunity to "check the black pawn." I introduced a new criterion into the balancing by pointing out that every program within OESE had a team leader except IAP. Since there was only one applicant (and a very good one) from IAP, and he was white, I said we had to have "program diversity," that is, team leaders should be selected from every program within OESE.

Janice challenged the need for program diversity, but I argued that the IAP was so different from all other programs that they needed a person in the team leader role to represent IAP whenever team activities were considered. I argued that the staff in IAP had been shunted to the periphery in OESE many times, because it was different from other programs. I asserted that IAP staff often feel like a fifth wheel.

Carroll Dexter supported my argument, saying that the lack of a team leader from IAP would just be another blow to their morale. Janice conceded that we had made our point. Carroll and I won the argument. Curtis Van Horn from IAP was now locked in, regardless of how the assignment of Ricardo came out.

Ricardo was finally reached and once he accepted an alternative team leader position, a final adjustment in the selection of team leaders was made. The selections included six males and four females, four whites, four blacks, one Hispanic, and one Native American.

On August 15th, Janice sent an e-mail to all staff announcing the selection and explaining the process. She reported, "Six people were assigned their first preference and one was assigned his second preference. The remaining three were assigned to meet the needs of balance and best fit."

I often thought back to those two long days selecting team leaders. There were many games played. And I felt that racial prejudice and lack of trust had compromised the reassignment process. I did not believe that it would have been possible to deal openly with racism in that room. Prejudice had been a long time in the making, and it would take a long time to undo. At times I felt helpless. When I saw how the whites were reacting, it seemed to me that some had become defenseless. I believed that the group leaders could have come up with a better selection of team leaders if only they could have had an honest dialogue.

Staff Assignments

In early September the selection of other staff was made. One hundred and fifty four people out of 195 were placed in their first or second choices. I was not present at the selections and learned later that the LMPC had been the key decision-makers in the selection process and that the union members got most of what they wanted.

Reassignments Announced. On September 12th, we had another All Hands meeting at which Janice announced that 110 persons received their first choice for program service teams and 84 persons had received their first choice for regional service teams. She also stated that the LMPC, the group leaders, and the team leaders had reviewed the assignments and had forwarded some recommendations to management, who had not yet met. She noted that the following principles were followed in the reassignment process:

- Employee preferences were to be honored whenever possible.

- Employees with greater seniority were to be given priority if more than one person asked for a given position.

- Employee narratives were to be taken seriously.

- All placements were to be lateral, in accordance with the personnel guidelines and the Collective Bargaining Agreement.

- Each program service team and regional service team must be capable of meeting customer needs.

- Each program service team and regional service team must have diversity among team members in areas of race, educational background and experience.

Janice was obviously attempting to convince the staff that the reassignment process had worked for the benefit of the staff and that it had been conducted fairly. Because most of the staff had not yet been told of their individual assignments, there was abundant apprehension in the room. It would be a few days later when they would learn of their specific outcome.

Changes Blocked. Two days later the program directors met with the Assistant and Deputy Assistant Secretaries, in the presence of the union representatives, to make any necessary changes in the reassignments. I had always believed that this would be the time when some sense would be infused into the process and the most grievous assignments would be rectified.

I received a distressed call from Cathy telling me that although she had been successful in getting some bad reassignments turned around, there were still some tough situations to solve to make sure IAP was not hurt too badly. (One indispensable staff member, Veronica Edwards, was going to be assigned to a regional team. In addition, IAP was going to end up with four vacancies.)

The major surprise to Cathy was the amount of pressure the program directors were receiving from Janice, Tom, and the union not to change any assignments. Cathy said that she thought the premature announcement at the All Hands meeting about the numbers of first choices honored was really a way to put pressure on the program directors not to change anything.

I was really surprised that Janice and Tom would not give the program directors the capability to carry out their program responsibilities. After all, it had taken one small section of OERI three years to make the adjustment in personnel assignments. Why were Tom and Janice trying to honor everyone's preference the first year?

The next morning, Cathy came into my office, closed the door, and sat down to update me on the continued negotiations. She explained that she had won a few battles and lost some, but in the end not much had been fixed. She was discouraged as she left with the following problems: she had lost Veronica Edwards to a regional team; people had been assigned to regional teams whom, she felt, could not do the work; and there were four vacancies in IAP that had to be filled.

The loss of Veronica Edwards, a property analyst, was especially devastating to Cathy and me. There were only two people left in the property section and neither had the knowledge and skills to handle certain complex properties, such as Indian lands. One of the two remaining property analysts was leaving on a buyout, and the other, I felt, could only do the most simple assignments. Veronica had talked to both Cathy and me about the situation before the reassignments, and stated that she would not feel bad if the reassignment to a regional team did not go through the first year.

I was also concerned about the quality and quantity of work that had to be done in the property section without any immediate help. This was my responsibility as Group Leader of the IAP Program Service Team. This could become a major bottleneck for the Program in the processing of payments to local districts.

My e-mail. For the next couple of days my thoughts kept returning to the reassignment of personnel at work. Reassigning Veronica would leave the IAP in almost desperate straits. I knew that there was little that Cathy could do. However, I knew that I had a voice that would get a response, and I could say things that Cathy couldn't. At least I could let Tom and Janice know what I thought. So on Monday morning I sent a lengthy e-mail to Tom and Janice outlining my thoughts and concerns. I said that I was "stunned" when Cathy informed me about the outcomes of the reassignments for the Impact Aid Program. I admitted that the more I thought about it the angrier I became. I let them know that I believed that they had made a serious mistake.

I wrote that I thought it was a mistake to charge the RRT with the task of designing a reassignment process without setting any boundaries. As a result, criteria were developed that all but ignored the knowledge and skills to do a job. People with no accountability for program outcomes were given the power to assign personnel and very capable and qualified people were passed over while some weak people were assigned to critical jobs.

"I realize that there is no way to get the genie back into the bottle," I wrote. "But I did expect that our program directors, together with our Assistant Secretary and Deputy Assistant Secretary, would deal with the most critically inappropriate assignments. 'After all,' I said to myself, 'our programs are at stake' . . . But obviously, that did not happen. We have not arrived with a reasonable accommodation of preferences. We have legitimized anarchy!"

I wrote about the situation with Veronica Edwards, explaining that although she had requested reassignment, she had told Cathy that she would understand if her first preference could not be honored. Cathy even assured her that although we preferred that she stay in her current position, because her immediate loss would be very harmful to the program, we would assure her an opportunity to change within the coming year.

I also wrote that "we are ignoring the fundamentals of our organization as a social institution. Every organization has a social structure, whether it is a tribe of aborigines in the bush of Australia, a Fortune 100 company, or a federal agency. All individuals are conscious of their roles and react in certain accepted ways to other individuals within their organization. Behavior varies according to the conceptions of relationships. Just as every employee has a particular physical location, so he has a particular social place in an organization.

"While there is nothing inherently wrong in changing where people or fundamentals reside within an organization, such fundamentals as power, authority, control, accountability, incentives, communication, and security must continue to exist in a viable alignment after a change as well as before a change. We have been changing these fundamentals similar to the manner in which we toss a salad. For example, program directors have been losers in such fundamentals as power, authority, and control while still being held responsible and accountable for their programs. The union has been a winner in these three fundamentals without any responsibility or accountability for programs. The evidence of these changes in the reassignment of personnel is obvious."

Finally, I suggested that the leadership of OESE must soon acknowledge that the fundamentals of the social structure must support our desired outcomes or the whole social structure of OESE would deteriorate.

Janice's e-mail. A couple of days later I heard from Cathy that Veronica would be sharing time with the Program Service Team for the purpose of processing Indian lands and training others in property certification. Then, a week or so later I received an e-mail message from Janice in which she explained her position: "We did pay great attention to the knowledge and expertise required to accomplish the work of OESE," she wrote. "The program directors have not been stripped of their power. They are, however, being directed to manage in a way that is fundamentally different than the management of the past. "Yes, managers are being held accountable for work with teams. Expertise will lie in the teams, not one individual."

"I agree that Veronica is very important to IAP. It is important to develop other employees with the same level of expertise. She is not leaving OESE, simply asking to do something different. Her expertise is not lost, it can be shared. Cathy has the situation under control."

She explained that she knew how difficult it was for an organization to change so radically. "I do not expect it to be easy. It took many years to build the culture. Our work must continue. We must deliver service to our external customers while working at our internal changes."

Of course, I did not expect Janice or Tom to agree with me. But I believed that my strong comments about Veronica Edwards had changed her work assignments. (Veronica gave about half of her time to the Property Section of the Program Service Team, working closely with me and with others to develop an exemplary training program for property analysts that was considered a model for the Department.) Ironically, during her experience in the Regional Service Team, she became more and more interested in returning to the Program Service Team full time and did so in early 1997 with an increase in grade.

On September 20th, Tom officially distributed the reassignments to all staff. On September 26-27, there was a Restructuring Fair for all OESE staff. This was the first time that the teams could meet as teams. Although they would not be co-located for months, they now started to get acquainted and do some work together.

Lessons Learned

Several preconditions contributed to the outcomes reported in this chapter. First, there was a long-term reduction in the quality of staff in OESE before the restructuring began, and the move to generic position descriptions in the restructuring contributed to this trend. Second, a wide open reassignment process was begun without criteria to distinguish the most competent for specific job assignments. This presented a threatening situation for program directors who were responsible for program outcomes. It also set up expectations for staff assignments that would be difficult to fulfill and still provide program quality. In an era when the emerging characteristic in the private labor force is the "knowledge worker," the Department of Education was moving in the opposite direction. Third, contending constituencies were established as organizational entities (for example, the RRT, the union, BIG, and the LMPC) to push for their objectives. Unfortunately, there was no ultimate authority, such as a steering committee, with the power to make and enforce an overall judgment. In addition:

- **When racial diversity problems are "swept under the rug" rather than constructively resolved, a single incident can turn an organization into a cauldron of anger and hatred.** Racial diversity problems are not limited to under-representation in the work force. A large overrepresentation of African Americans, according to the EEO and OPM criteria, existed in OESE. National-wide, 10.5 percent of the population are African Americans. In contrast, the Department had 36.7 percent and OESE had 48.9 percent. One program, IAP, had 67.4 percent.

Most African Americans found jobs in the lower levels of government service and aspired to move up in grade and status. This does not mean that highly competent and well-educated blacks did not find employment in the Department at higher levels. Nor does it mean that less competent and less-educated whites did not find employment at the lower levels. It simply means that an unusually large number of African Americans with fewer skills and less education found employment in OESE, predominantly at the lower levels. One simply needs to look at the EEO data of the Department to confirm these findings.

Prior to the restructuring, the problems of the diverse work force were apparent, but most of the time they would manifest themselves in subtle ways. However, there was nothing subtle about the response of the African Americans to Tom's *faux pas*—his explanation for appointing two white females as program directors. The anger, hatred, and enmity released by that event ignited a passionate wave of activity that consumed the energy of many people, energized a cadre of embittered blacks, forced morale to its lowest point in OESE, and called for understanding and patience that tested everyone.

It was devastating not only to the reassignment process, but also to the whole reengineering effort. Now everything would be seen in the light of race. Both African Americans and Hispanics fought for their ethnic representation in the reassignment process. Because of the size of their group, their dominating representation in the union and the LMPC, and their chapter of BIG, African Americans had more clout. Among other things, they challenged and successfully delayed the implementation of the restructuring effort and wrung out concessions.

There is little doubt that the ethnic diversity of OESE would have made the reassignment process a contentious experience without Tom's blunder. OESE was like a tinder box just waiting for the spark to ignite it. Yet, little had been done to confront the issues before the restructuring. When the restructuring did occur, the whole landscape was opened up for grabs. Many minority members saw this situation as an opportunity to correct the unfairness of the world of work as they perceived it.

- **When race-based criteria drive out knowledge and skill criteria, inappropriate and dysfunctional staff assignments result.** It was in the context of lowered standards for the labor force, an increased effort to recruit more minorities, and the eruption of racist feelings in personnel, that the criteria and processes of reassignment were prescribed and implemented. The RRT, dominated by vocal blacks that did not trust management, sought to make the selection criteria "objective" and "verifiable" by selecting *grade level* and *time in service* as their major criteria. These criteria would eliminate managerial judgment—or, in the minds of many of the African Americans, prejudice—about a person's knowledge and skill to do a particular job. Understandably, my advocacy for educational attainment, which could also have been selected as an objective criterion, was unacceptable to the African Americans since college attendance rates for minorities was lower than for whites. Ironically, education in the Department of Education would not be a criterion for the selection of staff!

The RRT also gave little consideration to knowledge or ability to do a job. In their preference statement, applicants were asked to state why they were qualified for a particular position in no more than one page of written comment. But after the grade and longevity criteria were applied, there had to be a *compelling* reason to deny any applicant a position, and there had to be a *consensus* about the reason. Since this would have been virtually impossible to obtain, the compelling reason did not come into play. The result of all of this procedure was the largely inappropriate and dysfunctional assignment of staff, mainly to the regional teams.

- **When procedural justice is not perceived in organizational decision-making, the organization is vulnerable to retribution.** In the *Harvard Business Review* (July/August:1997), W. Chan Kim & Renee Mauborgne describe what frequently happens when unfairness is perceived, causing employee complaints and uprisings. They write:

> But by then it is too late. When individuals have been so angered by violation of fair process that they have been driven to organized protest, their demands often stretch well beyond the reasonable to a desire for what theorists call *retributive justice*: not only do they want fair process restored, but they also seek to visit punishment and vengeance upon those who have violated it in compensation for the disrespect and unfair process signals.

It seemed to me that what many of the African Americans in ED wanted was retributive justice. Lacking trust in management, black employees pushed for policies that were inflexible and administratively constricting. They wanted to roll back decisions imposed unfairly, even when the decisions themselves were good ones. Although this was apparent in many actions, it was most perfectly displayed in the personal and vindictive report of the Diversity Task Force.

In OESE, the management of fair processes had always been seen as a system of *distributive* justice. Management allocated the resources, established the incentives and rewards, and prescribed the organizational structure. After all, they were managers, and it was their role to manage fairly. They believed that they were doing a good job of it, and assumed that most employees would agree that what they received they deserved.

In contrast, there is what Kim and Mauborgne describe as *procedural* justice. It involves engagement of the staff, explanations of what is about to take place, and clarity of expectations. It builds trust and commitment; trust and commitment produces voluntary cooperation, and voluntary cooperation drives performance. Managers who view fair process as a nuisance or as a limit on their freedom to manage must understand that a violation of fair process will do serious damage to an organization and its productivity. Managers don't abdicate all management decisions to their staff, but they must think through the decision-making demands upon an organization, work out viable, decision-making relationships with staff, clarify the expectations, and develop the feeling that the opinion of the staff does count.

Ironically, OESE was moving from a distributive to a procedural form of management when the whole thing exploded. OESE management really never thought through the decision making of the Office, so the transition resulted in unanticipated consequences. Neither did all of management accept what was taking place. Furthermore, they were making the transition in an atmosphere of racial unrest. When this unrest exploded, there was no way to constrain the outpouring of anger.

- **Organizations saturated with racial discontent require an infusion of leadership—not an avoidance of concerned interventions.** The avoidance of confrontation and a plethora of leadership mistakes characterized the situation in OESE. The racial discontent that existed in OESE and in the Department was obvious to everyone long before the restructuring of OESE was proposed. But it was not a comfortable or easy situation to resolve. Political appointees would rather put in their 18 to 20 months of public service and move on without stirring up a storm. Racial discontent is something that should be dealt with when the problem becomes evident, not after emotions explode.

In their book, *The Leadership Engine*, Noel M. Tichy and Eli Cohen write: "Winning leaders never take the easy way out . . . they face the hard facts and make the tough calls . . . [they] pursue the truth and can explain it to others" (1997:151). In other words, they have the courage to see reality and act on it. Tichy and Cohen also quote Dante as writing, "the hottest places in hell are reserved for those who, in times of great moral crisis, maintain their neutrality" (*ibid:* 261). While the racial discontent that was festering in the Department of Education will not go down in history as a "great moral crisis," there are important realities to acknowledge and decisions to be made by leaders every day. Sweeping this racial discontent under the rug and moving on without facing it is not a mark of responsible leadership.

Tom Payzant should have been prepared for the question from Ricardo at the All Hands meeting. He knew that racial diversity was a hot issue. He knew that he had just appointed two white women to program directorships. These two obvious situations should have told him that there would have to be a good explanation sooner or later. There were other reasons as well, which although he may not have known, his staff should have. The rumor mill had been spreading the discontent for a couple weeks. Tom should have known that if the appointments could not be justified, they should not have been made. If they were the right appointments, then he should have been prepared for a better explanation.

Perhaps an apology by Tom or the use of a mediator would have helped. A third party would certainly have tempered the emotions. But this was something that would have been difficult for Tom to accept. However, it is a viable option in many situations.

As for the reassignment process and criteria, why was there no charter for the RRT and no boundaries? Why had reassignment criteria assuring job competence not been prescribed by management? And why did management take on a total reassignment process for OESE when it was OERI's experience that it took three years with a much smaller staff? When the RRT got the job of prescribing the criteria and processes, they ran like a team of wild horses with the bit in their teeth from the program directors they did not trust.

One option would have been for the leadership to take the selection of the criteria out of the hands of the RRT and put it in the hands of a team of stakeholders charged with setting criteria best for the customers (instead of a particular group of staff) in OESE. The bottom line is that none of the top leaders in OESE had any experience with this type of reassignment process. And they did not seek any expert assistance.

Given the failure of early leadership, why did Tom and Janice allow these criteria to endure? Why did they constrain the program in making final changes of bad assignments? These were the questions that puzzled me. In retrospect, I reasoned that Tom was in no position to make another decision that would jeopardize his relationship with the black constituency in his work force, but I did not know for sure.

The reassignment debacle was bad enough in itself without Tom's goof. However, the problems which it spawned were legion. The consequences were evident in all that followed. My prediction, "The day that we assign everyone to his or her position in the new structure, we will see a marked drop in productivity," was about to come true.

Teams, Teams, Teams

Celebrating a Watershed

On Tuesday, September 26th, I walked six blocks with some of my colleagues from the Impact Aid Program to the Columbia Room of the Holiday Inn to participate in the "Restructuring Fair." The Fair was billed as the watershed between preparing for the restructuring of OESE and its implementation. Attendance was mandatory and the attitude of my colleagues wasn't upbeat. Most of them hadn't participated in the restructuring teams and didn't see themselves as stakeholders. Perhaps others were looking forward to the Fair with enthusiasm, but these colleagues of mine from Impact Aid were not.

At the entrance we each picked up a packet of material, and were asked to wear a colored button coded to the program we were now assigned. The room was larger than anything in our office building, but not large enough for what was coming. Many of the attendees found their assigned tables, others talked with friends, and a few looked with curiosity at the agenda in their packets. According to the agenda, the purpose of the two-day fair was (1) to meet with their teams for the first time, (2) do some team building, (3) obtain information about the restructuring,

(4) identify needed competencies, (5) reinforce the importance of communication, and (6) celebrate their accomplishments.

The activities of the first day included a motivational speech about restructuring OESE from the Assistant Secretary, a couple of ice-breaker activities, a presentation on managing change, and group discussions about staff expectations and customer needs. A special effort was made to legitimize the reassignment process—members of the LMPC talked about the fairness of the process, Bob Morgan, a union official, talked about the union's commitment to sustain change, and a program director who had previously been raising some serious questions about the restructuring, talked about management support for restructuring.

On the second day Mark Rhodes, a consultant, introduced the staff to the Organizational Systems Design (OSD) model and had us thinking about how it related to what OESE was doing. But most folks had fun with the competitive team exercises. Bob Pallone also came through with a very humorous interview of Tom and a rap that earned him the recognition as OESE's most humorous person. His self-designated title for the occasion, "Main Man," would stick with him until the day he retired.

But what did it do for the staff? The Fair reinforced the intention of the top (politically appointed) leadership in OESE to proceed in the restructuring. The Fair proved that the staff could have fun together. They were able to share information. It also created a lot of flip chart lists that were typed up and turned in, and, I suspect, never used. If there was any benefit from the discussions it would come from the thinking that occurred, the enjoyment of having some fun together, and from getting better acquainted.

The staff were now assigned to their teams. But the members of the regional teams would not move to their new locations for about six months. Whatever momentum for the restructuring effort was picked up soon became minimal. There would be team meetings each week, but people's work stations were the same as before—scattered over two floors of their office building. Most members of the program service teams did not get reassigned, and they continued to work at their assignments much as they had done previously. For them, not much changed. In fact, most members of program service teams never did see

134

themselves as teams in anything but name. They continued to work much as they always had.

Union Disenchantment

Although many new problems emerged with the implementation, many old problems took on even more importance. One of them was the disenchantment of the union with the whole restructuring effort, especially the feasibility of teams. The union had still not anointed the restructuring, in spite of what was said by Bob Morgan at the Fair. In fact union leaders entertained a lot of doubts.

Questions and Answers. About a week prior to the Fair, Sandra Stead, President, AFGE, Local 2607, sent a memorandum to Janice Jackson requesting answers to about two dozen questions. This was an initial step leading up to mediation. The questions had to do with the status of team leaders, evaluation and appraisal of employees on regional service teams, and the distribution of work load. To me, some of the questions reflected petty gripes, others had to do with unresolved problems in the transition from former personnel procedures to the new ones, and some dealt with fundamental problems.

Leslie Harris, in the Labor Relations Group of the Office of Management, responded to the union's list of questions for OESE. But it was impossible to provide the union with satisfying answers to all questions. On October 30th, with questions and answers in hand, the union and management met to see if they could come to an agreement. Phyllis Barajas informed a meeting of group and team leaders that significant progress had been made, but four sticking points remained and would go to mediation:

1. **The roles of team and group leaders.** The major issue was who reported to whom? Who made the work assignments and who was responsible to whom for staff accountability?

2. **Performance appraisals.** The responsibility for performance appraisals was still being debated. What role, if any, did the team leader have in the performance appraisal process?

3. **Structure supporting grades.** The problem of generic position descriptions was at the heart of the matter. Members of the union

apparently believed that there would be grade drift within the classification system. (Human resource people dealing with classification were back in the picture trying to sort this one out and developing a monitoring plan.)

4. **Current work assignments.** Lack of clarity in the current work assignments of team and group members was confusing. Apparently some team leaders were expecting more work than others, and some team members were not supporting current team work. What could be done under current authority and what will be done in the future?

Phyllis summarized by stating: "We are currently working through issues. This is what we should be doing. Let the floor know that there is no crisis." As I listened to the issues being discussed by my colleagues, I could tell that the emotions with which these issues were argued indicated otherwise. And I knew that these issues could not be easily resolved.

Mediation. On November 6th, a representative from Federal Mediation and Conciliation Service convened a group comprised of OESE's LMPC, representatives of the Executive Committee of Union Local 2607, and staff from the Office of Management's Labor Relations and Human Resources Groups. The mediation dealt with the (1) maintenance of grades, (2) communication and reporting relationships, and (3) lines of authority regarding work assignments and performance evaluation. In the end, the union agreed that OESE could implement its restructuring. However, it was agreed that a monitoring and evaluation process would begin immediately through the LMPC, and no structural changes would be made for at least a year unless there was a major, compelling reason. Twelve recommendations for monitoring the three issues were specified.

This mediation also captured the elements of a memorandum of understanding between AFGE Local 2607 and the Department of Education. The memo was drafted and debated extensively within the union. But there were many who were not happy with it and a variety of issues were raised. So, on December 7th, union and management representatives met and hammered out a revised memo, which the leadership of the AFGE supported. The next day, the AFGE distributed the revised memo with comments, and set up an additional meeting to discuss it. Among the comments were the following key acknowledgments:

> Management has the legal right to unilaterally determine OESE's organizational structure, regardless of whether or not the union agrees with it; OESE [management] is not willing to reconsider the structure at this time.

> It is important to understand that if this memorandum of understanding is not signed, employees will lose the benefits it provides. To be certain of management's continuing commitment to this agreement, it has been written as a formal collective bargaining agreement, so that it is legally binding and enforceable, no matter who is the Assistant Secretary.

Despite the fact that the union signed the memo, a lack of trust between the staff (especially the African Americans) and management persisted. The LMPC continued to be a battleground, although not the only one. The feasibility of teams, especially the RSTs, remained in doubt.

Charterless Regional Teams

The regional service teams, which were to serve a specified group of states with "one face to the customer," became the focal point of most problems and issues. I had expressed my opinion on a number of occasions to my peers and to Janice that two of the mistakes made with the restructuring teams were that they never had a clear charter and they never had boundaries. I argued that these failures resulted in wide-ranging assumptions, expectations, disappointments, and inevitable problems. I said that if these mistakes were repeated with the initiation of the regional service teams, we could expect the same results.

Six months earlier, on May 11th, there had been a very discordant meeting of the so-called "Steering Committee," in which the reassignment of staff was the subject of the meeting. (See Chapter 3.) The more I thought about the meeting and the anguish over the reassignment process, the more troubled I became. On May 16th, I wrote to Janice and recommended establishing a charter with boundaries for all teams against the background of the recent troublesome meeting. I attached a format for creating a team charter that contained five sections with key questions related to each section. The five sections of the charter were (1) purpose, (2) responsibilities, (3) boundaries, (4) ground rules, and (5) meetings. I stated that it was the responsibility of management to set boundaries and establish charters. In a comment about boundaries I wrote: "In my judgment it would be a mistake not to set boundaries, to allow the teams to establish false expectations, and then say that for the lack of trust, we have to allow full empowerment over management responsibilities to prove management's fairness." This was my interpretation of what had taken place.

The memo had gotten Janice's attention. My meeting with her a week later was the most open, frank, and honest sharing of information we ever had. To support my argument that teams can take on more responsibility as they gain experience and mature, I gave Janice two additional handouts. One was an example of a team responsibility chart that planned the phasing in of more and more responsibility until a team became self-directed. The other was a matrix format for increasing team responsibilities over time. I also brought material from the *OSD Model Guidebook* (1994) about organizational decision making and an example of a responsibility chart to analyze it. Janice was pleased by what she saw and asked me if I could help the teams work through their charters, incorporating the components of increasing responsibilities and decision making. I agreed to do this, but said that I would have to involve management. Janice said she wanted me to plan on doing it.

As the two of us left Janice's office, Phyllis Barajas was waiting to see Janice. Janice said that Phyllis had recently been officially transferred from the Office of Management to OESE to help with the reengineering. On three occasions, during the next several months, Janice asked me if Phyllis had talked with me about my role in helping the teams develop charters. On each occasion, I had to answer no. Janice would look puzzled, but wouldn't say anything. I assumed that Phyllis had been given the responsibility for involving me, but was reluctant to share the leadership. I never heard anything from Phyllis about it. The charter and other features proposed by me were never developed.

Failure at Roles, Functions and Responsibilities

Several months later, after Tom and Janice had left for new jobs in the Boston Public Schools, the new Assistant Secretary, Gerald N. Tirozzi, arrived. Although obligated to support the restructuring effort of his predecessor, he discovered that OESE was not operating as expected. Since he did not have the same vested interest in the restructuring as his predecessor, and had no experience in reengineering, he had the OESE assessed by a third party.

From "Tweaking" to "Roadblocks." The new Assistant Secretary contracted with the firm, Coopers & Lybrand, to assess the situation and recommend some "mid-course corrections." To use his word, he wanted to know how to "tweak" the organization. Coopers & Lybrand's assessment of the OESE organization was made public on August 9, 1996. The report revealed that OESE's reengineering would take a lot more than just a tweak. Among other findings, they identified six primary "roadblocks" to success. One of these roadblocks dealt with roles and responsibilities, about which Coopers & Lybrand had the following to say:

> OESE staff are not clear about what is expected of them in the new environment. There are no means by which success of the new operation can be measured. Reporting relationships and accountability are unclear. The roles of supervisor of record, RST group leader, and team leader are especially confusing.

> There are many mixed messages given to teams that impact performance. Regional service teams (RSTs) are said to be self-directed, but decisions are reversed with sometimes inadequate explanation. Program support teams (PSTs) are called teams, but do not function as teams. RSTs and PSTs have not established a clear working relationship.

These findings were no surprise. No one would doubt that there was major trouble with the interfacing of roles, functions, and responsibilities. These topics had been discussed and debated, defined and redefined, written and revised, disputed and refuted, and complained about again and again. My files on the roles and functions of team leaders, group leaders, and program directors were jammed full of material. These problems emerged repeatedly, meeting after meeting. Each time a committee or task force would be delegated to work on them, the drafts would get circulated, revised, and eventually adopted. Still, OESE could not make them work.

Early Attempts to Define Roles and Functions. There were a number of attempts to define and clarify roles and functions. Chuck Hansen and his team did the first thinking about roles and functions in the conceptualization of the restructuring. The next major effort was when OESE drafted its official reorganization plan. Before OESE could implement its restructuring, it had to submit a plan to the Office of Management that included position descriptions. The three most essential position descriptions in the plan were those of the group leader for the regional service team, the group leader for the program service team, and the team leader.

A third early effort to think about roles, functions, and responsibility came when Joe Colantouni, Director of the Human Resources Innovation Group, facilitated a meeting on August 8th to think about the problems and issues involved in implementing the restructuring plan. Joe opened the meeting to the identification of problems and issues. The issues and problems the group was most concerned about were those of roles, functions, accountability, and responsibility.

After the meeting, Joe and his staff prepared a report that showed the prioritized and categorized list of roles and functions the group had worked on. To my knowledge, nothing was ever done with this report.

Team Leaders and the Leadership Team. Despite all the other efforts, the most extensive discussions of roles and responsibilities were usually held at the weekly meetings of the Leadership Team. In the beginning, the Leadership Team, as distinguished from the Senior Leadership Team, included the group leaders and team leaders. The Leadership Team, itself, was a good example of the inability to work out roles and responsibilities. They soon discovered that they could not work out their problems without the participation of the program directors. Reluctantly, the program directors began to participate in meeting of the Leadership Team. At one point the Senior Leadership Team (made up mostly of program directors) decided that team leaders should not be included in the Leadership Team, because they were not officially a part of management. This rankled the team leaders and a compromise was worked out. They were soon reinstated one meeting per month, for the purpose of facilitating communication, not decision making.

Unable to develop a constructive working relationship between program directors, group leaders and team leaders, the Leadership Team was destined to fail. The Team continued to meet for several months until the meetings eventually faded away due to the excuse that they were in conflict with other more important events. However, while they met there was seldom a meeting without a discussion of roles, functions, and responsibilities. Ironically, even they could not develop a cooperative working relationship.

Informal Discussions. There were also many informal discussions. One particularly frustrating effort, took place on August 8th with two of my colleagues, Harris Taylor and Curt Van Horn. At one point in the conversation, Harris stated that regardless of how interrelationships and work characteristics were spelled out, little would change. "The work will not change, because the organizational structure is not going to change the functions. Regional teams will be an extension of the core programs and will be directed from the core program base," he said. For clarification, I asked him, "Are you saying that the work will not change because the authority, responsibility, accountability, and status of the key persons are not going to change?" Harris responded, "Exactly!"

Roles vs. Positions. In August, a series of meetings for program directors, group leaders, team leaders, and selected individuals from the front office was begun. The series was named the "Learning through Change Series." In each of these meetings, there was a lot of time devoted to roles and functions of program directors, group leaders and team leaders.

At one point when considering the role of team leader, I took a contrarian point of view. I asserted that OESE was not delayering by assigning team leaders to teams and designating them *roles* instead of *positions*. I went on to say:

We spent two long and difficult days selecting 10 team leaders. There was keen competition for these positions. We have been giving them special training. They have important work to do, and we all consider them critical to the success of our reengineering effort. They are responsible for the success of the integrated review teams that review state programs, the assessment of consolidated state plans, solving a host of problems, and meeting the needs of our customers. Any analysis of their roles will reveal that they do have power, exert authority, control activities and events, and have considerable influence. Others aspire to their positions and they have status and prestige.

I then concluded my remarks with this reference to the behavioral sciences:

In the behavioral sciences, it is *human behavior* that defines the situation, and any analysis of the human behavior of team leaders, and their colleague's relationship with them, assures us that we definitely have a management layer at this level . . . In research we often find that conventional wisdom, rationale, and even theory is wrong. If we were to collect data that we knew were valid and reliable, but did not support our theory, we would not throw away the data. We would throw away the theory!

My comments were too much for Janice to take sitting down. It was time to defend the administration's position that the Department of Education was delayering. She stood up and said, "There are a number of ways to look at the team leader role, and behavioral analysis was only one." She did not suggest another way or give any examples. This was the second time that I had said essentially the same thing in a meeting, and this was the second time Janice had given the same short— and to me—inadequate response.

Integrated Review Teams

Goals 2000 and State Reform. On March 31,1994, President Bill Clinton signed into law *The GOALS 2000: Educate America Act.* The Act enjoyed the backing of almost every major national parent, education, and business organization. Both houses of Congress passed this legislation by roughly a three-to-one vote with bipartisan support. Most of us in OESE were excited about the legislation. It attempted to forge a new partnership with the states, based on the assumption that public education works best when parents, educators, taxpayers, and policy makers at the local schools and state levels decide how to make their schools better. It focused on improving the education system for all students, rather than on supporting specific categories of students with identified "disadvantages." It reflected a commitment to raising the academic expectations for all students.

Under *GOALS 2000,* each state had to develop its own academic standards for all students, its own comprehensive plan for school reform, and its standards and reforms with broad-based, grass-roots involvement. The Department of Education issued no new regulations, but it did say that at least 60 percent of the federal funds had to be passed on to the local districts in the first year, and 90 percent in subsequent years.

Piloting the IRTs. Before *GOALS 2000* became law, the Assistant Secretary of OESE was moving in a collaborative direction with what he assumed would be enacted into legislation. In December of 1993, he established an Integrated Review Team (IRT) as a pilot project. The IRT (later referred to as the "core team") represented OESE programs and was charged with the task of "developing strategies for integrated program reviews that support system reform." A central component of the core team's development work was to launch pilot reviews in six states. The goals of these pilot efforts were to explore approaches to (1) examining states' use of federal resources to support systemic reform, and to (2) providing technical assistance to enhance states' efforts to serve disadvantaged students effectively. Previous program reviews were done by each program office, and they focused primarily on compliance issues related to its specific program.

In addition to the core team, there were also six state teams made up of members of each program and some of the members of the core team. Each team had six to nine members, including the team leader. Some team members represented more than one program, but not all programs were represented on each team.

Drawing from official OESE documents and discussions with senior staff, the core team drafted its own charter. It identified five tasks for the integrated review process:

1. Examine the educational curriculum and services provided to all children, including recipients served by federal funds.

2. Consider the extent to which a state's high standards and programs are effective and students are achieving.

3. Assist the state departments of education and school districts to use their federal funds to enhance service to the targeted populations.

4. Identify institutional barriers to using federal funds to support state educational initiatives.

5. Monitor for essential program integrity requirements.

An Observer Contract. Not long after the core team began its work, the members acknowledged their limitations in observing, documenting, assessing their activities, and requested an outside observer. This resulted in a contract with Policy Studies Associates, Inc., (PSA) to become an outside observer. PSA not only looked at the activities of the OESE staff, but also assessed the involvement of state and local staff in the process.

As I read PSA's report, *The Integrated Program Review Process*, it appeared to me that PSA was trying to get their messages across without burning any bridges. For example, when they wrote "this set of tasks posed significant challenges." they could have been more straightforward about OESE's lack of competence for this task. The real message I read between the lines was that the staff did not have the technical assistance capacity, an understanding of standards-based reform, or the ability to alter their compliance monitoring approach. PSA issued a report with four recommendations:

1. Clarify expectations and requirements for the major elements of the integrated review process: examining state systemic reforms, monitoring compliance with essential program elements, and providing technical assistance.

2. Define leadership roles for the integrated review process.

3. Expand training for all staff assigned to conduct integrated program reviews.

4. Define and support teamwork.

Of course, this was a pilot project, but thousands of hours of work would be committed to IRTs in the future, and the report did not forecast any warning with the IRT approach when staff do not have the competence. The IRT approach rolled on to the next phase, which was to spell out more specifically what was involved in the implementation of the IRT process in the newly established RSTs, and provide training for RST members. The task was given to the Special Integrated Review Team of ten members, chaired by the Director of the GOALS 2000 Program. The report that was distributed to the staff on August 26, 1996 was fairly comprehensive and demanding, but, I felt, not very realistic, given the abilities of our staff. To me, the outside contractor had ignored a major problem.

Perceptions of Team Inadequacy. Indeed, during the pilot testing and the implementation of the IRT process, I tested my understandings and perceptions about what was taking place with some of the participants. I engaged Julia Lesceux, one of the members of the core team, in conversation a number of times about how the pilot was working out. In one conversation I had with Julia, not long before they closed down the pilot, she said, "We still don't know what we're doing . . . and how it is coming across." She was convinced about a few things. For example, she warned that OESE management would have to have some "integrated control" of the ten RSTs. "If not,' she said, "we'll be like an octopus without any communication between its tentacles. We will have ten 'tentacles' [regional teams] out there doing their own thing. This shouldn't be!"

Julia reported that in the beginning, the core team wanted to send "first line" people into the field, but the program directors wouldn't let them. She felt they needed credibility with the states. The states were putting up their first line people while OESE wasn't.

I thought Julia was specially insightful when she said, "There is an assumption behind the restructuring that everyone can be trained for IRTs, but this is wrong . . . We need a description of what is needed for team members. Without descriptions, how do we know what the training should be? And not everyone with good training will ever be able to do a good job on an IRT . . . The team leaders in the RSTs will have to orchestrate their teams. Not everyone can contribute. Some staff may be able to contribute very little. The team leaders will have to facilitate the use of appropriate people for a lot of things."

About training she said: "We had formal training as an IRT core team. This was helpful, but it didn't meet what we needed. Don't assume that newly formed IRTs will be able to hit the ground running . . . Our most important learning was how to become a team. One day we stopped 'peacocking' and discovered that we had become a team. We now could trust one another. This took a year and a half."

Another highly credible reporter was David Kanthak. Dave is an experienced school administrator, and it is doubtful if anyone in the Department knew more about school finance across the 50 states than Dave. He was especially interested in how systemic reform was working out in school finance. He had drafted some specific questions to ask, from which he could easily determine how far a state or school district had gone. He reported that his questions allowed him to cut to the heart of the reform issue and helped him make a constructive contribution.

He did complain that the most difficult part for him was the drafting of the report. He stated that he couldn't make any suggestions or recommendations, because the IRTs could not "dictate" to the states what they ought to do. He complained, "I had my part of the report returned to me and couldn't negotiate even a very bland suggestion based on my observations." He concluded, "I don't understand how the IRT visits are going to have much usefulness. I can see that it's a learning experience for the OESE staff. I don't know what use OESE, or the regional teams in the restructuring effort, can do with visits conducted and reported in this fashion."

Curtis Van Horn, a former school superintendent, was especially concerned with the level of ability of the staff. He asked: "They keep talking about providing technical assistance, but what do we have to give in the way of technical assistance? Nobody knows anything about learning around here. Nobody knows anything about teaching around here. Nobody knows anything about standards and assessments. Nobody knows anything about school reform." He continued, "It is kind of embarrassing to go out on an IRT with the people in this Department, sit across the table from the people who are running the schools of this country, and have nothing to contribute to the discussion but compliance requirements."

I caught Curt on a roll. He had other questions and complaints: "What can you expect from this Department that has no respect for education when they hire staff?" he asked. "We have wiped out nearly all educational requirements for personnel in this Department. Anybody can get a job here, whether they have had any higher education or not. Anybody can get a job here, whether they have taught or not . . . This Department should not be called the Department of Education. We should call it the Department of Giving Out Money for Education." He concluded by saying, "I am not saying that this [the concept of the restructured OESE] is not what we should be. That's for somebody else to decide. But we ought to admit what we are and what we are not. We shouldn't try to fake it!"

I found many of the same themes repeated in the discussions I had with other colleagues. One day, when I was on a coffee break with a few of my colleagues, we discussed the effects of the series of ten training lectures on systemic reform that the Assistant Secretary had made mandatory for all staff. Harris Taylor said that the series would not be sufficient to prepare anyone for technical assistance at any depth. I asked, "What percentage of our RST staff would ever be able to provide technical assistance?' Harris replied, "Not many!"

When I asked, "Why do you say that?" Harris answered: "Our staff have not been hired to do this type of work. Most don't have college degrees, especially studies in education. They do not have practical experience in schools. Some don't even have any interest in it." He continued by saying, "We have to change our employment and our promotion strategies. We've taken all the relevant criteria out of our position descriptions, and we no longer employ people with the relevant education and experience. He also said that "We have to stop placing people in career ladder positions that move secretaries into professional positions that require professional work of this kind."

Oral Reports Reveal Team Weaknesses. The oral reports of the IRTs on their visits to the states also revealed striking weaknesses. I sat in on a number of them. In spite of the desire of the team leaders and others to put their visits in a good light, the teams were having difficulty with basic issues such as standards and their assessments. One team member said that prior to going on their trip, he asked one state official how they might help them. The official said they needed help with the key concepts of systemic reform. This team member then worked hard to learn as much as he could about reform. But, he admitted, the state administrators were so far ahead of him that he didn't even take the material he had brought with him out of his brief case.

Another common phenomenon was the reaction of team members who had never taught or worked in a school in any position. The local school staff would show off their special programs for the federal visitors and the inexperienced OESE staff would be greatly impressed with the "dog and pony shows" put on for their benefit. This was undoubtedly a learning experience for many of the IRT members, but it certainly was not analysis or technical assistance.

The day after the report of a team's visit to Kentucky, Carroll Dexter and I discussed the report. Carroll pointed out that Ricardo Sanchez, who presented the report for the team, really had no idea what Kentucky had done about the reform of their educational system. Carroll, who had followed the reform events in Kentucky with great interest, highlighted for me what had been done. He stated, "Nothing that Ricardo said gave any indication that he knew about any of it." This was one of the nation's most significant reform efforts and the IRT had nothing to say about it.

Carroll said: "If the academic minds in our universities ever caught on to the fact that the Department of Education knows so little about the systemic reform they are purporting to promote, they would have a field day [exposing ED's ignorance]."

The state plans also came in for a good deal of discussion. The IRTs did not assess state plans; that was done by a panel of readers. But technical assistance with the development of state plans was part of an IRT's domain. In one oral report, a team member who had been to Idaho stated that there appears to be little agreement on what constitutes a state plan. Mary Jean LeTendre was clearly irked by the comment. She spoke up from the audience asking, "Do you want any answers?" Then she took a hard line and said, "Idaho should be told that they are not in compliance and how they can get in compliance!"

A Commissioner's Response. One of the most thoughtful responses concerning an IRT visitation was provided by Dr. Shirley J. Holloway, State Commissioner of Education, Alaska, in a letter to Assistant Secretary of OESE, Gerald Tirozzi, the Commissioner observed that the IRT did not have any standards for the review and suggested the following:

- In order to move from a subjective, individual program, process review to an objective, consolidated review-driven review—standards need to be established.

- The consolidated review standards would represent the common elements across programs.

- If the rubric is designed for the standards, the expectations would be clear to the U.S. Department of Education (USDOE) reviewers and the State Department of Education (SDOE) staff.

- This approach would facilitate communicating how proficient the SDOE is in relationship to the standards.

- A road map is needed to get from the old structure to the new one. Why ask for an overview of the reform efforts and then not look for those in the review?

Dr. Holloway described the exit conference between state officials and the IRT team as follows: "At the exit conference, the USDOE team described their experiences and observations during the school site visits, provided praise, and hinted at problems." In the middle of the exit conference, she interrupted the meeting and reported making the following remarks:

- I realized that this is a new process for all of us. We are still learning and just as I felt I needed to be told the major elements of the review prior to receiving the written results, I felt they needed to know from me how I felt about the conference.

- The points in the first part of the letter on standards were covered.

- I told them I had not learned anything from the presentation, thus far, other than their visits to the different sites were enjoyable. There was no substance to their comments.

- Since Dr. Buell, Director of all the reviewed programs, and I were not part of the individual meetings between USDOE and SDOE program representatives, we were virtually in the dark.

- In my opinion, the exit conference is the appropriate time to bring to our attention the areas needing improvement and give us an opportunity to ask clarifying questions.

- If, in fact, the substance was given program-by-program, then this was not a consolidated review. USDOE staff is still talking about "program integrity."

- Basically, we observed the team talking privately about individual programs and talking publicly about consolidation.

She concluded her letter saying, "It is my belief that we are all professionals trying to do the best job possible for children. We do not have to waste time with 'feel good' conferences. Talking honest, caring, constructive criticism is part of what we need to do with children, with individuals we evaluate, and programs we review. If the conference were then followed up with *technical assistance* and support, positive changes can occur."

The contents of the letter were no surprise to me and most of my colleagues with professional backgrounds. The IRT could not make the transition from a program-by-program monitoring mode to which they were accustomed, to a system analysis of their consolidated approach to education. They had no format (standards) for this type of analysis. There was no substance to their comments. They could not provide technical assistance. Not being able to contribute on this level, they provided "feel good" reports of their experiences.

Controlling the Regional Teams

The Management Dilemma of Program Directors. The goal of having program work done in regional teams was a problem for the program directors from the beginning. Although they had to go along with the restructuring of OESE, there had not been wholehearted buy-in from them. They felt it was going to be difficult to manage programs with staff assigned to regional teams and spread over two floors of the building. Furthermore, the reassignment of OESE staff would exacerbate the problem. The program directors were not only disenchanted with the structure, they had very little to say about the assignment of their personnel. Therefore, it was not surprising to see the program directors exerting influence over the teams once they had been formed. For example, I attended a regional team meeting in which their IRT travel plans to Oregon were discussed. The team became upset about the intrusion of a group leader from the Title I program, who they felt tried to dictate who would go on the IRT trip to Oregon. She wanted another person outside the team to go in the team member's place. She also objected to two other persons who did not know enough to function well on an integrated review. The team reacted negatively to the intrusion and proceeded with their original plans. Nevertheless, they acknowledged that they would probably get their travel orders denied.

There was also a discussion at this meeting about the fact that 18 persons would be involved in travel related to the IRT. Those who attempted to justify the travel of 18 people explained that there were really three separate trips involved. The first trip involved a few staff that would travel to the Northwest Laboratory in Portland, because the Lab had been providing technical assistance to the state. A second trip would be made by a few staff to plan for the review with officials in the state. The final trip would be made by IRT itself. Cathy Schagh, who was also sitting in on this meeting, warned the team that they had better have a back-up plan, because they would not get approval for 18 travelers.

Bob Palone, a member of another regional team, spoke to me on several occasions about the Group Leader, Dan Bonner, who came to every meeting and interjected his comments and directions into their deliberations. Bob said that the team leader and some of the team members would defer to his suggestions because of his position. Bob pointed out that if you want to move up in responsibility and grade, you go along with those above you in the hierarchy. "But Bonner," he said, "has become the team boss."

Elizabeth Whitehorn, a former school principal and member of this team, was more direct. A couple of months later she said: "Dan Bonner still does not get it. He is still imposing decisions made by the program base [SIP Program Service Team] on the team, and attempting to control it in every way he can." She added, "He is voting on team issues, even though he had been informed that his vote does not count."

Program Director Interventions. One day I noticed that Curt Van Horn, Team Leader of Team #8, was upset. He had just come from a meeting of his team. I followed him into his office and we sat down to talk. Curt stated that Mary Jean, program director of CEP, had assigned a new person to their team from her program, without conferring with him or the group leader to which he reported. The new team member suddenly appeared. Curt said, "We already have two persons from CEP, and a third was not needed." It also upset the other two persons from CEP. To make things worse, the new person was very rigid. She arrived after plans for an IRT had been made and insisted that they change their plans to accommodate her opinions. Curt complained, "She has no flexibility. She kept insisting that there was only one way to do things . . . My team is really upset."

Team Leader Response. One morning during a coffee break, Randy Kingsley, another team leader, was very depressed. He complained that their team members were getting work assigned to them by everyone—program directors, group leaders, and others. He said: "What steamed my rice was the fact that my team has so much work to do, and they get no help from the program service teams." He added, "It should be the other way around. Some of the work that is being loaded on to the regional service teams should be distributed to members of the program service teams."

Randy continued to analyze the situation. He argued: "We should be made supervisors equivalent to the branch managers in the old structure." "And," he added, "we are not going to be successful as long as the team leaders don't have any authority to assess performance." At that point, I pointed out, "That won't happen because the Department is out to eliminate middle management, and if they say that team leaders are really supervisors equivalent to branch managers, they'll be back to where they started on the span of control numbers."

The discussion then turned to the role of the program directors. The consensus was that in the long run, the program directors will be judged by the way that they run their programs, not the success of the restructuring effort. Programs are a *specific* responsibility; restructuring is an *overall* responsibility. Program directors won't get hurt when the restructuring plan fails, but they will get hurt if their programs fail. As a result, program directors and their "lieutenants" will continue to interject their will on the regional service teams. Empowerment for the regional service teams is a fiction.

Randy said, "I'm going to give them another couple of months to get this situation straightened out. If not, they are going to get my team leader position back in their laps." Curt added, "I'll be right behind you."

Forcing Round Pegs . . .

Most people in the Impact Aid Program (IAP) and the Indian Education Program (IEP) thought it was a mistake to include them in the RSTs since these programs were different from the other programs in OESE. They both interacted directly with the local school districts and did not work through the states. As a result, both programs had many of the same problems with the restructuring. For one, they both had distinctly different work to do that would be very difficult, if not impossible, for other staff to do. Secondly, there were certain periods in the yearly schedule during which work would overwhelm their staffs and keep them from working on team tasks. And thirdly, both had heavy concentrations of applicants in certain regions and states, not spread evenly throughout the country. The idea that cross training could teach other staff to do the work of people in these two programs was not realistic.

IEP Dysfunctions. Not knowing much about how IEP was faring under the restructuring, I paid a visit to Amos Goodfox to learn more. Amos reiterated the difficulty of anyone but the staff of the IEP doing the work of the IEP. But the biggest problem of all was the inequities that resulted from the reassignments of staff to RSTs. In IEP, for example, RST # 6 had 400 applicants and only two staff from IEP to serve them, and RST # 7, 275 applicants and only one IEP staff. In contrast, RST #8 has only 27 applicants in the region with one staff. "The ridiculous thing about this situation," he reported, "we are not allowed to do the work of IEP staff in other teams." He stated that those with light loads would be glad to help out those with overloads, "but they won't let us."

Amos charged that there would be a great cost to the Program when the surge of telephone inquiries come. During these periods, a lot of phone calls will have to wait a long time to get answered, and some will get no answers at all. Also, some of IEP staff are going to get way behind in their team work responsibilities. They can't do it all.

As for IAP dysfunction, the issue of integrating the staff into the regional teams was a contentious issue from the very beginning. At one IAP staff meeting, a conscientious employee complained that she had to give an inordinate amount of time to the assessments of the state plans and the IRTs, in spite of the fact that Impact Aid was not included in either. Others agreed, feeling that IAP staff were doing the work of the other programs while the Impact Aid work was not getting done. We get no help on our work because nobody but Impact Aid staff know how to do it." In other words, there was no reciprocal assistance.

Carroll Dexter, a group leader, stated that Impact Aid staff should be teaching people from other programs how to do the work of the Impact Aid staff, but they receive no support to do so. Another staff member responded, "Who here is willing to take responsibility for the product of other team members who have never done our work before? That is the heart of the matter! When the work gets screwed up, it takes extra time to get it corrected, and it could involve a lot of money." From my point of view, I felt that the problem would not go away. "Impact Aid does not fit well with the other programs, and it is doubtful if it will ever be integrated with the other programs," I told the IAP staff.

Cathy Schagh, the Program Director, could not let the discussion end on this note. She had to support the restructuring. About all she could say, without denying the problems, was that: "There are times when the other programs really need our help."

Indeed, the workload problem for the IAP staff was a constant bone of contention. As the problem continued, the costs began to enter into the discussions. One morning when Carroll and I were sharing observations, Carroll looked worried and said, "The team structure for OESE isn't working and won't work." He pointed out that there were a number of costs that really were not being calculated. For example, Impact Aid made only 200 field reviews during 1996, while in the previous year they had done 900 reviews. Since the restructuring, they could now only do field reviews for some special or urgent reason."

Although IAP processed their payments by computer, the Program maintained an "Official" file in hard copy for each applicant, which included such things as the application, correspondence, payment vouchers, and supporting documents. Arnett Smith, a senior IAP employee, was very concerned about the status of the files. He reported: "With the official files being distributed to staff spread over two floors in this building, many of them are lost . . . and I pick up files all the time which are incomplete. Many are missing vouchers. You can't trace a payment history with the official files any longer."

On one occasion Curt Van Horn confided to me that he thought the restructuring of OESE was not working for IAP. "Our work tasks can never be integrated with the other programs," he said. "Think of what we've done. We've taken a cohesive working group and scattered them over two floors of this building. We've broken up the filing system and scattered it all over the building. And we've made it very difficult to manage people by spreading them all over the landscape. As a consequence, the Impact Aid Program is going to suffer. That's for certain."

Curt predicted: "We've cut down on the number of field reviews we do because of lack of time and travel money. As a result, the program will be administered with more errors in payments. Funds will be unfairly distributed—giving some districts more money than they should have, and other districts less money than they are entitled. In brief, the quality of the program will suffer."

Curt concluded by saying that personally he couldn't do anything about it, so he wasn't going to worry. He said that from now until he retires, he would be there to do what they tell him to do, and he wasn't going to get upset as long as they kept paying his salary.

Program Service Teams

The Coopers & Lybrand report stated, "PSTs are called teams, but do not function as teams." I knew that this finding was true for IAP, and had been told that it was true for the other programs as well. I knew that the historical pattern of OESE management had not changed, and without a change, self-directed teams could not possibly emerge and survive. Obviously, the RSTs were not allowed to become self-directed teams. Interventions into their activities were daily events. Why would anything be different in the PSTs?

The PST Stretch. As I considered the PST members and their work, I questioned if they could work as a team, especially a self-directed team. First, there would be the culture hurdle. The membership of the PST after the reassignment was almost identical to the membership of the Program Support Branch prior to the reassignment. They worked on the same jobs at the same desks as before. The Program Director continued to manage much as she always had. Instead of supervising me as a branch chief, Cathy now supervised me as a group leader. She informed me that she would continue to manage her immediate staff as before, even though they were now members of the PST. So little had changed. In brief, because of only modest changes in the personnel and the way they continued to work, the culture would not change.

Second, most work assignments were specialized and not directly dependent upon the labor of others. This was not entirely true for a few people who expedited the computer payment processes, and two persons who certified property. But most of the time, the staff worked independently on specialized tasks without a dependency on others.

Third, this was not work that could be bundled into a self-directed team effort. The team members did not want that type of interrelationship, nor would the Program Director relinquish any of her decision making to a team.

Consequently, it would really be a stretch to make a self-directed team out of the IAP Program Service Team.

Thinking Styles that Inhibit Change. Furthermore, the thinking styles of most of the program directors would not be comfortable with change. It was obvious to me, and to some others as well, that the program directors worked mainly from the left (risk adverse) side of their brains. I confirmed this one day when talking to Mark Rhodes, a consultant who had administered the Herrmann Brain Dominance Instrument (HBDI) to members of the Senior Leadership Team. I asked Mark a general question, "The program directors are primarily left brain dominant, aren't they?" Mark responded, "Yes, and some of them are *very* left brain dominant."

Ned Herrmann, the designer of the HBDI, explains that "the core of the Whole Brain Technology is a metaphor of how I believe the brain works. It is founded on my brain-based research and on observable evidence that thinking styles can be best described as a coalition of four different thinking selves." (1996:6) He identifies these selves as follows:

- The A-quadrant Analyzer: Logical thinking, analysis of facts, processing numbers.

- The B-quadrant Organizer: Planning approaches, organizing facts, detailed review.

- The C-quadrant Personalizer: Interpersonal, intuitive, expressive.

- The D-quadrant Visualizer: Imaginative, big picture thinking, conceptualizing.

Ned Herrmann illustrates these four quadrants with the whole brain model depicted in Figure 3, and explains that because of our individuality we display specific dominating characteristics in our thinking styles. There is nothing right or wrong, good or bad, about having a particular thinking style. But as illustrated in Figure 4, our thinking characteristics turn us on to certain types of work preferences. It is not surprising that left-brain dominant people become program directors.

In the HBDI, upper left brain dominant people do well with analysis. They are comfortable with numbers, statistics, and data. They understand technical elements and do well at critical analysis, financial analysis, logical problem solving and arguing rationally. People who have a strong upper left dominant thinking style are commonly found in scientific, technical, financial and legal occupations.

In the HBDI, lower left brain dominant people do well with organization. They are good at organizing and keeping track of data, developing detailed plans and procedures, approaching problems practically, and providing stable leadership and supervision. People with these thinking styles are usually in managerial, administrative, supervisory and service occupations. One should not conclude that left brain dominant people cannot deal with change. It simply means that it is more difficult and less common.

Figure 3. Whole Brain Model

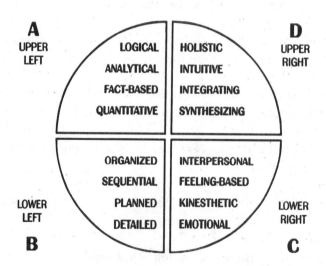

Source: Herrmann, Fred (1996). The Whole Brain Business Book: Unlocking the Power of Whlle Brain Thinking in Organizations and Individuals. New York, NY: McGraw-Hill, p. 21.

Figure 4. Turn-On Work Indicator Map

A

D

Working Solo
Applying Formulas
Accomplishing
Analyzing Data
Putting Things Together
Making Things Work
Solving Tough Problems
Making the Numbers
Being Challenged
Analyzing & Diagnosing
Explaining Things
Clarifying Issues
Logical Processing

Taking Risks
Inventing Solutions
Providing Vision
Having Variety
Bringing About Change
Opportunity to Experiment
Selling Ideas
Developing New Things
Designing
Having a Lot of Space
Playing Around
Seeing the End from the Beginning
Excitement

Building Things
Being in Control
Having an Ordered Environment
Preserving the Status Quo
Paperwork Tasks
Establishing Order
Planning Things Out
Stabilizing
Getting Things Done on Time
Attending to Detail
Structured Tasks
Providing Support
Administrating

Getting Groups to Work Well Together
Expressing Ideas
Building Relationships
Teaching/Training
Listening and Talking
Working with People
Persuading People
Being Part of a Team
Communication Aspects
Helping People
Expressive Writing
Coaching
Counseling

B

C

Source: Herrmann, Fred (1996). The Whole Brain Business Book: Unlocking the Power of Whlle Brain Thinking in Organizations and Individuals. New York, NY: McGraw-Hill, p. 26.

My program director, Cathy Schagh, acknowledged the obvious—she was left brain dominant. I believe she typified the thinking style of other program directors. She was a good analytical thinker who was skilled at working with program details and regulations. But it was difficult for her to visualize, develop, and implement a participatory management mode that would facilitate the development of self-directed teams. It was also difficult for her to visualize and accept some of the creative training and other kinds of group processes proposed by her staff. In a moment of introspection, Cathy said to me that she found it difficult to interact with those who were not left brain dominant, and this was something on which she had to work. Unfortunately, the managers of OESE were never given the opportunity to work on a whole brain approach after the HBDI was administered.

I often thought about Cathy's thinking and leadership styles. Although I was the designated Group Leader, in practice I shared the leadership of the PST with Cathy. On several occasions, I had moved into some new ventures only to sense that I was being observed, not supported.

On one occasion I moved the team into a consideration of an environmental scan for IAP. But after doing a good job of defining our environment, the team decided they were not enthused about the added work of carrying out the scan itself. Cathy showed no interest in the plan so I let it go. On another occasion I convinced the team to study our interaction with our "customers," both internal and external, so we could improve our services. The data were gathered and codified, and a "points-of-contact" plan was drafted to better interact with the program's customers. But the plan never received a response from Cathy so I let it drop. On still another occasion, I asked if I might lead a team in the reengineering of the application/payment process, which was the core business process of the IAP. I stated that I would not attempt it without a strong demonstration of her backing. Although she knew that I previously led a team that successfully reengineered a portion of the process she never picked up on my offer. From these experiences I concluded that Cathy's risk adverse thinking style was not comfortable with reinvention.

The PST for the Impact Aid Program never did function as a team. I did not have much first hand knowledge of the other PSTs, but my guess is Coopers & Lybrand were correct about them, too. There was little change in the personnel of the PSTs. They were the same people, with the same work, at the same desks, with the same culture, working under the same management with the same expectations. What else would one need to know to indicate that PSTs had not become teams? It would be impossible with the structure, management style and culture of OESE to have self-directed PSTs.

Lessons Learned
At the time of the Restructuring Fair, when the team structure of OESE was to be implemented, certain preconditions were already established that predetermined the character of the teams. Not the least of these was the conception of the restructuring that placed the ill-defined outcomes of the teams beyond the competencies of the staff and attempted to integrate programs that could not be integrated. Another was the way the organizational architecture was constructed, by putting structure first with little thought about how the elements would be aligned. A major factor was the culture of OESE, in which traditional management style was not compatible with self-directed teams. Program leaders were skeptical of the restructuring effort, the union

fearful, and the African Americans charging the management with racism. The lessons to be learned are:

- **Conceiving a high-performance organization and attempting to implement it without the distinctive competence to deliver the desired outcomes is folly.** As we stated earlier, "personnel policies that determine the character of the labor force will eventually determine the character of the organization." The conceptions behind the restructuring, in which OESE would present one face to the customer by bringing all programs together for the customer, and would provide technical assistance in the systemic change of the nation's schools, were impossible to accomplish. Those who conceived of a high-performance organization for OESE did not work from a performance model. They did not consider the requisite outcomes of the teams and the competencies that would be necessary to deliver them. The leadership moved ahead without the critical knowledge base they needed about the organization they attempted to change.

  Nor was it helpful for Policy Studies, Inc., to talk about "challenges" rather than insurmountable problems when addressing the work of the IRTs. Discussions I had with Julia Lesceux, David Kanthak, and others involved in the pilot testing revealed quite plainly that OESE did not have the staff to perform the prescribed functions or assist the states in obtaining systemic reform.

  The staff was basically unable to give any technical assistance. Nor was it really possible to provide them with adequate training to overcome this deficiency. The oral reports of the IRTs following their state visitations confirmed the limitations of the staff. As the letter from Commissioner Holloway revealed, the IRT from the Department could not give them any significant assistance. "We do not have to waste time with 'feel good' conferences," she said. The IRTs had no standards to apply. They talked consolidation, but dealt with individual programs. IRT visits are events the states must endure to get their money. IRTs are completely out of character for OESE.

- **Combining dissimilar outcomes and work processes into the cross-program results in dysfunctional teams.** Another failure of the conceptualization was the attempt to integrate all OESE programs. Forcing IAP and IEP into the regional teamwork structure was like forcing round pegs into square holes. The other programs of OESE work through the state education agencies, while IAP and IEP work through the local education agencies. They cannot be included in the consolidated plans of the state agencies, nor could they integrate their program work with their colleagues in the IRTs.

Essentially, the core work of the IAP and IEP staff can not be done by other program staff. Any significant work in these two programs takes years to learn and experience to perfect. Consequently, when IAP and IEP staff work on the consolidated plans in the IRTs, they are giving away precious time they previously had to do their unique work. Yet they received no reciprocal assistance in return. In practice, this additional work resulted in less time to serve the IAP and the IEP customers. Including IAP and IEP in the regional teams was a mistake in the original conception of the OESE structure that management refused to acknowledge.

Again, when the restructuring was conceived nobody made an examination of the desired performance outcomes of the regional teams or the competencies necessary to deliver them. If they had, the inability to integrate the work of the IAP and the IEP would have been obvious.

- **When the organizational culture does not support teams, they fail.** Throughout the entire restructuring process, the culture of the management never really changed. From the beginning, it was difficult for the program directors to fully buy into the restructuring, and most of them never did. Even under ideal circumstances it would have been a momentous change for them to move into a participatory style of management and empower self-directed teams to make decisions and carry out a work plan independent of their direction. This had never been a management format in the Department of Education. The Department was a traditional bureaucracy in which managers were expected to take charge and manage the details. The Department in general, and OESE in particular, was the ideal place for left brain individuals to move into management positions. Here managers would exercise their logical, rational, planning skills, and deal with the facts and details of program implementation. They would not be comfortable in a participatory, team oriented organization.

The events that transpired did not help the transition. The reassignment process was a contentious struggle by the staff to overcome their perceived management constraints. The intense racial tensions emphasized the differences between the African Americans and management. And during the whole process, the program directors felt vulnerable. Often they were under attack.

Nor was it easy for the staff. The fact that they were struggling with management was a constant emphasis of the we/they orientation in the work environment. This was further emphasized by the LMPC.

Consequently, the culture never changed. As Janice Jackson said, she had never been in an organization with so little trust. This was not a culture in which self-directed work teams could flourish.

- **Teams fail when the organizational architecture does not support them.** OESE did not perceive the nature of the change they were making, the inadequacies of their restructuring effort, or the necessity of bringing into alignment all the organizational elements of institutional change. One of the major consequences of this failure was the undermining of the teams. The organizational design did not support them.

Consider, for example, the instability of roles, functions and responsibilities as they related to teams. These issues had been defined and redefined, written and rewritten, discussed and debated, disputed and refuted, and complained about over and over again. Why was it that the roles of the regional team leaders, group leaders, and program directors came up over and over again? Why was it that these three groups could not even work out among themselves who would be included in the Leadership Team? Certainly a major reason was that they could not do their business according to the structure that had been prescribed, so they constantly disregarded it and intervened in the process. This was the outcome of a dysfunctional design.

Program directors felt that they could not allow certain staff assigned to the regional teams to represent their programs in the field. Consequently, they intervened in the activities of the regional teams, not allowing certain team members to represent them, and assigning others to do the job. Group leaders, at the direction of program directors, were actively involved in influencing regional team activities. On at least one occasion, a person was arbitrarily assigned to a regional team without any discussion with the team or its leader. With the power and authority of program directors over one's career, many employees offered no resistance. The teams had little chance to plan and mature on their own.

Consider the regional team leaders who had to provide leadership amid these interventions. They and their teams were circumvented time and time again. They were told who could represent certain programs in the field, who could travel, who could work on their team efforts, and who would be diverted to other assignments. At the same time the team leaders were considered essential to the success of the restructuring effort and the programs. They were given critical responsibilities to perform and special training. They were expected to get the work done with whatever power, authority and control they could exert. They competed for their positions and they had status and prestige among their colleagues. But, in theory they had *roles*—not *positions*. Because the Department was delayering, they would not be counted as supervision or management.

The regional team leaders were in fact the "marginal men" of OESE. They were like the foremen on the shop floor who were expected to supervise the workers, but were neither considered supervisors by management, nor employees by employees. They were like the warrant officer that I once reported to in the Navy. When he came aboard ship the first time, he moved into the officers' quarters, but the other officers did not accept him. He then moved in with the chief petty officers and was only partially accepted there. The team members did not consider their team leaders as merely staff, and the senior leadership did not consider them as part of the Leadership Team.

Consider the program service teams. According to Coopers & Lybrand, none of the PSTs became teams, except in name. Again, they were not aligned with the rest of the organization and many preconditions determined their character. The transition from the branch chief operation to the program service team operation did not essentially change the management perspective or the staff perspective. Neither the culture nor the management style supported the change.

Although the team went through the exercises of setting ground rules and developing vision and mission statements, they did not come through on a number of promising activities that would have been constructive. For example, there was no environmental scan, no points-of-contact plan, nor was there any reengineering of the core business process of the IAP. Although the management of OESE hired a consultant to help the IAP act more like a team, there were too many preconditions for training to make any difference.

Teams do not become empowered and self-directed unless the organizational architecture supports them. They need goals they can buy into and support. They need an organizational structure that allows them to take responsibility and be accountable. They need trust and rewards for good performance. They need to be trusted. They also need time. But in the restructured OESE they had none of this.

So, what could have been done differently? Once the design of the restructuring effort was prescribed and implemented, probably not much. I believe it would have taken a return to the beginning and a redesign with a different approach. To become an organization that supports teams, rather than work groups, OESE would have had to redesign their decision-making systems and change the allocation of power, authority, and control. They would have had to reexamine their structure and technical systems for alignment of effort and outcomes. They would have had to change their people systems and their reward systems to find competent team members who could do the work and reward them. And they would most certainly have had to adjust their values and their guiding principles.

Strategy Fiasco

Legislating Results

Over the last 20 years or so, the federal government has adopted a number of planning and budget approaches. None could be considered an unqualified success and none lasted very long. In recent years, public interest has forced the federal government to reinvent itself in a more businesslike manner. Just as companies are accountable to their shareholders, many citizens reasoned, the federal government should be accountable to the taxpayers. The American "shareholders" have been insisting that their legislators cut the costs and make the federal agencies accountable.

For the most part, the reform of government agencies has been by executive order or administrative action. The reform efforts have focused on inputs rather than results, that is, what should be introduced into government agencies to change them rather than what should come out of them. In the 1990s, however, government reform was launched by the legislation of performance results. No congressman expressed more frustration with government's focus on inputs rather than results than Senator William V. Roth (R-DE). In the age of the National Performance Review (NPR) Senator Roth and his colleagues

167

were able to join forces with Democrats and pass legislation that did, finally, focus on results. Three of their congressional actions undergirded the NPR of the Clinton administration with federal law:

- The Chief Financial Officer Act of 1990 provided for chief financial officer positions in 24 major agencies and required annual reports on the financial condition of government entities and the status of management controls.

- The Information Technology Management Reform Act of 1996 required, among other things, that agencies set goals, measure performance, and report on progress in improving the efficiency and effectiveness of operations through the use of information technology.

- The Government Performance and Results Act of 1993 (GPRA) provided for the most fundamental changes of all. Every major federal agency now had to ask the basic questions, What is our mission? What are our goals and how will we achieve them? How can our performance be measured? How will the information be used to make improvements? The act forced a major shift in the focus of federal agencies—the single overriding issue now became the measurement of results!

The role of the Office of Management and Budget (OMB) was also a very significant factor in budget reform. Donald F. Kettl, professor of public affairs at the University of Wisconsin and senior fellow at The Brookings Institution, asserts, "The most promising source of glue to hold the movement together and promote the right incentives lies in the reorganization of the Office of Management and Budget . . ., launched in March 1994 under the banner of 'OMB 2000,' and the Government Performance and Results Act . . . which seeks to link budget inputs with performance outcomes" (1995:60). OMB Director at the time, Leon Panetta, and Deputy Director Alice Rivlin, restructured OMB to strengthen the linkage between budgetary, management and performance issues. The reorganization was designed to support GPRA. "In the long run," speculates Kettl, "the GPRA may well prove to be the keystone of the federal government's reinvention movement. It defines performance as the critical touchstone of the government's programs; it defines the linkages among the government's activities; and it provides important incentives for government managers to focus on results."

Under the act, each federal agency had to prepare a five-year strategic plan updated every three years; a comprehensive mission statement that links the agency's current operations with its long-term goals; an identification of the goals and objectives, along with the resources, systems and processes required to achieve them; a description of the most important external factors that could affect the agency's success in achieving them; and explain why goals might not have been met, and revise the goals if necessary. The OMB did not expect the transition to performance-based management to come easily. The act called for pilot projects in the beginning.

In 1993, the General Accounting Office (GAO) came to the following conclusion after its study of the Department of Education:

> The Department charged with managing the federal investment in education and leading the long-term effort to improve education itself lacks a clear management vision of how to best marshal its resources to effectively achieve its mission. Past Education Secretaries have not built an organization that could implement major policy initiatives. Moreover, the Department's history is replete with long-standing management problems that periodically erupted, became the focus of congressional and media attention, and subsequently diverted attention from the policy agendas (1993).

The GAO also acknowledged that the previous Secretary, Lamar Alexander, "inherited a management infrastructure weakened by past political leadership that had not given priority to building and maintaining an organization that could implement major policy initiatives" (1993: 7). And it reported that "Secretary Alexander recognized the need to improve the way ED is managed and took initial steps to enhance departmental leadership, transform agency culture, and improve operations. However, GAO is concerned that this momentum, already dissipating, not be lost" (1993: 2).

The GAO report made the following major recommendations:

- Articulate a strategic management vision for ED that demonstrates how its management infrastructure will be developed to support its mission and such Secretarial policy priorities as the national Education Goals.

- Adopt a strategic management process in the office of the Secretary for setting clear goals and priorities, measuring progress towards those goals and ensuring accountability for attaining them.

- Enhance management leadership throughout ED and strengthen agency culture by (1) implementing a Department-wide strategic management process, (2) identifying good management practices within ED and supporting their adoption, (3) rewarding managers for good management and leadership, and (4) filling technical and policy-making leadership positions with people with appropriate skills.

- Create for information, financial, and human resources management, strategic visions and strategic plans that are integrated with the Department's overall strategic management process.

Bottom-Up Approach

With both an administrative and legislative mandate in place, and a GAO report that recommended needed strategic management, the Department of Education made its first attempt at strategic planning in early 1994. It was a "bottom-up" approach. In March, a set of "Guidelines to Strengthen Office-level Strategic Plans" was issued by the Performance Management Reinvention Team of the Department's Reinvention Coordination Committee (RCC). Each of the offices (formerly known as bureaus) of the Department was directed to develop a strategic plan for their office according to the "Guidelines." I first learned about the Guidelines when I received a draft of the OESE strategic plan in early April. The covering memo requested feedback from any person who had an interest in the plan. Upon inquiry, I was told that a team had been assembled to develop the plan on a short time frame and submit it to the RCC.

I examined the draft of "The Strategic Plan for O.E.S.E." It had a vision statement more than one page in length, a mission statement with 46 words built upon the Department's statement, and three definitions of the "customer," "systemic reform," and "staff accountability." It also contained 4 goals, 11 objectives, 15 strategies, 15 performance indicators, and 19 action steps containing 36 sub-steps. I thought the plan had the look of an urgent product put together by a committee that had not done anything like this before. I did not understand the reason for the urgency. Since the cover memo asked for responses from anyone with an interest, I immediately forwarded a number of recommendations, with hopes that I could have some influence on the plan.

Shortly after the distribution of the draft strategic plan, a memorandum invited all OESE staff to discuss the strategic plan with Assistant Secretary, Thomas Payzant, in one of a number of small group meetings. I attended one of the meetings prepared to discuss the plan. Tom came to the meeting late and distributed what he referred to as the "final version" of the strategic plan. My colleagues and I were told that the strategic plan would be revisited annually and that changes could be made in the future, but there was no longer any opportunity to make changes in the current draft. Although there had been a few changes made in the earlier draft, none of my suggestions had been adopted. Several of us asked questions about parts of the plan, but it was clear that Tom did not really want to talk about the plan.

What Tom did want to talk about was himself. He took up over half of the meeting talking about his experiences in the school districts he had served as superintendent. He pointed out that the staffs of the school districts he managed were much larger than the staff of the OESE. He also made a number of statements about his philosophy and style of management. Those in attendance listened politely. A few raised non-threatening questions and comments. After it was clear that Tom was not really interested in discussing the strategic plan, and that there was no longer any way to influence it, I sat back and observed what was occurring. To me it appeared that Tom, who was a new personality to many in the room, was trying to legitimize his role and leadership, and the staff were tactfully not raising any obstacles for him at this meeting.

The first strategic plan of the OESE was developed by a small group of people, then distributed, reviewed and forwarded to the RCC—all in just a little over one month. Although it was supposed to be a "bottom-up" plan, I never was able to find out who drafted the plan, despite inquiries. It turned out that it really didn't matter since, in the months to come, there was little attention given to the plan. The staff immediately forgot about it, I'm sure, in part, because they had no part in its development.

In February 1995, when the second attempt at strategic planning was initiated, there was a weak attempt to legitimize the first plan with a one-page "OESE Strategic Planning Update" with seven accomplishments credited to it. But nothing was listed that would not have happened without the plan, and there was no attempt to measure anything with performance indicators. When I was involved in the second attempt to develop a strategic plan for OESE, I had a lengthy telephone discussion with Nancy Rhett in the Office of the Undersecretary, Planning and Evaluation Service, who summarized the outcome of the Department's first effort at strategic planning. She told me that the first attempt to develop a plan in which each of the principal offices developed separate plans that were then sent on to the RCC did not work. She explained that there was no way that the Department could bring together all of the separate plans of the principal offices into one integrated, coherent plan. She asserted, "The bottom-up effort was not successful."

Departmental Plan

In December 1994, the Department released its plan, entitled "Strategic Plan for the U. S. Department of Education: Working Document." In my conversation with Nancy Rhett, I told her that I believed a strategic plan should start with strategic thinking at the top of an organization. In the Department of Education that should come from the President, Secretary Riley, and those he wished to involve in the strategic policy. Nancy agreed and told me that was how the departmental plan was developed. She said that the strategic direction for the plan took place over a six-month period, involving a retreat for the top people in the Department. "Then," she said, "Alan Ginsburg (Director of Planning and Evaluation in the Office of the Undersecretary) reminded them of the necessity of performance measures, and this stopped further activity on the plan for awhile. It was at this point that those drafting the plan really began to agonize over the plan. During the next eight months, they worked on identifying objectives, strategies and performance indicators."

The Department plan had three goals: (1) achieve the national education goals, (2) ensure equity, and (3) build partnerships with customers. It had four priorities:

1. Help all students reach challenging academic standards so that they are prepared for responsible citizenship, further learning, and productive employment.

2. Create a comprehensive school-to-work opportunities system in every state.

3. Ensure access to high quality post-secondary education and life-long learning.

4. Transform the U. S. Department of Education into a high-performance organization.

The plan was comprised of 22 objectives, 67 strategies and 79 performance indicators grouped into 27 categories. Of course, it also included the mission statement: "To insure equal access to education and to promote educational excellence throughout the nation."

With the strategic plan came this promise: "By adopting the goals, objectives, and performance indicators in this plan, the Department of Education is entering into a performance agreement with the President of the United States and the American people. The measure of our success will be the progress we make toward our goals."

New Charter for Strategic Planning

On February 6, 1995, I received an e-mail from Ted Parker, who worked for Deputy Assistant Secretary Janice Jackson, requesting my participation on the Strategic Planning Team of OESE. The message stated, "The purpose of the team is to develop on or before May 1st, an OESE strategic plan that is aligned to the priorities and objectives of the ED Strategic Plan: Working Document." With the support of my boss, Cathy Schagh, I accepted the assignment and walked down the hall to Ted's office to obtain more information.

When Ted said that he was the designated team leader, I was eager to talk with him about getting the team off on the right foot. I talked about the necessity of having a charter for the team and Ted promised me that one was coming. We talked about the work of strategic planning and the fact that it had fallen out of favor in much of the private sector. I mentioned that I had just purchased Henry Mintzberg's book, *The Rise and Fall of Strategic Planning* (1994). We talked about the time limitation on the work, and Ted acknowledged that he was concerned about that also. He felt certain that they could get an extension, because, as he said, "nothing was ever done when it was due in the government." I stated that I thought it would be difficult getting measurable performance indicators from the team members, and recommended that the team get training. I also recommended that Ted ask Alan Ginsburg, Director of Planning and Evaluation Services, to meet with the team up front to describe the development of the Department plan and talk about the role of OESE in the plan.

Although Ted said that he wanted to have his first meeting on February 20th, time went by and no meeting was called. Finally, I walked down the hall again to ask about the delay. Ted was eager to talk. He complained, "I have been trying to get an appointment with Tom since January, but it always gets canceled." He explained that Tom had an unrealistic time frame for the work, but without a meeting with Tom to settle this and other critical issues, he could not get the team started. Ted also brought up the problem that Tom perceived the strategic plan to be a work plan and not a strategic plan. I expressed the need to obtain somebody like Alan Ginsburg to meet with Tom and the Strategic Planning Team to get some of the confusion worked out of people's perceptions. I pointed out that misperceptions would continue and time limits would not change without an understanding of what the team was all about.

Finally, Ted got his meeting with Tom and scheduled a meeting of the team for March 16th, over a month after the establishment of the team.

Because of a schedule conflict, both Janice Jackson and I were not able to attend until after most of the business was completed.

Nevertheless, I was able to get a copy of the team charter, which I read with great interest. I did not know how important it would be at the time. Later, I would become very upset because the charter would not be followed. The purpose contained no surprises.

> The mission of the OESE Strategic Planning Team is to develop an OESE Strategic Plan that relates to the goals, priorities, objectives and performance indicators of the Department's "Strategic Plan: Working Document" (December: 1994). The team's effort will focus on the various priorities of the Department's plan and specifically priorities 1, 2, and 4 and their related objectives and performance indicators.

It was to be a five-year plan with short and long-term objectives. There would also be performance measures to indicate progress in achieving priorities and objectives. The team would be closely involved in the restructuring of OESE in priority 4, so that the plan would reflect the progress of restructuring OESE. I knew that the members of the team were novices when it came to strategic planning, but there would be only a brief orientation, no training. That concerned me. I was glad to see that the due date was now set back to April 15th, two weeks later than Tom had originally set, but I knew that unless the team would gave this task its top priority, it would not get done.

Rough Start
The charter clearly stated that "Although formal training will not be provided, the Planning Team will receive an orientation about strategic planning, goals, objectives and performance indicators." However, the team did not have an orientation either. So the members started coming to the meetings with different perceptions about what they were supposed to do and how they would do it. In my prior discussion with Ted, I had expressed my concern about developing a plan with an inexperienced team. Although I was not involved in much of the first meeting, I did reiterate my request for training. The lack of any training or orientation undoubtedly contributed to the confusion and the different perceptions of the team members.

175

At the second meeting, both Ted and I came prepared to help with a needed orientation. Ted led a brief discussion with the Planning Team about SMART objectives, which are (1) Specific, (2) Measurable, (3) Attainable, (4) Related to mission, and (5) with Time commitments. He also passed out a copy of a magazine article by Tom Peters entitled, "Attention Strategic Planners: It's Time to Search for New Jobs" (*Monday,* April 4: 1994). Coincidentally, I came prepared with a handout about SMART goals and objectives that included examples. I also came with two handouts from the *Harvard Business Review,* "The Fall and Rise of Strategic Planning" (January/February: 1994), and "Changing the Role of Top Management Beyond Strategy to Purpose" (November/December: 1994). I also brought a copy of Henry Mintzberg's book, *The Rise and Fall of Strategic Planing,* and urged everyone to read the book. I cautioned, "Our strategic planning could very easily be a big waste of time, but Mintzberg's book could help us avoid the pitfalls and make strategic planning a productive effort."

One of the early debates centered on whether the Planning Team was to do strategic thinking and make strategic decisions, or if the team was only to do planning. When I heard Ted and Ed Smith, a member of the team, talking about making strategy for OESE, I challenged their assumptions. I stated that the Secretary and those at the top of the Department had developed the strategy and that a departmental strategic plan had been developed based on that strategy. I asserted that it was the job of the Planning Team to extend the departmental plan where the programs of OESE were involved. Janice spoke up to support my perception.

By the end of the second meeting, we all agreed that we needed an outside authority to provide instruction on how to generate performance indicators and to measure them. At the third meeting, Joanne Wiggins of the Planning and Evaluation Services, appeared. I assumed that she was there as the trainer on measurement that the team had requested. She explained that she had experience in working with measurement problems for research and evaluation projects, but she was not there to train anybody. She was there to listen. I continued to request the training we all agreed upon, and I continued to request that Alan Ginsburg be invited to the meeting to give the Planning Team background on the departmental plan and provide training.

However, after the third meeting, still no one was brought in to train the team on performance indicators and measurements. So, at my suggestion, we began work on one of the objectives in priority four, hoping that working on performance indicators would give us a better understanding of what we needed to know. My plan was to use this for a discussion, or perhaps as a model.

One continuing discussion concerned the utility of any private contracts that had been awarded for the evaluation of OESE programs. At this time, work was being done on the Safe and Drug Free Schools Program because the evaluation of it had been mandated by the authorizing legislation. Many thought that these data would be a bonanza for the Strategic Planning Team, but the problem was that they were not designed to answer the objectives of the departmental plan. The evaluations had been independently designed to answer different questions. I acknowledged that some of the data might be appropriate, but the team would not know that until we had decided upon our own performance indicators.

It was a rough start for the team, and it got worse when the political motivation for what the team was doing came to the surface. At one point, Janice stated that the team ought to be aware of both primary and secondary measures of success from a political perspective. She defined the primary measures as measures of student learning, and secondary measures as how many grants were made or how many administrators were trained. She explained that the politicians would look for measures of learning, not how many grants were made. She asserted, "If children do not learn more, we would be considered a failure, and then the money for education would go to the states. Any measures short of this were politically inadequate."

"Beating a Dead Horse"

On April 6th, the team held a meeting that I will not soon forget. Joanne Wiggins stated that priority 1, objectives 2 and 5, were the sole focus of the team. (At this time the department's plan consisted of 4 priorities and 22 objectives.) She explained that each of the assistant secretaries had been given special responsibility for particular portions of the department plan and this was the responsibility of Tom Payzant. At the earliest opportunity, I corrected her. I stated that priority 4, objectives 2 through 6, were also the team's responsibilities. Priority 4 was to "Transform the U. S. Department of Education into a high-performance organization. This, too, was a part of our charter."

At that point, Ted and a few other members of the team corrected me. Ted said, "Tom had limited our work to priority 1, objectives 2 and 5, and other priorities had been assigned to other offices." And he stated, "We would be addressing priority 4 anyway if we did priority 1."

I was dumbfounded. My main interest in working on the team was to work on priority 4 which was directly related to the restructuring of OESE. The argument that OESE could accomplish priority 4 by working only on priority 1 made no sense. I read from the charter, "The team's effort will focus on the various priorities of the Department's plan and specifically priorities 1, 2, and 4, and their related objectives and performance indicators." (Priority 2 was later dropped by mutual consent as not related to OESE activities.) I also reminded Ted that he had previously stated the same. Ted responded: "There was no relationship between strategic planning and the restructuring effort."

I then stated that I had been laboring under a gross misperception and that I was really not interested in doing strategic planning limited to the Safe and Drug Free Schools Program. I stated that I thought that by working on this team I would be contributing to the extension of priority 4 into the restructuring effort of OESE. When I continued to press the issue, Ted said, "Bruce, you're beating a dead horse. We are not going to work on priority 4." I then gathered up his materials and left the meeting.

I learned later that after I left the meeting, Janice joined the group and was asked about the team's priority responsibilities. Harris Taylor, a member of the team, reported that Janice had said exactly what I had said. I was distressed and puzzled. When I returned to work the following day, I opened my computer and wrote a memo of resignation to Ted with a copy to Janice.

When I returned to my office on the close of business that day, I found Ted sitting at my desk waiting for me to arrive. We talked for about 30 minutes about my resignation from the Strategic Planning Team and my reasons for it. By the end of the discussion, I understood Ted to be saying exactly what he had said at the team's meeting. Namely, Tom wanted the team to limit its work to priority 1, objectives 2 and 5, and that is what the team would do. And by working on priority 1, the team was doing the work of priority 4. In addition, Ted wanted me to reconsider resigning from the team and to join a subgroup headed by Bill McCoy working on objective 5 of priority 1.

For me, Ted's argument was very confusing and irrational. I could understand that Tom wanted priority 1 to be addressed, because he had a special responsibility for it. But how could Ted think that priority 4 would be addressed by working on priority 1? Why was he still insisting that nothing else would be addressed, when Janice had stated, unequivocally, after I left the meeting that the team would address priority 4?

I seldom had a conversation with Ted without his wanting to talk about other things as well. The conversation drifted off on a number of additional topics. Finally, I stated that it was now one hour after I had planned to leave and had to go. It was late on Friday, and I was anxious to get home and start my weekend. Ted pressed me about staying on the team, and I said I would sleep on it.

The following Tuesday, Janice approached me at an All Hands meeting and asked me to stop by her office in the afternoon. She wanted to talk about my resignation. At their meeting, I informed her about the discussion at the meeting of the Strategic Planning Team, Harris's report of her clarification of the team's work, and my meeting with Ted. I stated that if the work of the Strategic Planning Team related only to priority 1, they did not need a strategic cross-cutting team to do the job.

Janice assured me that I was absolutely correct in my perception of the team's work, and she wanted me to remain on the team. She also assured me that she would get Ted back on track. As a result of this conversation with Janice, I decided to return to the team and continue working on priority 4.

This whole episode was a puzzlement. Ted knew what was in the charter. He had been involved in drafting it. Did Tom really tell him that he wanted it limited to priority 1? Were Tom and Janice at odds over the team's scope of work? Was Ted playing some kind of game? Did he have an ulterior purpose? Why did he make an irrational argument about priorities 1 and 4? The whole thing did not make sense. I knew that there were answers to my questions, but I did not have them.

Team Termination

The next meeting opened with further discussion about the team's scope of work during which I did not speak. Ted reluctantly acknowledged that the team would have to work on all the relevant priorities and objectives, but suggested that we would have to concentrate on priority 1, objectives 2 and 5. Near the end of this discussion Harris Taylor spoke up to say that there was a lot of work to do on priority 4 and that we had to get moving. He suggested that a subgroup be set up with me as leader to work on priority 4. He reported that I had already done some work on priority 4 and felt strongly that it was an essential part of the strategic plan. So I was pleased and hopeful when I was given the assignment to lead the work on priority 4.

I still wanted very much to get the assistance of Alan Ginsburg and after several attempts, I made contact with Nancy Rhett of Alan's staff. I briefed her on the confusion over the work of the team and learned that she already knew about it from the staff of the Planning and Evaluation Services who attended the team meetings.

I also mentioned the late start and the short time the team had to do the work. Nancy said she did not know where the urgency was coming from. She said that she did not know of any group within the Department that would be pressing OESE for the plan and thought that it had to be coming from Tom. I also talked with her about how to approach the objectives in priority 4, and found her in agreement with what I was doing. We closed our discussion talking about recent books on strategic planning and the NPR—primarily the work of Henry Mintzberg, and the works of Donald Kettl, John J. Dilulio, and others from The Brookings Institution. As I rested the phone on the receiver, I felt validated and secure in my knowledge and actions. I had gained some additional information, been reassured that OESE should be working on priority 4, and that I was approaching the objectives of priority 4 in an acceptable manner.

Attendance at the meetings of the team became smaller and smaller as time went on. Originally, ten people had been selected for the team. One person dropped out because of illness. Some never attended after the first few sessions. On two occasions, I was the only person who came to the meetings. Sometimes legitimate reasons, such as sick leave or annual leave, and travel, limited the attendance. More often, absent members cited program work and other teamwork as the reasons. Until it came time for the submission of the report, Ted saw his responsibility as that of facilitator of meetings, not a participant in the planning. All of these limitations meant that the work of the team was done by a very few people.

Nobody worked any harder than Gael Beumont from the Safe and Drug Free Schools program. She did not begin with any special knowledge about constructing strategic plans, but she patiently brought draft after draft to the team for review and critique. She worked on objective 2 of priority 1, "Help create safe, disciplined, healthy, and drug-free environments for learning." She had a rough problem to solve. How could she measure the results of the federal intervention through the schools when she could not control or measure the environmental factors in the community, especially when all the research indicated that drug use and violence would increase?

In addition, she had the problem of not having enough information to measure accountability when her program provided local agencies with flexibility to implement their own programs on the basis of unique needs. When flexibility is given, the types of activities carried out vary from locality to locality, as do program objectives, information, and measures of success. The Safe and Drug-Free Schools Program allows a wide range of activities by state agencies and local schools. In testimony before the Subcommittee on Labor, Health and Human Services, House of Representatives (March 24, 1998), Cornelia M. Blanchette summarized the situation thusly:

> In carrying out its mission, the Department of Education has a careful balancing act to perform. While elementary and secondary education is largely the states' responsibility, this federal department [Department of Education] is expected to provide leadership at the national level. For example, in the preschool, elementary, and secondary education areas, it is expected to give state and local education agencies flexibility in using federal funds and freedom from unnecessary regulatory burden, yet it must have enough

information about programs and how money is spent to be accountable to the American taxpayers.

There was a mandated research project awarded to an external contractor that would produce some relevant data, but it was not designed with the strategic plan in mind. The Department plan had three strategies and two performance indicators. Gael ended up with 18 OESE strategies, 15 performance indicators, and a caveat to acknowledge her inability to obtain valid data.

On April 20th, Ted opened the meeting by announcing again that the team had until May 1st, six more working days, to complete the plan. I reported that I would be on annual leave until after the due date and that left only Harris Taylor to finish the development of the five objectives of priority 4. This was impossible.

Nobody seemed concerned about the time limitation. But still curious about where the urgency was coming from, I asked Ted about it. Ted responded that the strategic plan was an unfinished, working document and that I needn't worry. I surmised that Ted was only interested in a plan for priority 1, not priority 4, which he had made quite clear weeks before.

The May 1st deadline for completion slipped and nine meetings were scheduled throughout May and June. During that time, two of us, Harris Taylor and I, worked on objective 3 of priority 4, "Empowering our employees." Harris took on the "diversity strategy" and "employee recognition and rewards," while I focused on making OESE a "learning organization" and the "encouragement of teamwork."

The Department's plan equated learning with training, two clearly separate concepts. In addition, the Department's performance indicators of a learning organization were (1) "an increase in employee satisfaction with training on an annual survey," and (2) "a decline in the unused portion of the training budget." I couldn't believe that anyone could consider these two measures as indicators of a learning organization! It was obvious to me that the people who wrote the performance indicators for the Department plan had no concept of a learning organization. Didn't I work in the U.S. Department of Education? Didn't my colleagues know the difference between training and learning?

So instead, I introduced the concept as presented by Peter Senge in *"The Fifth Discipline"* (1990) and *"The Fifth Discipline Fieldbook"* (1994). I developed five strategies and five performance indicators and, at a meeting, introduced the concept of a learning organization through them. For over two hours, I led a discussion about vision, mental models, individual skills, systemic learning, etc. Harris had worked on his assignments too, but he was never given an opportunity to discuss them with the team. The time was given over mostly to the objectives of priority 1, and the issues and problems related to its measurement.

Then a new concern began to emerge. What would be done about the strategic plan when and if it was finalized? It began to dawn on some members of the team that getting the data and making the measurements were going to be an enormous and costly task. Members of the team began to doubt whether management had any commitment to the strategic planning effort and whether they would ever do anything about it when it was completed. On June 1st, I wrote the following note after one of the meetings:

> I believe that the confusion and lack of commitment from management about what we are doing is killing this team right now. Furthermore, our 'leader' isn't providing any leadership to solve our problems. I keep raising questions, but nobody is providing any answers. Right now, other things appear to be of more importance than strategic planning, and that says a lot about its priority and future use.

On June 22nd, Ted told the team that Tom had directed him to close down the Strategic Planning Team and turn in what they had done. I was flabbergasted. We had just begun and now we were being shut down. Clearly this whole exercise was a sham. The next day I sent off another e-mail to Janice to see if she could shed any light on Tom's decision. After receiving no response from Janice I sent an e-mail to Ted with a copy to Janice resigning for the second time, indicating that I had lost all faith in a commitment to strategic planning in OESE.

In my e-mail to Ted I said, "The GAO report of May 1993 hit the Department hard on the lack of a strategic planning framework. Then, the Government Performance and Results Act (GPRA) made strategic planning mandatory for all federal agencies. In addition, Tom was given a special responsibility for objectives 2 and 5 of priority 1 in the ED plan. Consequently, I believe that having a plan is driven much more by the necessity of having a plan than doing anything about it. Further, Tom only feels the need to have his special responsibility covered and, therefore, sees no need to spend any more time on the OESE plan . . . The bottom line is this: I am not going to put any more time in this fruitless exercise."

Five days later I received an e-mail from Janice that stated:

> Bruce, I would like to talk about this because some of the info is not correct. I asked Ted to talk with you. I would also like to talk with you about what might help to clean up the shortcomings.

I responded that I would be glad to talk with Janice at her convenience, but never heard from her. Even though we continued to work together in a variety of ways in other restructuring efforts, Janice never brought up the topic.

Ted took a draft of one strategy from me and one strategy from Harris, altered them, added them to the work on priority 1 so he would have something on priority 4 as well, and submitted the report to the Senior Leadership Team on July 11, 1995. The Senior Leadership Team thought the report was excellent. About a year later, when Ted and I were having a coffee break, Ted said to me, "You were absolutely correct about the [OESE] strategic plan . . . and, nothing will ever be done about it."

The Deputy Secretary and the Department Plan

A subsequent handout provided some of the answers I had been seeking. The handout included a cover memo from Deputy Secretary Madeleine M. Kunin, to senior officers of the Department praising the plan. There was also a one-page draft implementation plan, and an attachment of lead assignments for the Department's strategic plan. The attachment indicated who was responsible for the priorities and the objectives. The draft implementation page specified the steps and reporting dates.

The attachment did confirm that Tom was indeed the responsible person for objective 2 and 5 of priority 1. It also confirmed that all principal offices were directly involved in priority 4.

The draft implementation steps for the strategic plan called for the following schedule:

Confirm leaders	May 31,1995
Performance indicators due	June 22, 1995
First priority leader's report	July 10, 1995
First report by objective leaders	July 10, 1995

These reports would be made monthly at the senior officers' meetings and the Deputy's meetings with assistant secretaries. The urgency question concerning Tom's lead assignments appeared to be answered. He undoubtedly knew this was coming. However, it did not answer the question of why additional time was not given to priority 4 objectives.

The covering memo from the Deputy Secretary placed the following paragraph in italics:

> *I am asking each of you to support the process leaders as they coordinate implementation of their parts of the Department's plan. It may be necessary for you to adjust your office plan to ensure that specific activities are accomplished. You may need to assign staff to support particular objectives and strategies, in collaboration with other offices, or to collect performance information data for the plan's indicators.*

The collecting of performance data had me puzzled. Very little data would be available. Most of the data sources on the OESE plan were a real stretch. There was a paucity of benchmarking data. Most data would not be available for years. Acquiring most the data would require a research effort and be very costly to obtain. Tom did not have the resources to get much data.

About the time she wrote this memo, the Deputy Secretary presented testimony before the House Subcommittee on Labor - HHS - Education Appropriations (May 16, 1996). Amid the praise she lavished this day, she said: "For example, program staff for the $7 billion Title I program are currently using 28 specific performance indicators, grouped under five broad goals outlined for the program in our Strategic Plan." But I knew that there was nothing like this in the Department's plan, and I knew that it did not exist in the OESE plan, where Title 1 was administered. Why would the Deputy Secretary make such a claim?

I then wrote to Deputy Kunin by e-mail, citing the quotation and saying:

> Since I had never recalled such performance indicators, I went to my copy of the Department's strategic plan and could not find them. I then went to the OESE strategic plan and could not find them there either. Finally, I called Mary Jean's [Mary Jean LeTendre, Director] office and was told that she had no knowledge of the 28 performance indicators to which you were referring. However, I was told that some performance indicators would be coming from her in the future.
>
> So, I am still left with my question. Where are the 28 specific performance indicators, and to which priorities, objectives and strategies are they related?

Deputy Kunin responded with a brief note that they had been developed by Alan Ginsburg's shop, and she had asked him to send them to me. In the end I received two drafts of performance measures—one from Ginsburg's shop and one from the Title 1 office. Neither draft was a part of a strategic plan for the Department. Nor were they in current use in that capacity. They were still very rough drafts.

Finalizing a Departmental Strategic Plan

On June 17, 1997, the Department released another draft of its strategic plan for the years 1998-2002 for consultation and review. The plan was primarily the work of the Planning and Evaluation Service in the Office of the Under Secretary, who had the responsibility of preparing the Department's plan in compliance with the Government

186

Performance and Results Act (GPRA) that was due by September 30, 1997. It was an update of the plan released in December, 1994, and the design that OESE had worked from to develop its plan. It now contained additional performance indicators that were not required by GPRA. Three major resources were used to modify the 1994 draft:

1. Recommended updates to the Department's strategic plan prepared by the assistant secretaries.

2. Performance plans prepared by task leaders for the Secretary's initiatives.

3. Individual performance plans for major programs.

In January 1997, the assistant secretaries were asked for their recommendations to update the 1994 plan. These recommended updates were not the strategic plans of the various offices of ED. The plans of the offices, such as the strategic plan of OESE, were considered of little use in updating the Department's plan.

President Clinton's ten-point "Call to Action for American Education," issued in February, 1997, was prominently included near the front of the plan. Ten task forces were established by the Secretary to implement the initiatives. Some material from their reports were incorporated in the Department's plan. Material from individual program indicator plans was also used in this draft. Some of these plans had been developed by or with the help of contractors.

On July 18, 1997 the General Accounting Office (GAO) published a review of the Department's Plan entitled, *The Results Act: Observations on the Department of Education's June 1997 Draft Strategic Plan.* It stated that "Overall, it is a useful document and included all but one of the six elements required by the Act – it did not discuss how the agency's long-term goals and objectives will be related to its annual performance goals." The GAO review also stated that the Department's plan lacked a complete description and schedule of program evaluations and adequate description of the Department's statutory responsibilities. The review also stated that some of the components lacked clarity and context.

Two months later, on September 30, 1997, the Department submitted its first official five-year strategic plan to the Congress, in compliance with The Government Performance and Results Act of 1993. It stated in bold type, **"At no time was any contractor involved in the drafting or other development of this plan."** (This was puzzling to me because I knew that contractors had been engaged in the evaluation of OESE programs.) The draft was a further refinement of the previous plan that was released on June 17, 1997, by the Planning and Evaluation Service of the Office of the Undersecretary.

In the final document, the Department now claimed to have "consulted extensively with outside interested parties . . . and made changes on the results of those consultations." The reference here was to the GAO, the Office of Management and Budget (OMB) and the Council for Excellence in Government who all reviewed the draft plan.

As far as I could see, the plan was basically the same as the one released in June with just the addition of an objective in Goal 3. However, the wordsmiths had revised numerous statements and expanded the supporting narrative. President Clinton's "Call to Action . . . " was dropped from the plan, and in its place could be found "The U. S. Department of Education's Seven Priorities" and a page of "Facts about the Department of Education." There was also an enhancement of the accomplishments of the Department in relation to legislative reforms, streamlining the agency, improving performance, and strengthened partnerships.

The contribution of OESE was not readily discernible. Although assistant secretaries and the heads of other major programs were credited with consultations, and a number of them were mentioned, OESE contributions were not cited. When comparing the OESE strategic plan with the final Department plan, the evidence of contributions was nil.

As I reviewed the final plan, I was impressed with the amount of work that had gone into it in the last couple months before the due date. I had been in contact with personnel in the Planning and Evaluation Service and knew how hard they were working on the document. I also knew that Alan Ginsburg and his staff were the best people to put the plan together in the Department.

In January, 1998 the GAO made favorable comments on the final version of the plan. In general, they now found the Department's strategic plan in more complete compliance with the Results Act. I now wondered about the implementation of the plan and if it would really make a difference.

At the same time the Department submitted its five-year strategic plan, it also submitted the *Fiscal Year 1999 Annual Performance Plan*. It consisted of two volumes: Volume 1 consisted of performance measures, performance goals, and key strategies for fiscal year 1999 for each of Education's 22 strategic objectives. Volume 2 consisted of 99 individual program performance plans that cover Education's programs. According to the Department, this volume links to its program activity structure presented in its budget request.

On June 8, 1998 the GAO responded to a request from Representative William F. Goodling, Chairman, Committee on Education and the Workforce, to an assessment of the Department's *Fiscal Year 1999 Annual Performance Plan*. The GAO found that the Department's plan provided an incomplete picture of the intended performance across the agency, could more fully have discussed the strategies and resources to be used to achieve its annual performance goals, and—although it adequately discussed how it planned to validate and verify some performance information—did not provide sufficient confidence that all of its performance information would be credible. Specifically, the GAO found that:

- Education's performance plan could provide a more complete picture of its intended performance across the agency. While many of the performance goals and measures in volume 1 are generally objective, measurable, quantifiable, and useful in addressing progress, many in volume 2 are not.

- Education's plan could more fully discuss the strategies and resources to be used to achieve its annual performance goals. The plan has a limited discussion of how Education's strategies and resources will help achieve its annual fiscal year 1999 performance goals. For certain performance goals and measures, however, the plan does not clearly convey how the strategies and resources will achieve the plan's goals.

- Education's plan does not provide sufficient confidence that its elementary and secondary education performance information will be credible, even though it adequately addresses how it plans to validate and verify performance information for its post-secondary—and to some extent its elementary and secondary education—programs. Volume 1 of the plan discusses how Education will ensure that its performance information is timely, valid, and reliable. However, the plan does not sufficiently recognize limitation in the agency's data for its elementary and secondary education programs. In particular, the plan indicates when elementary and secondary education performance would come from sources external to Education but does not state or recognize known limitations to these external data. Without recognizing and addressing significant data limitations, Education's plan cannot provide sufficient confidence that its performance information will be credible.

Lessons Learned

Assuming that they have been responsive to the Government Performance and Results Act, all federal agencies had just gone through the development of strategic plans. For most of them, it was the first time. It is not possible to know what went on in all the other agencies, but the experience of the Department of Education provides some valuable lessons about the development of strategic plans in all government agencies. Above all, we learned that successful implementation of the Results Act is not easy.

- **Federal bureaucracies need external pressure to effect major change.** Strategic planning came to the Department of Education because of external pressure. The GAO report of 1993 lowered the boom on the management of the Department of Education and hammered home recommendations about the need for strategic management. The Congress said that it was not enough for federal agencies to say how much money they spend on their promising programs. Congress wanted to know what results these programs were having. So they wrote legislation hoping to get evidence of results. The administration, trying to build a reputation on the reinvention of the federal government, endorsed the legislation. The key legislation, GPRA, called for strategic planning.

One of the lessons to be learned from this political pressure is that institutionalized federal bureaucracies, such as the Department of Education, need external pressure to effect change. They are not likely to change much from internal motivation alone. (This is true of the private sector as well. It receives external pressure from customer response, which directly affects a company's bottom line.) But not even the GAO report was sufficient to motivate ED to make strategic plans. It took an act of Congress, in the form of the GPRA, to mandate strategic planning. Donald F. Kettl, of the Brookings Institution, might be correct when he stated, "In the long run, the GPRA may well prove to be the keystone of the federal government's reinvention movement" (1995).

- **Strategic planning requires knowledgeable leadership.** Another lesson is that it takes a knowledgeable and committed leadership to successfully implement strategic planning. At the top, the President, and the Secretary of the Education provided the mission, the vision, and the general goals of the Department. At the next level down, however, the knowledge of how to proceed with strategic planning was not adequate and meant that the effort would not succeed. The Department sprung out of the starting gate to get a lead on the other federal agencies by trying to assemble it from the bottom up, but the effort was a dismal failure. Assembling a variety of strategic plans, developed by the separate and independent offices of the Department, could not be combined into a unified plan for the Department. What came together did not go together.

The second example of the lack of knowledge was evident when it was necessary for one of the ED leaders to point out that they had to have performance indicators that could be measured. How else could you tell the Congress what their results were? Then the work began on indicators and measurement. Finally, over a year after the effort started, there was a plan that could be moved down to the office level and be distributed to the rank and file.

- **The plethora of individually legislated programs makes it difficult, if not impossible, to develop a focused strategic plan.** At the office level, the leadership was expected to extend the Department plan to their programs. One problem they faced was the Balkanization of the Department from the plethora of legislated programs. Even after a marked reduction of individual programs in the reinvention effort, the Department still had 197 different programs in 16 different offices. Over the years, politicians had enacted law after law establishing new programs for the Department to administer. The Department assigned them to whichever office appeared the most appropriate at the time. For example, OESE ended up with the Impact Aid Program, which deals with school finance for elementary and secondary schools, but has nothing to do with either teaching or learning. It was a round peg for a square hole when it came to strategic planning. Only a small portion of the programs were ever considered in the strategic plan of the Department. Like a host of other programs there is no reference to the Impact Aid Program.

- **Committed leadership must be involved in the development of an agency's strategic plan.** When the plan came to OESE, the Assistant Secretary showed little commitment to strategic planning. He assigned it to a team of staff volunteers who knew little about strategic planning and who received no training to help them. In a multitude of ways, the Assistant Secretary indicated that it was not a high priority for him: the team's leader attempted to get a meeting with him for over a month, but it kept getting canceled; he was scheduled to meet with the team at their first meeting, but never appeared; he allocated a very brief time span for the work, and he made it clear that he was only interested in the part of the plan for which he had special responsibility. He never conceived of the plan having anything to do with the major restructuring effort in which OESE was involved. Team members did not feel that he understood what they were doing. Then, and in spite of an inadequate plan, the Assistant Secretary praised the team for their product, which contributed very little, if anything, to the final Department plan. Like most of the other office plans, it was ignored when the Department plan was written.

- **Requisite expertise is needed for the development of a strategic plan.** Another lesson to be learned from the OESE experience is that special expertise is required to develop a strategic plan with measurable indices. Among the volunteers on the Strategic Planning Team in OESE, only a couple had any expertise in that area. This was typical of all of the offices in the Department that worked on the plan. There was a small staff of planners in the Office of the Under Secretary and a few with research background in OERI. In the end, they were the people who developed the Department's strategic plan. Most offices had nobody with the desired expertise. Yet this planning effort was cascaded down to the offices. Those who attended meetings of the team from the Planning and Evaluation Service said they were only there to listen, not to provide guidance and training. No training was provided. The idea that any willing novice could do the job is just not valid.

- **Strategic planning requires a committed, skilled, and clearly focused team.** Planning requires a committed and cohesive work group with clear and purposeful leadership. There never was much commitment to the effort by the majority of team members. Many of the members did not participate and most did not have the requisite skills. Also, many were confused about what was expected of them. It wasn't long, therefore, before the members found that they had other things to do, rather than attend another meeting.

The team also suffered from divided leadership. Ted was the designated leader, but I also made my presence felt, as did Janice Jackson. I challenged the abandonment of the charter, spotlighted the inadequacies of the work plan, and forced some critical discussions and decisions. I even resigned at one point to demonstrate my frustration with the direction the effort have gone. Ted and I worked in close harmony on several other aspects of OESE restructuring and became good friends, but Ted's leadership was a big problem for me and often a mystery when it came to strategic planning.

The most significant leadership came from Janice, who was greatly overworked. She made as many meetings as she could and was essential in the resolution of disputes and in keeping the team working on its charter. Unfortunately, her leadership appeared to be out of sync with the Assistant Secretary.

- **Strategic planning can become confused with tactical planning.** The work of the Strategic Planning Team was to develop an OESE plan that extended the Department Plan into the distinctive work of OESE, with refined strategies and measurable outcomes. This placed definite boundaries on their work. The OESE team did not set the direction of the Department of Education. They did not do any strategic thinking, set the goals or priorities, or administer programs. They did not make decisions about the strategic use of the Department's staff. All these things had presumably been done already.

  Furthermore, the Planning Team did not plan how OESE programs would be carried out or how the restructuring would be done. When the Department Plan came to OESE, it was the Planning Team's job to find ways to measure the results of key programs that were already operational. Programs such as Title 1 or Safe and Drug Free Schools had to be administered according to the authorizing legislation and administrative direction. Most of the programs in OESE would not be a part of the plan. The restructuring of OESE was mainly prescribed by administrative direction, and there was little in the plan that related to it. In no instance did the Planning Team have anything to say about how these programs would operate. It was their job to examine the programs and activities, and to identify performance indicators that could be measured. In brief, they were to identify the means of measuring results.

- **Strategic planning must be supported by adequate resources.** This is true for both the planning and the measurement of outcomes. The OESE strategic planning effort was never a high priority for management. One important component of GPRA is that agencies provide annual measurement of goals and reporting of results. Few people, if any, expect that the resources will be available to measure the outcomes of the OESE strategic plan, to say nothing about the programs of OESE that were not included in the plan. What the Department reports about the work of the agency is another matter, but what is included in its plan is a small part of what actually goes on in OESE or the Department. Since the Department has to report to Congress on its annual performance goals and measures, it must come up with resources to do the reporting.

Contractors will most certainly be used for much of the measurement of outcomes.

Did the OESE team do its job? In my opinion, barely! Since Tom was only interested in priority 1, that is what got the attention. Obtaining measurement data from the sources identified would be a real stretch, and it would be difficult to make any cause-and-effect connections from them. It would take extraordinary resources to obtain the data identified and make the analyses, and the OESE would never spend the effort or the money. As a result, the data would be nil and the assessments superficial. Where it is relevant, the best data will probably come from external contractors employed to evaluate programs.

What was the effect of Congress upon the Department's strategic planning process? On the one hand, the legislators made the process extremely difficult by passing laws to deal with specific problems and sending a potpourri of programs to the Department to administer. A federal agency is not like a private enterprise that can decide what products and services to keep and which to spin off in order to meet a strategic goal. The Department had no choice but to take what it was given and administer the programs according to the law as best it could.

For the small staff of the Planning and Evaluation Service in the Office of the Under Secretary the situation was much different. After the failed attempts to get a plan developed from the bottom up, and then from the top down through the offices of the Department, it fell to them to meet the September 31, 1997, deadline to fulfill the responsibilities of GPRA. Under great pressure, and having made many mistakes, they did, finally, submit the strategic plan of the Department of Education.

7

seven

Sheep Dipping

During the whole time the restructuring process was going on, I seldom attended a meeting in which the subject of training was *not* raised. Whenever something went wrong with the restructuring effort, someone would call for training. If staff did not know enough about OESE programs, cross training would be suggested. If the regional teams were having problems, it was because they did not have sufficient team training. If there were problems with the integrated review teams, then training in systemic reform was the cure. And if there were not enough African Americans in the higher grades, then African Americans ought to be placed in higher positions and trained to perform at that level. Training was a reflex response—the universal remedy for every problem. Yet training as the ultimate solution was never challenged.

The training reflex is certainly not unique to federal agencies—one has no trouble identifying it in the private sector as well. The major problem is that training is commonly considered the only solution for a performance need. Yet the correlation between training and performance in a job is quite low. In their book, *Training and Transfer*, Mary Broad and John Newstrom assert: "Most of [the] investment in organizational training and development is wasted because most of the knowledge and skills gained in training (well-over 80 percent, by some estimates) is not fully applied by those employees on the job" (1992: ix). Moreover, Timothy Baldwin and Kevin Ford report, "Not more than 10 percent of these expenditures [in training] actually result in transfer to the job" (1988:63).

Leaders in the field of human resource development have been writing and speaking about the disconnect between training and performance on the job for over three decades. In 1970, Joe Harless coined the term "front-end analysis" (Dixon 1988: 65-68) to focus on what people are expected to accomplish on the job instead of what they are expected to learn. In 1978, Thomas F. Gilbert wrote a classic and provocative book based upon the rigorous examination of exemplary performers, entitled *Human Competence: Engineering Worthy Performance* (Republished 1996). He argued that it is not enough to ask performers what they do; the analyst must observe their performance. Geary Rummler stated that "training alone is almost never an appropriate cure" (1989: 43- 44).

The point is this—training is never the simple way to fix a performance problem. Geary Rummler and Alan Brache provided a systemic view of performance improvement in the context of the total organization in their book, *Improving Performance: How to Manage the White Space on the Organization Chart* (1990). In this work they look at the whole organization including the overall organizational level, the work process level, and the job level. They have observed, "Most training attempts to improve organization and process performance by addressing only one level (the job level) and only one dimension of the job level (skills and knowledge). As a result, the training has no significant long-term impact, training dollars are wasted, and trainees are frustrated and confused" (*ibid:* 26). Elsewhere in this work they state: "Our experience has led us to a bias: most people want to do a good job. However, if you pit a good performer against a bad system, the system will win almost every time" (*ibid:* 64).

Dana and James Robinson in their book, *Performance Consulting: Moving Beyond Training*, sum it up very well in these words:

> Traditional training approaches in support of performance change are not working, primarily because they are not system-oriented in their approach to resolving performance

problems—this despite the fact the significant leaders in the field have been writing about performance approaches for thirty years (1995: 5).

As you proceed through this Chapter, reflect upon the lessons learned in Chapter 1, "Putting Structure First," and Chapter 2, "The Restructuring Deficit." The leadership of OESE did not realize that the early decisions made in the restructuring caused problems. They did not think of its restructuring as a systemic effort in which all of the design factors were considered and kept in alignment. When performance problems arose, training was considered a "fix." Given the *melange* of unaligned restructuring efforts, the training fix would never help much.

Professional Development Team

It was to be expected that one of the restructuring teams would be assigned to prescribe the requisite training when the OESE restructuring plan was initiated. It was charged with the task of developing "a professional development strategy to support restructuring and reengineering. The plan should look at the needs of four layers in the organization: staff, team leaders, group leaders/coaches, and senior leadership. The plan could include such things as understanding the change process, chaos management, team leadership and facilitation skills, team building and working in teams, conflict resolution, program/customer service, and methods of joint monitoring and evaluation."

Edward Smith, a person who had some experience as a trainer and who perceived himself as an authority in the field, became the leader of the Professional Development Team (PDT). Twelve others, including Alicia Coro, one of two program directors who volunteered for restructuring teams, was also on the team.

First Clues to the Training Plans. It wasn't until the All Hands meeting on January 24, 1995 that I learned what kind of strategy the PDT was developing. I listened with interest as Richard Kress, a member of the PDT, spoke for the team. Richard emphasized the need for OESE to become a learning organization and that the PDT had developed a long list of training programs. However, it seemed to me that there was an absence of any coordination of their planning with the needs of other restructuring teams. In addition, it seemed naive to assume that

OESE would support the overwhelming list of training events the team had prescribed.

After Richard's presentation I wondered whether they had equated a learning organization with an organization that supported a lot of training, instead of one that supported employee learning. I was also puzzled how the team had arrived at the long list of programs. Were they based on performance needs? If so, how would they identify the competencies needed? The team was charged with "developing a professional development *strategy*," but I did not hear any strategy mentioned for determining competencies. I also wondered if they had discussed their training strategy with other teams (as far as I knew nobody had talked with the Reengineering Team.) Finally, I wondered whether the team thought that the Senior Leadership Team would commit OESE to the time and resources to make their plan a reality. The Reengineering Team had been unequivocally told that the Senior Leadership Team would *not* devote the time proposed as necessary to adequately consider the reengineering effort which they had launched, so I didn't think there was much hope for the PDT.

Personality Obstacles. I knew I would have to meet with Ed Smith, if for no other reason than to begin to coordinate training between the PDT and the Reengineering Team. Ed was on leave and I immediately phoned Lorraine Wise, who was acting for him. She saw no purpose in a meeting and stated: "The Professional Development Team was taking into consideration all the training needs of all the teams." I knew that they were not taking into consideration the needs of the Reengineering Team, so I insisted on a meeting and one was arranged.

When I met with Lorraine, she seemed unreasonably hostile. I began with general questions about how they were developing their strategy and plans. Lorraine seemed confused and her responses were vague. I followed with a few specific questions about a learning community and the basis for selecting the training programs on their lists. Lorraine seemed to know nothing about learning organizations or competency based performance improvement. With no foundation for an informed discussion of these topics, I moved on to discussing some of the learning that the Reengineering Team had identified. I requested that the two teams meet together in the near future, but she rejected that idea.

So I expressed my desire to meet with their team. Although she saw no need for this, she did promise to pass on my request to Ed.

Ed returned to work the next week, but there was no word from him. About a week later, I ran into him and asked about coordinating the interests of the two teams in training. Ed told me there was no need to get together, but that if I sent him a memo about the training needs of the Reengineering Team, they'd consider the request. When I asked if they were using a competency based approach to determining training needs he said, "Yes, of course." When I asked how they were planning to identify competencies, Ed excused himself and said that he had a meeting to attend.

I did not need much more information about the Professional Development Team to remind myself to keep my expectations low. Richard's presentation at the All Hands meeting raised more questions than it answered. Lorraine's hostility, inability to discuss their work intelligently, and reluctance to work cooperatively didn't improve my perception of the team's competence and their willingness to work together. And Ed's unwillingness to discuss his team's work convinced me that the PDT did not want any external viewpoints and was not going to make much of an impact upon either the restructuring effort or the professional competencies of OESE staff.

I was dismayed about Ed's unresponsiveness and wondered what prompted their lack of cooperation. Ed openly referred to himself as an authority on training, yet he did not wish to answer my questions and seemed defensive. So from that time on, I only engaged Ed in friendly small talk that included no comments about the work of the Professional Development Team. However, at open meetings the rules were different. I spoke about training issues when they came up, sometimes differing with Ed's point of view.

Data Gathering. Early in their work, the PDT separated into three subgroups for data gathering. They took note of the *Improving America's Schools Act* (IASA) of 1994, which provided different relationships with the educational establishment. They also took note of the *1993 Employee Survey of the United States Department of Education,* (Synetics For Management Decisions, Inc., and Price Waterhouse, 1994), which broke out and reported the data for OESE. Eight questions on the survey that dealt with training were particularly interesting to me. About half of the OESE staff "mostly agreed" or "strongly agreed" that the training provided by the Department was satisfactory, with the exception of training for higher positions and preparation for moving into management. To such questions, only about 22 to 23 percent rated them with the same degree of satisfaction. The overall scores clearly told the team that in the opinion of the OESE staff, the Training and Development Center (TDC)—the training facility of the Department—was doing a mediocre job at best.

The team brought in a number of resource people. Charles (Chuck) Hansen, who headed up the conceptualization of the OESE restructuring format, was brought in to talk about the restructuring and its intent. Bette Novak, TDC's liaison person for OESE, was brought in to talk about existing and potential services from TDC. The team also met with Phyllis Barajas, then employed by OM and later transferred to OESE, to help with restructuring. Finally, they interviewed a number of division directors and branch chiefs.

All of these individuals were internal to the Department. Chuck Hansen was undoubtedly helpful in describing the purpose and format of the restructuring effort. I did not know Bette Novak or Phyllis Barajas at the time, but later gained a lot of respect for Bette Novak's knowledge of training. Later, when I worked with Phyllis, I realized that she had little to offer in the way of training knowledge. The division directors and branch chiefs would have undoubtedly been concerned about knowledge of their programs and cross training. Unfortunately, no one inside understood the importance of focusing on performance, and there was no external consultant to help them with a performance improvement approach to training.

The "Findings." The final report of the PDT lists 45 findings in three categories: (1) external environment, (2) internal environment, and (3) people. It is upon these findings that their professional development plan was based. When I read the findings, I wondered how they could refer to them as "findings." Rather, they seemed to me to be a large number of very biased statements. With the exception of the data from the 1993 employee survey, there was no methodology followed to assure the validity and reliability of their data.

One of the things that particularly interested me was the way the findings were worded. For example, the findings repeatedly read *"Only 36% . . . , Only 53% . . . , Only 27% . . . , Only 35% . . . ,"* as if they were making an argument, not reporting findings. In addition, there were other places where their findings appeared to have little validity. For example, they argued that clerical workers should be moved into professional positions because they would "require less learning time," and that hiring through the Outstanding Scholars Program or the Presidential Intern Program would create an "ivory tower mentality." I questioned how they could call such an argument a "finding." To me these so-called "findings" could more appropriately be called "assumptions" or "opinions."

One of the things that struck me was that the training plan was related to the team's findings, not strategic goals, and the findings also covered the whole waterfront. For example, there were findings on the number of people who signed off on memos, and judgments about adequate workspace and the appraisal system. There were also findings about the future which, in hindsight, never materialized. When I read them, I wondered how they related to a strategic professional development plan. When I asked a team member about this, I was told that "There were many issues that had to be resolved before training could be effective." I thought to myself, "At least they see training in an environmental context. But this warped view is not something related to strategic goals."

Data taken from the 1993 employee survey placed them on firmer ground because the survey had been conducted by survey professionals. From that data, they found that the morale of staff within OESE was the second lowest in the Department. In 72 percent of the questions on the survey, OESE's staff gave the questions lower ratings than the Department average.

The PDT may also have been prophetic about the problems of race. They stated, "Racial [in]equity is the most serious equity problem in OESE." While one could argue about the *fact* of racial inequity in OESE, they were correct in identifying it as one of the *perceived* problems.

The equity issue was a significant part of the larger morale issue. Equity was sometimes addressed directly and sometimes indirectly. For example, employment policies and upward career mobility practices are equity issues when they are seen as adversely effecting an ethnic group. So are management practices. Many of the PDT's short- and long-term morale enhancers were rationalized from both direct and indirect references to the equity issue.

Management also received a big hit regarding racial equity. The PDT found that management in several offices was "dominated by individuals of European origin" and that management's relationship with staff "fosters cronyism and conflict." The PDT stated that "intense conflict exists between some managers and their staff." They charged that there was "flagrant abuse of the performance appraisal system by supervisors." And there were several findings related to the failures of managers to communicate.

The study presented ten findings about the future. These findings were really perceptions about what would happen in the future, given the restructuring plan that was being pursued at the time. There were findings about the need to develop generalists, rather than more specialists, the phases that the teams would pass through as they moved to maturity, the future role of the team leaders, and the nature of adult learning and training adults. They also "found" that it would take an "extraordinary investment in time and financial resources" for professional development in OESE.

Recommendations. Based upon these 45 "findings" (as opposed to strategic goals), the PDT made 58 recommendations:

- 5 short-term training topics

- 15 short-term morale enhancers

- 14 long-term training topics

- 9 long-term morale enhancers

- 15 employee self-improvement resources

Both the short- and long-term training topics were traditional training programs, to be delivered by OESE staff, Department staff, external trainers employed by the TDC, and a consultant. Two of them would be delivered by an institution of higher education. Some would be targeted at all staff, but most of them were for specific staff in leadership roles, such as senior staff and team leaders.

Because of the impelling concern for morale, both short- and long-term morale enhancers were planned. A few were related to training, such as an upward bound program for support staff and activities to promote training programs. Most of them were activities such as rewarding success, rewarding loyalty, diversity in promotions, a new policy of compensating non-duty hour work, and election of team leaders. Plainly, the team did not see training as the only way to address this problem and was going beyond professional development to address it.

The PDT should be commended for viewing performance as more than training. When an organization has performance problems it must look at the barriers to its performance and ask themselves if and how they might be reduced or eliminated. Although some persons would argue about the barriers the PDT identified or the way they arrived at them, I believe the team inadvertently hit upon a very good concept. I would not argue that there were not barriers that training could not address.

Finally, employees were seen as responsible for their own learning. I felt certain that this emphasis could be traced to Bette Novak on the staff of the TDC. Bette had been advocating this type of learning and TDC was developing instrumentation and other resources for self-directed learning. In addition, the TDC was listed as the providers of such learning in most of the categories, along with institutions of higher education and peers. Employee self-improvement included such topics as mentoring, action reflection learning, peer teaching, satellite technology training, and team empowerment. This was another useful learning concept.

Outcomes. On February 16, 1995, Ed Smith sent a prioritized schedule of short-term training activities to Assistant Secretary Tom Payzant in response to a request for immediate decision making. Under the heading of "Professional Development in a Learning Environment," Ed listed the following:

1. **Paradigm/Model Training**—(Three days) March 1995. If we are to work in a more effective way, we need to mentally prepare ourselves to propose new solutions and approaches. A pilot session will be held OESE-wide.

2. **Coaching/Team Building Overview**—(Three days) April 1995. Managers need to learn quickly the new skills needed to implement the new team procedures. A pilot session will be held OESE-wide.

3. **Cross-Program Overview**—(Two days) May 1995. This workshop will inform all OESE staff about the basic elements of all OESE programs.

4. **Cross-Program In-depth Training**—(Five Days) June/July: 1995. These sessions will provide staff with a working level of knowledge on OESE programs.

5. **Stress Management**—(These skills/strategies will be systematically incorporated into training schedule.) March/July: 1995. Employees need strategies to help them cope with the turbulent work environment. Skills in effective time management will be included.

Some of the programs mentioned in this memorandum did take place, but most of them were not conducted until much later. There was a one-day, mandatory cross-program overview for all staff held in May 1995. But there never was any in-depth, cross-training program. The high priority paradigm/model training that was proposed for March did not take place until almost the end of 1995. There was some stress management and some coaching and team building, but with the exception of the mandatory cross-program overview training, attendance was voluntary and small.

As for the report of the PDT, it went the way of most other reports from restructuring teams—the PDT never received a response from the Senior Leadership Team. However, all teams were asked if they wished to continue working after the reports were submitted. Some of the team members continued for awhile, but quit when they found that their programs were not going to be implemented and that they would be used to implement other people's programs.

When Gerald Tirozzi replaced Tom Payzant as Assistant Secretary, he instituted a "Professional Development on Systemic Reform" series of training sessions described below. A couple of the former PDT members assisted in this series.

Although the term "learning organization" was used throughout the report, it was never clearly defined. Nor did the report explain how OESE could become one. I could not go along with the assumption that a learning organization would evolve from what was presented in the report. Judging from the report, I could only assume that this was a rhetorical term.

Of particular concern to me was the unwillingness of the PDT to work with the Reengineering Team or with other teams in the restructuring process. There were no subtleties in the reactions I received from either the team leader or his designate. From my view, it made a lot of sense for the PDT to involve the other teams in the planning of the professional development of OESE. There is no evidence this was done.

The most fundamental failure of the PDT's plan is that it did not address the performance needs of the staff; it did not provide a way to find out what those performance requirements were. Although front-end analysis of work roles had been advocated for over three decades, the staff of the Department of Education, including the TDC, has never approached professional development from this perspective. The team did not work from job models or recommend the strategy to develop them. No systematic inquiry was ever made into what individuals would be doing to further the goals of the restructured OESE.

However, the team should be commended for viewing training as taking place within an organizational environment that had both positive and negative factors that influenced performance. They also recognized that it took more than training to develop a high performance organization.

Leadership Training

Ignoring the recommendations of the PDT, the Senior Leadership Team launched a series of meetings, which they named "Leading Through Change." The meetings involved program directors, group leaders and team leaders. The overall plan and number of meetings were never specified, but the series resulted in three meetings. The first was held on August 17, 1995, prior to the Restructuring Fair for group leaders. The other two were held on October 11th and November 7th for program directors, group leaders, and team leaders.

First Training Session. Carroll Dexter and I walked six blocks to the Mary E. Switzer Federal Building, a weathered edifice that the Department of Education shared with the Federal Drug Administration. We arrived at room 1014 a few minutes prior to the beginning of the meeting to find the door locked, a group of people gathering in the hall, and none of the leadership for the meeting present. Since I had had been in the room several times before, I wondered how we were going to hold the planned meeting in this small room.

A small crowd waited outside the locked meeting room when, finally, 15 minutes after the scheduled meeting time, Phyllis Barajas showed up with Craig Polite, a consultant. Apparently, the room had been reserved, but nobody had obtained the key. Finally, after Phyllis made some telephone calls, somebody was dispatched to go after a key. When the key arrived, everyone moved into the room, only to discover that it was much too small. Everyone was really frustrated at this point and snide comments were being exchanged about the lack of planning and preparation. Phyllis and members of the group began making telephone calls to friends in the building to inquire if there were any conference rooms in the building that were not being used. Finally, one was obtained and the group moved to a larger space. It was well over an hour after the designated meeting time before the participants settled into their seats.

The meeting began in the traditional manner. There was a statement of purpose, a review of the agenda and time frame, which had now been blown. Ground rules were listed, and an icebreaker was used in an attempt to enhance communication. The purpose of the meeting was described as defining the change agenda for OESE and explaining how the restructuring initiative related to that agenda. Craig Polite came with a set of overhead transparencies which he had obviously prepared for use with private sector organizations. The transparencies had references to business, industry, corporation, profits, stock and pay systems.

Most federal employees believe that the public sector is quite different from the private sector and that their agency is unique. To his credit, Craig did present some material that was relevant to those in the public sector, and he apologized for the private sector references. He compared the "doer" manager and the "facilitating" manager. He spent considerable time going through his transparencies about "the horizontal corporation," which would have been more appropriately labeled "the horizontal *organization*." He presented the seven key elements as (1) organize around process, not task, (2) flatten hierarchy, (3) use teams to manage everything, (4) let customers drive performance, (5) reward team performance, (6) maximize supplier and customer contact, and (7) inform and train all employees. He summed it all up by saying, "You must manage across, not up and down!" There wasn't much discussion about the key elements. I detected a "We'll wait and see attitude."

Another part of Craig's presentation concerned the five types of power that he identified as (1) reward power, (2) negative power, (3) legitimate power, (4) expert power, and (5) referent power. At this point, I asked him to make some distinctions between power, authority, influence and status, but Craig had trouble with these. Craig and I had a short dialogue about these terms, noting some differences between power and authority and different types of status. Following the discussion the group broke for lunch.

The afternoon was devoted to management competencies. Although the term "competencies" was never defined, the discussion was focused on a matrix that distinguished the "know that" from the "know how" in 10 categories. Craig's categories were:

1. Principled leadership

2. Action orientation

3. Team development

4. Strategic orientation

5. Learning orientation

6. Communication

7. Collaboration and negotiation

8. Systems thinking

9. Business orientation

10. Program related: technical and analytical

Given these competency categories, the participants were directed to prioritize them in the restructured OESE. I thought that the group had a general perception of these terms but did not understand them in terms of competencies. The session ended, referring to these competency categories as a personal matter for each individual to embody as best he or she could.

When the meeting was concluded, I headed for the Metro train to ride back to Vienna, Virginia, where I lived. While on the train, I reflected upon the experiences of the day. The training had a bad start, and, as a result, some of the agenda had to be dumped. Secondly, Craig had brought too many concepts to the meeting that were new to most participants and the limited time meant we could not discuss them in any depth. When I queried him about the meanings of the terms on his transparencies, he appeared to be beyond his depth. I felt that the meeting had provided a good overview of some important things for the group leaders to think about. But I questioned what it would mean to my colleagues in a week or a month. Were these generic categories of competencies what group leaders really needed? How did they identify the ones in which they were weak or strong? Would the group leaders work on any of them in the months to come? Would any of the other sessions in the "Leading Through Change Series" pick up on concepts presented?

Second Training Session. The second in the series of "Leading for Change" training sessions took place on October 11, 1995. The program directors and the team leaders also attended this session, along with the group leaders, since one of the outcomes of the meeting was for people in these three roles to think of themselves as a "Leadership Team." The stated purposes of the session were to develop facilitative skills and to follow up on the training given at the Restructuring Fair. Two external consultants, Mark Rhodes and Craig Polite, facilitated the meeting, along with Phyllis and Janice.

After a late start and a series of unrelated announcements that took up precious time and seemed to annoy many of those present, we finally got under way. The rest of the morning was devoted to helping the participants see the Organizational System Design (OSD) Model in terms of the realities of the OESE restructuring. The OSD Model had been presented to the rank and file the previous month at the Restructuring Fair. Unfortunately, many of the participants needed more than the quick overview Mark gave. And I thought that Mark should have used a diagram of the Model as a handout to refresh their memory. Mark grouped the participants together by programs in which they worked, and then directed them to identify what they ought to be doing to implement the design choices of the Model.

The IAP team consisted of Cathy, Carroll, Curt and me. I was the only person in the group that had any significant knowledge of the OSD Model, so it fell to me to describe the assignment we had been given and lead us through the Model. In the available time, we developed a fairly comprehensive list that addressed goals, technical systems, decision-making, people systems, reward systems, and renewal systems.

The afternoon was devoted to role-playing problem situations. Each of the small groups identified two problem situations, and then developed a scenario. It was felt that because the problems identified for the role playing were real problems, the participants could identify and learn from them. It was both enjoyable and instructional.

Some descriptions of group leader and team leader duties were distributed that did not appear to be related to any agenda item. This led to a discussion about delayering OESE by making team leaders a role rather than a position, which prompted me to assert again that this was more fantasy than fact. I reiterated my previous statements that any behavior analysis of the team leader role indicated it was a distinctive supervisory layer even though it was in a weakened state. I asserted that it was a myth to say we are delayering.

211

Having now made my point for the third time in Janice's presence, Janice rose to her feet to take the position of the administration and asserted that OESE was eliminating middle-management positions and increasing the span of control. She said there were a number of ways to look at the team leader role, and the behavioral analysis was only one. Without giving any specifics, she stated that OESE was delayering and the team leaders had a role and not a position.

But now I was not alone in my opinion. I pointed out that there were others in the Federal government asserting that the establishment of teams was not really eliminating middle managers in their agencies. For me, the issue was the contrast between organizational reality versus political correctness.

Once again, too much was included in the agenda. The group was to receive the findings of the Herrmann Brain Dominance Instrument and have a session interpreting them, but there was no time for this. There was also going to be some time devoted to management of teams in change, but there was no time for this either. And there was to be a professional development planning period that never materialized.

Near the end of the meeting, Phyllis asked for feedback on the meeting. When it was my turn to speak, I stated that I would prefer to give her a memo rather than make my comments at the meeting. Two days later, I sent Phyllis an e-mail in which I first stated my frustration that neither of the meetings got started on time and that too much time was spent on irrelevant lengthy announcements. I also said that they should be more realistic about what might be accomplished in the time allotted. In addition, I told Phyllis that I did not think that they were using their consultants appropriately. I pointed out that they paid the fees for two consultants, when Mark could have easily provided the services Craig provided, (although not vice-versa.) I suggested that future training be planned around the expertise of the consultants as well as the needs of the participants.

Third Training Session. Although the third meeting again started late this time it was because of the participants, not the facilitators. The stated purposes of the meeting were "to continue evolving group and team leaders and program directors into a leadership team," and "to define and clarify the differentiation of roles and responsibilities" of the three groups. The agenda was planned around the problems that the restructuring effort was experiencing. The discussion of the roles and responsibilities of the three groups of participants was scheduled for the morning because the program directors had only committed one half-day to the meeting. Phyllis would be the primary facilitator.

After reviewing the meeting's stated purpose and setting the ground rules for the day, Janice provided a debriefing of the LMPC mediation meeting with the union. (At this time very difficult negotiations were underway with the AFGE, and the previous day the negotiations had lasted from 9:00 a.m. to 7:00 p.m.) It was announced that the major accomplishment of the previous day's meeting was that the AFGE had decided that OESE could implement the proposed restructuring (which it was already doing), but a long list of issues still had to be resolved. For example, AFGE demanded that there must be a 12-month trial period in which the union would monitor the activities. Janice distributed a two-page handout listing the controversial issues and concluded saying, "If problems occur, we will deal with the issue, but will not change the structure."

There was obvious concern about the status of the negotiations and the unresolved issues, and a number of questions were asked for clarification. Janice responded as objectively as she could, even though she represented management. I asked her a different type of question. I inquired, "When is the LMPC going to provide the minutes of their meetings?" Janice responded that they had. I pressed back saying that I had not seen any minutes. Janice then admitted, "The outcomes have been distributed, not the minutes." I responded, "Everyone in OESE has a right to the minutes of the LMPC meeting, not merely the outcomes." Others in the room expressed their agreement. Janice assured everyone that minutes would be distributed but few were.

With this report over, the remainder of the morning was devoted to a further defining of the roles and responsibilities of the program directors, group leaders, and team leaders—an exercise that would be replicated over and over. Each of the three groups were assigned the task of defining the roles and responsibilities of each group from their perspective. The program directors were reluctant to buy into this assignment, but they finally agreed. In the end, their effort, as compared to the effort of the group and team leaders, was modest.

The group agreed that redefining roles and responsibilities should be combined and synthesized for further refinement. When volunteers were requested, an awkward situation emerged. Group and team leaders responded in adequate numbers, but there were no volunteers from the program directors. After a direct request was made to the program directors, there was a long silence. Finally, one person broke the unsettling silence, saying: "Some of the problems we have now are because of the lack of communication with program directors . . . they needed to be involved to solve them." Her indicting comment moved Bayla White and Cathy Schagh, who were embarrassed by the situation, to volunteer to work on synthesizing the roles and responsibilities.

Before the meeting began, Janice had stated to me that with the exception of the OESE/AFGE mediation report, she was going to sit this one out as an observer. I jokingly said, "I am sure that I can say something that would provoke a comment from you." She laughed and said, " I don't think so." At the lunch break, she called to me and said: "The program directors nearly succeeded in getting me involved when they wouldn't volunteer to work with the group and team leaders on the synthesis of the roles and responsibilities." "But," she added, "I intend to say something to them at another time." She was obviously quite disturbed by their behavior.

After lunch there was a lengthy presentation by several people involved in moving the integrated review teams (IRTs) from the trial period into the implementation stage. Again, I felt that this whole lengthy discussion was out of place in a training program that had been planned for another purpose. There was an attempt to legitimize the effort as a major activity of OESE, to discuss many technical problems, to link it to strategic planning, and to justify the IRTs in terms of the vision for OESE. There was an urgent, almost desperate character, to the discussion because the implementation of the IRTs was behind schedule and there were many problems to be solved. Clearly, the training had been preempted by urgent problem solving. However, many of us in the room who were not involved in IRTs resented the intrusion into our training time.

Nevertheless, I did not play a passive role in the discussion. I knew that the strategic plans had nothing to say about the IRTs. So, when one of the presenters stated that the IRTs were included in the strategic plan I asked, "How do the strategic plans of either the Department or OESE support the integrated reviews? Can you tell me what objectives, strategies, and performance indicators in either plan relate to the IRTs?" After a brief discussion, the presenters admitted that the IRTs were not a part of the strategic plans.

I again upset some of the presenters by challenging the relevance of the IRTs to the vision of OESE. I was quite certain that Chuck Hansen's team, who conceptualized the restructuring of OESE, had never envisioned a dozen or more people going out to a field site at one time. In particular, I wanted to know "how they could justify the tremendous resources expended on the IRTs with the original vision of Chuck Hansen's team." The justification came in what I perceived to be weak anecdotal stories. What I really saw in the development of the IRTs was an evolution of the original restructuring plan because of the unperceived problems in the conception.

In the evaluation at the end of the session, the major positive feedback of the group was that they had dealt with practical, every day problems—not theoretical concepts. Those who were involved with the IRTs thought that the time spent on this topic was good, and those who were not involved thought it was out of place. The major negative perception was the lack of participation by the program directors. They were criticized for not wanting to participate in the group work on roles and responsibilities and for their reluctance to help with the synthesis of the group outputs. I said, "They sent the wrong signal to the group leaders and team leaders and perpetuated the perception of some people that the program directors were dragging their feet in the restructuring process." I was certain that Janice would be bringing a strong message to the program directors at their next Senior Leadership Team meeting.

A Retrospective View. The "Leading Through Change" series was another in-house attempt to facilitate the restructuring of OESE by what the leadership thought appropriate. In hindsight, the planning and preparation for the sessions, especially the first two, were inept. Much of the training was seen as the presentation of generic material to the participants on the assumption that it would sink in and make a difference. But there was no follow through. The third meeting was an exception in that the leadership focused this meeting on current, practical problems, namely, the roles and responsibilities of the three groups of mid-level managers (that is, team leaders, group leaders, program directors), and the IRTs.

The group leaders and the team leaders were very supportive of the training and demonstrated this by their attendance and participation. And although they were often part of the problem, the program directors were reluctant to get involved. They appeared to set themselves apart from group leaders and team leaders.

The race issue also affected our training by leading to the use of two consultants—one Caucasian and one African American. Some blacks were objecting to using only Mark Rhodes, a white consultant. Shortly after that, Craig Polite, an African American consultant, began appearing. To me, both were not needed.

OESE/TDC Partnership
On August 3, 1995, exactly two years after Tom was confirmed by the Senate to serve as Assistant Secretary of OESE, he was selected to become the Superintendent of the Boston city schools. He stayed long enough to participate in the Restructuring Fair in September, which officially marked the implementation of the restructured OESE. He was not gone long before it was announced the Janice would leave at the end of the year to work with him.

A New Assistant Secretary "Gets Serious." Dr. Gerald N. Tirozzi arrived to take the helm of OESE in December 1995, at a time when most government agencies were furloughed by political disagreements over the budget, and an unseasonable blizzard kept employees home. In February, he named Jim Kohlmoos as Acting Deputy Assistant Secretary for External Affairs, and Phyllis Barajas as Acting Deputy Assistant Secretary for Staff and Organizational Development.

As one would expect, Gerry was sizing up the situation that he inherited during his first months in office. He had not had much experience with organizational change and Phyllis did not have the expertise to help him. But he was a good observer and listener, even if he did not always take the advice of others. He most certainly heard about the many problems the teams were experiencing in the new OESE structure. I had a couple of sessions with Gerry, in which we discussed the characteristics of the OESE work force and some of the resource people who could provide assistance in professional development.

One of Gerry's early initiatives became apparent on April 23, 1996. At a Leadership Team meeting, attended by group leaders and team leaders, he announced an "Organizational Development Plan." He reported that OESE had developed a partnership with the Department's Training and Development Center (TDC) to provide training to strengthen OESE's team structure, enhance the level of service provided to its customers, and advance the use of technology. He declared that it was a time of transition from a program orientation to a team orientation. He talked about an ongoing systemic approach to professional development.

Gerry further stated: "It was time to get serious." He explained that he had discussed the plan at length with the program directors, and was now presenting it to the group and team leaders. He then turned the meeting over to Ingrid Kolb, Director of TDC. He remained with the group for a few minutes, and then left to attend to other matters.

Ingrid's Plan. Ingrid announced that TDC would be implementing the goals of the Assistant Secretary:

- Strengthen new team structure,

- Improve customer service,

- Increase use of technology, and

- Enhance professional skills.

She organized her presentation around each goal and it was clear that she saw training as the solution to Gerry's goals, not simply an enhancement of professional skills. After she talked "training" for some time, I asked, "How are you going to determine the content and the approach to training?" Her response was, "That is a very good question, but please hold it until later when I plan to talk about that." So, I sat back to listen for the answers to my questions.

She then turned her presentation to "the TDC approach to training" and said that because the teams have a variety of needs, the training would be customized to each team. She explained that the instructors would meet with the teams to determine their unique needs. Then both management and staff would give consideration to what was needed. She said she knew that finding time would be a problem, and that the instructors would work with the teams to schedule training. She also explained that the instruction would be "facilitated" instruction, based on the needs analysis that had been conducted. She then opened the meeting to questions.

I started the questioning, which developed into an argument. I said: "Training is expensive. In North America, we spend 50 billion dollars a year on training, and that is just direct costs. If we add to that the indirect costs; such as the time we spend away from work, travel to training sites, and per diem; training probably costs us somewhere between 300 and 400 billion dollars per year. It sounds to me that what you are proposing for OESE is going to be costly as well."

After bringing up the Broad/Newstom and Baldwin/Ford research on transfer of training which report that very little training actually transfers to the job, I asked, "Given the costs and small results obtained, what will you do to break the mold?"

Ingrid responded, "We will be breaking the mold by using instructor interviews with teams prior to the training, in which the team needs will be identified, and for which custom training will be designed." Unfortunately, she did not mention coaching, the one factor which the research cites as making a major difference.

I responded, "Why are we not studying the jobs people do in the newly structured OESE? For more than 30 years HRD people have been talking about front-end analysis . . . What we really need around here are some job models or competency models so that the training will be directly related to the knowledge and skills our staff need for the jobs they must do."

Ingrid answered me by saying that Phyllis was going to provide her with the job models shortly, and they would be ready to start in about a month.

At that point, it occurred to me that Ingrid probably did not know what a job model was. So I said, "We have no job models. The only thing we can give you are some generic position descriptions, and some lists of roles and responsibilities of team leaders and group leaders. We do not have anyone who knows how to build job models. We need external help for this."

Ingrid responded by saying, "We have external help. We have contracted with instructors, and if they do not perform their jobs, we will get rid of them."

Realizing the futility of the argument, I made one last rebuttal. "We need more than instructors," I said. "What this whole restructuring effort needs is some performance consultants. We have never had a close up, realistic analysis of what our leaders and our staff must do to accomplish our objectives. Without determining what we need to know and do to perform our jobs we will not have training that is worth the cost. And without identifying and eliminating the barriers to our performance, we will never attain our goals." It was obvious that Ingrid had little understanding of the performance improvement approach to training.

As I was leaving the meeting, Ed Smith, Team Leader of PDT, walked down the hall with me, asking questions about performance consulting and developing job models. After months of small talk, I was now having a substantive discussion with Ed. We stopped in front of the IAP suite of offices, continuing our discussion. Finally, I said to Ed, "I happen to have Dana and Jim Robinson's most recent book on performance consulting in my office. It should answer most of your questions. Would you like to borrow it?" Ed said he would, so the two of us walked to my office, and I gave Ed the book. Several weeks later, I found the book on my desk. There was no note attached, and Ed never mentioned it.

During the next few days, several people who were at the meeting came to me to comment about my dialogue with Ingrid. Some people who were not at the meeting also had heard about it. In general, most said they admired me for speaking up and some were impressed with my knowledge of the literature and the research. Yet I knew that confronting Ingrid was not appreciated by OESE leadership.

I had not known Ingrid very well. I knew that people had respect for her and I could understand this. Though small in stature, she had a commanding presence when she took over a meeting. She was direct and articulate. She had come to her current position through administrative roles, having once worked in OESE's front office. I had no doubt that she would be a respected manager in any federal bureaucracy. But I speculated on what it would take to bring the state-of-the-art to TDC. I did not think they would get there with Ingrid at its helm.

Implementing the Plan. For the next couple of months, team training instructors from several consulting organizations fanned out over OESE, conducting interviews with team members and the OESE leadership. No job modeling was done. I decided that I would cooperate with anyone working with TDC's team training program. I concluded that if this was the best they could do, I would go along with the training, even if it was useless.

Impact Training Systems, Inc. (ITS), of Springfield, Virginia, was given the contract for training the Program Service Team of the IAP, for which I was the group leader. During the next couple of months, all of the team members were interviewed. ITS identified what they termed the "team strengths" and the "opportunities for improvement" based on participant opinions, and made its recommendations. Their recommendations were (1) clarify how the team should function and its relationship with RSTs, (2) develop strategies for strengthening team dynamics, and (3) provide more opportunities for cross training within IAP.

The training consisted of three half-day training sessions. The sessions dealt with the first two recommendations and consisted of components that, for the most part, are found in stock training programs for teams. Follow up, such as developing a mission statement and vision statement, was left to the team. The opportunities for cross training were also left to the PST to identify and implement.

I knew that making a mature team of IAP's Program Service Team was going to be a real stretch. In fact, the structure, the decision making, the culture, and most everything else worked against the success of the teams. The OESE/TDC training partnership was not going to create teams out of work groups in this situation.

Training on Systemic Reform

Gerry Sees the Need. When Gerry Tirozzi assumed the leadership of OESE, he made professional development in the traditional mode one of his goals and demonstrated his interest in it. He had most recently held a professorship in the Department of Educational Leadership Development at the University of Connecticut. Prior to this post, his varied career in public education involved him in various aspects of professional development.

The first strong indication of Gerry's interest was the nature of the All Hands staff meetings. Instead of allotting the major portion of the meeting to the activities of OESE, he assigned most of the time to a distinguished authority, who spoke on some aspect of education.

I also discovered Gerry's interest in educational matters in a couple of our private discussions, during which I recommended future speakers and other resources. We also had a good dialogue about some of the relevant literature on the contemporary work force, knowledge-based learning organizations, and the Herrmann Brain Dominence Instrument. Gerry also asked my opinions about professional development and study groups he was thinking about. When he asked if I would be interested in leading a study group I said "yes," but no invitation was ever extended.

I was encouraged to see Gerry express this kind of interest in professional development of the OESE staff because I felt it was a serious staff deficiency. But, I wondered if Gerry really understood the challenge he had accepted. I told him that I thought he had taken on a real challenge by attempting to bring the staff of OESE into the present age in teaching and learning. I pointed out that much of our labor force had little education and very few had any experience in schooling. I informed him that in Impact Aid, for example, we had a few who had been school administrators and a few more who had been teachers. The majority of our staff in professional positions did not have four-year degrees.

The next time Gerry and I had a one-on-one discussion, Gerry brought up the characteristics of the OESE staff. Immediately after the discussion, I gave him a copy of some of the EEO data on OESE staff, and suggested that he obtain the whole packet of data that the Department files with OPM every year. I was later told that there was a discussion at the Senior Leadership Team about the data, so I assumed Gerry had obtained them.

Training on Systemic Reform. In early May, ten professional development sessions on systemic reform were announced, and all staff were expected to attend. The announcement read:

> As part of OESE's efforts to provide ongoing professional development, we are providing the following series of seminars and discussions on various aspects of systemic reform. We will be bringing in outside speakers/presenters who will talk about each topic from its broad perspective, including trends around the country, as well as those who are from the field—superintendents, principals, and teachers.

The series started on June 21st and consisted of a presentation by one or more presenters, followed by break-out sessions of small groups. The series consisted of the following sessions:

1. Origins and Development of Systemic Reform Model

2. Standards

3. Assessment

4. Professional Development

5. Governance/Accountability

6. Managing Change

7. Mobilizing Community and Parental Support

8. Technology

9. School-to-Work

10. Change

The announcement of the series received a mixed response from the OESE staff—it would meet the needs of some and bore others. In general, I believed that those persons who had some work experience in schooling went to the sessions fairly regularly. Those who had some need for knowledge about school reform, such as those on regional teams that would be traveling to the states, attended the meetings whether they had ever thought about school reform before or not. Many of the staff in IAP did not attend because they felt their program had little to do with either learning or teaching. Their customers were the "show me the money" school administrators who focused on financial issues because their districts had been financially burdened by federal activity in their districts.

Participant Criticism. The reviews of the first session were mixed. When I asked Carroll Dexter what he thought of the first session he said, "The presentations were interesting, but the break-out sessions were a flop." When asked why, he said, "because our staff do not know anything about teaching and schools. A discussion about systemic reform was really way beyond them."

When I asked Curt how the session went, Curt said: "It was just something else to talk about. Schools are always in some kind of reform: they reduce class size, they raise teachers' salaries, they introduce accountability systems. They are always doing something. This, too, will pass."

After the second session, Harris Taylor said he thought making it mandatory was a good idea but it would be necessary for the staff to go way beyond what they are getting in this series. "This series is insufficient to prepare anyone to function in the area of reform because it does not have the necessary depth."

I asked Harris how he saw it working out if the staff could get more training. Harris thought that it would be best for the staff to try to become experts in one area, such as standards, assessments, teacher training, parental involvement, and that it would be wrong for them to think that they could provide technical assistance across the board. I then asked Harris, "What percentage of the regional service teams would ever be able to provide technical assistance?" Harris replied, "Not many."

When I asked him why, Harris responded: "Our staff had not been hired to do this type of work and most don't have college degrees, studies in education, or any practical work experiences in schools. Some don't even have any interest in it." He continued by saying that we would have to change our employment and promotion criteria. OESE should ask itself what it can realistically provide with the type of personnel we have.

In the early afternoon of September 19th, Genevieve Cornelius, a staff person in the front office, stopped me in the hall after an All Hands meeting. She was going out of the building for lunch with some friends when she spotted me, and evidently thought that she had found somebody who would listen to her locked-up emotions about the systemic reform series. I could hardly get a word in edgeways. She had expressed some of her muted opinions at the All Hands meeting, and now she wanted to express some unrestrained opinions to me.

Genevieve insisted that these lectures were not going to turn OESE staff into people who could constructively interact with educators across the country. She talked about people going out to talk with educators who had never taught anything, or had anything to do with schools. She insisted: "The lectures are in vain. They won't prepare our staff for anything." She said: "It is getting worse with each person we hire. We don't hire people with the knowledge and skills we need." She illustrated her point with several names.

Weak Staff Support. After the sixth session fewer and fewer of the staff were attending these "mandatory" training sessions. Kathy Silva and her committee, who were responsible for the series, gathered the attendance data and wrote a memo to Gerry about the "attendance issue." Their attendance data indicated that only 13 of the 230 staff had attended all six sessions, and only 130 had attended three or more sessions. In addition, only half of these attended the small group discussions. They pointed out that staff who were supposed to provide technical assistance in systemic reform were not attending the professional development program. They proposed that Gerry exert his authority and make the staff accountable.

On September 9th, Gerry wrote a memo to all staff, and made the group and team leaders responsible for the attendance and small group discussions. The attendance picked up somewhat, but it still left much to be desired. I wondered what the people learned who were ordered to attend. What did they take away?

Advice from the Cheshire Cat. At the end of October, an additional meeting was added to the series. Its purpose was to involve the staff in determining what kind of professional development should follow the series. Should they follow the format of the sessions just concluded, or should they approach their training differently? I could understand the benefits of staff feedback, but I felt the design of training should be done by professionals. Frustrated, the next day I sat down at my computer and sent Gerry an e-mail with copies to Kathy Silva and Jim Kohlmoos. I wrote:

> The fact that we had that kind of meeting reveals that we are still *muddling* through our training. Because we have not decided what we want as outcomes, we have no plan. So we just open it up and brainstorm. Then somebody picks and chooses from the input and we go into something different. This is no way to design professional development.

In the memo, I talked about the model of The Rummler-Brache Group (1990) that provides for the outcomes from the organizational level, the process level, and the job level. I talked about goals, design, and management at each level. I recalled a discussion I had with Gerry about developing job models, and the fact that Gerry was going to order Dana and Jim Robinson's book entitled *Performance Consulting (1995)*. I then emphasized the main point of my memo with capitalization:

> My point in telling you about the Rummler-Brache model and job modeling is this: IF WE HAD DEFINED THE OUTCOMES AT THE ORGANIZATIONAL LEVEL, THE WORK PROCESS LEVEL, AND THE JOB PERFORMANCE LEVEL; AND HAD WORKED TO DESIGN AND MANAGE THESE LEVELS TO ATTAIN OUR DESIRED OUTCOMES, WE WOULD NOT BE MUDDLING THROUGH OUR TRAINING NOW. IF WE HAD JOB MODELS, THEY WOULD BECOME THE FOUNDATION UPON WHICH WE BUILD OUR

TRAINING. THE TRAINING WOULD BE DESIGNED
TO ATTAIN THE DESIRED OUTCOMES.

Finally, I pointed out that there was no definitive statement about what we want our staff to deliver, no work processes have ever been reengineered, and no job models have ever been created. I closed my memo with this reference to the Cheshire Cat:

> As I left the discussion on Wednesday, I thought of the Cheshire Cat in "Alice's Adventures in Wonderland." I recall the Cheshire Cat saying to Alice that if she didn't care where she wanted to go, it didn't matter which way she went. This is a good commentary on where we are now in planning training.

Lessons Learned

As the restructuring of OESE was rolled out, there was the assumption that training would be necessary to make it work. Consequently the Senior Leadership Team set up the Professional Development Team (PDT) to develop a training strategy. The work of the volunteer PDT was largely ignored by the Senior Leadership Team with good cause. In the place of the PDT program of training, a three-session mid-management training program plus various other training sessions were provided that were largely devoted to general generic content and the role problems that were emerging.

By the time that Tom and Janice left and Gerry arrived, it had become apparent that the restructuring was not working as planned. The problem of roles—team leaders, group leaders, program directors—was not abating. Teams were not working out well. The IRTs were over their heads. Work was not getting done. When the new Assistant Secretary brought in Coopers & Lybrand, Inc. to look at the situation, they declared that it would take more than "tweaking" to fix.

The new Assistant Secretary turned to training to fix the problems. He established a series of 10 mandatory training sessions on systemic reform of schooling and developed a partnership with the Training and Development Center (TDC) to provide team training. He did not realize that TDC could not give him the help he needed and that training would not *fix* the problems. Coopers & Lybrand, Inc., had confirmed some of his problems, but they did not identify the causes. Nor did they provide a performance consulting service. The Department of Education was not becoming the "high performance organization;" it envisioned!

For the Department of Education to develop competent staff to service public education and support reform with knowledgeable participants, it must change its basic approach to professional development. It should stop the "sheep dipping" (Carlene Reinhart, 1997), that is, disregarding individual learning needs and dunking everyone into a single training program whether they need it or not. The Department continues to spend large amounts of money on consultants to deliver packaged training programs in an out-dated, inefficient system of training delivery. Here are some of the lessons to be learned from this experience:

- **The Department should replace the traditional approach to training with a learning support system that identifies the critical performance results required to successfully accomplish the strategic and tactical goals of the Department.** The Department should have developed a learning support system that identifies the knowledge and skills of current performers and assesses them against the critical results that are required for a high performance organization. The learning support system should have included:

    1. Performance and competency modeling,

    2. Competency assessment,

    3. Resource identification,

    4. Analysis of barriers,

    5. Individualized development plans, and

    6. Ongoing evaluation and feedback.

- **The Department does not have the expertise internally to make this transition.** It was clear that neither the Director of TDC nor the top-level leadership of OESE had the expertise to provide the desired change. And it was clear that the staff, as exemplified by the Professional Development Team, did not have it either. All of these contributors to the training programs for OESE produced a marginal training effort at great cost.

- **Training is not the solution to all problems.** For example, we should have learned that mature, self-directed teams cannot be developed in organizations whose structure and design characteristics do not support them, regardless of the amount of training that is expended. Training will not fix a structural or environmental problem.

- **The Department can not develop the knowledge capital it needs for leadership if it does not recruit and promote staff on the basis of competency.** If the Department continues to reduce the knowledge and skill criteria for employment and promotion, it will not have the expertise to go head-to-head with educational leadership in the field, regardless of the training efforts expended.

- **Improving performance and creating a "learning organization" means more than providing training courses based on someone's perception of what people need to learn.** One must start with strategic goals, figure out what the critical results are that various players must achieve that will enable the organization to achieve its goals, then assess what people don't know and can't do (against the critical results). Once these gaps are identified, the organization can prioritize the learning needs based on the gaps that have the most effect on the organization and address the top priorities first.

  Improving performance also means identifying all of the other factors in the work environment that prevent employees from achieving the desired performance. For example, one must ask "What are the barriers to the achievement of results?" Does the organizational structure facilitate the desired goals? Are the reward and recognition systems supporting desired behaviors? Do people have the information they need to do their jobs? Do people have the technical support they need, etc?

Improving performance can only be accomplished by taking a systems approach, that is, by taking all of the factors in the work environment into consideration. Performance goals cannot be achieved in the traditional training mode!

Part III

*A Call for
Institutional Leadership*

eight

From Administrative
Management to Institutional
Leadership

America is becoming a nation of suspicious strangers, and
this mistrust of each other is a major reason Americans have
lost confidence in the federal government and virtually every other major national institution. Every generation that
has come of age since the 1950s has been more mistrusting
of human nature, a transformation in the national outlook
that has deeply corroded the nation's social and political
life . . . The reason our politics is behaving badly is because
the whole country is behaving badly.

This description of the decline of public confidence by Richard Morin
and Dan Baltz (*The Washington Post,* January 28: 1996), based on a
joint project by *The Washington Post,* the Henry J. Kaiser Foundation,
and Harvard University (1996), describes the social context in which
the federal establishment is undergoing change. It is in this context
that presidents have won elections by bashing the federal government
and that angry voters veered in different directions in the elections of

231

1992 and 1994. It is in this context that the federal government focused on "total quality management" movement during the Bush administration and the National Performance Review during the Clinton administration. It is in this context that the Congress passed The Chief Financial Officer Act of 1990, The Government Performance and Results Act of 1993, and The Information Technology Management Act of 1996, as well as others. It was in this context that federal agencies moved headlong into reorganizations, restructuring, and reengineering, referring to it all as "reinvention." And it was in this context that push came to shove in the Department of Education, and OESE fundamentally reconfigured its organization and attempted to radically restructure it.

The Department of Education is expected to deliver a melange of individual programs enacted by different Congresses, and is held responsible for the educational achievements of the nation's schools administered by local boards of education. Any attempt to bring this potpourri of laws together for the systemic reform of the nation's schools is a non sequitur. The leadership of the nation's schools understands this far better than the Congress.

This book has reported the specific events and described the responses of its personnel in one agency from the internal perspective of one participant observer. It is now time to consider these events in the light of what they reveal about the problems of change in the leadership of federal agencies. In this chapter, we now stand back from my experience and break away from my narrative to consider the overall story rather than the individual events.

The "Logic" of Institutional Leadership

In a profound essay on *Leadership in Administration,* Philip Selznick wrote:

> As we ascend the echelons of administration, the analysis of decision making becomes increasingly difficult, not simply because the decisions are more important or more complex, but because a new 'logic' emerges. The logic of efficiency applies most clearly to subordinate units, usually having rather clearly defined operating responsibilities, limited dis-

cretion, set communication channels, and a sure position in the command structure (1957: 3).

Selznick believes that "The executive becomes a statesman as he makes the transition from administrative management to institutional leadership."

With few exceptions, OESE had administrative managers—not institutional leaders. And for the most part, there was little understanding of what it would take to move a long-standing, established federal agency from its current state into a radically new way of doing business. The managers did not understand how the restructuring would impact institutional characteristics. They did not consider how changing an organization's structure would throw other institutional elements out of alignment. Nor did they take into consideration the resources—both human and nonhuman—to make the concept a reality. Basically they did not think of OESE as a social institution. The managers may have been caring and sensitive to human trials and tribulations. Indeed, they knew that change would be difficult for their staff. But they did not understand the internal dynamics of organizational change. In Selznick's words, they did not have the "logic of institutional leadership."

Emphasizing the type of leadership needed to make change happen, John P. Kotter, in *Leading Change (1996)* identifies eight critical mistakes that bring failure to organizational change efforts:

1. Allowing too much complacency

2. Failing to create a sufficiently powerful guiding coalition

3. Underestimating the power of vision

4. Under-communicating the vision by a factor of 10 (or 100 or even 1,000)

5. Permitting obstacles to block the vision

6. Failing to create short-term wins

7. Declaring victory too soon

8. Neglecting to anchor changes firmly in the corporate culture

These eight critical mistakes made by the leaders of organizational change reflect a need for institutional sensitivity—a sensitivity that OESE's leadership did not have.

It is also of interest to note that James Champy, one of the authors of *Reengineering the Corporation* (1993), laid the failure of reengineering efforts at the feet of leaders. In a subsequent book, *Reengineering Management: The Mandate for New Leadership* (1995), James Champy asserts that leaders are responsible for four broad issues: of purpose, culture, process and performance, and people.

These four broad issues call for an institutional perspective. There is a place in the reengineering of an organization to be concerned about structure and management, but these issues are not a preoccupation with structure and management. Champy believes that as one ascends toward the top of an organization, there is the need to go beyond the organizational restructuring and administrative management that was the preoccupation of OESE's management. Rather, there is a need for a different type of thinking—a different logic and a different sensitivity.

Some Problems of Institutional Leadership

In the story of the reinvention of OESE, we can identify ten major problems. They are not drawn from a theoretical textbook on organizational change, but from the actual problems encountered in this practical experience. They are not unique to OESE —they are common in the reinvention of federal agencies. They all deal with institutional perspective.

The Problem of Mission and Role. What shall we *do*? What shall we *be*? These questions can be hard enough in matters of personal purpose; they can be enormously complicated when trying to define the character and direction of an institution. Yet it is one of the most difficult and indispensable tasks of an institutional leader. As Philip Selznick stated, "He must specify and recast the general goals of his organization so as to adapt them without serious corruption to the requirements of institutional survival" (1957: 66).

It is the task of the top leadership of an organization to respond to the organization's *internal* character: the strivings and competencies that exist within it. Among these internal elements, nothing is more important than the distinctive competence of an organization, for it determines the organizational character. It must reflect the unique strength of an organization. It is what an organization wants to emphasize about itself. It is what makes one organization different from another. It is how an organization wants to be known. Clearly, the shift from an individual program monitoring role in OESE, to providing cross-program technical assistance in the systemic reform of the nation's schools, requires a shift in organizational character.

The distinctive character desired by the leadership of OESE is revealed in its statement of mission and guiding principles. The mission statement claims to "improve the quality of teaching and learning by providing leadership, technical assistance and financial support." And among the guiding principles is the statement, "We intend to more closely align our compliance monitoring and technical assistance in order to provide better support to our customers as they embark on local systemic reform initiatives." Instead of serving the states, communities, and local school districts along direct programmatic lines, "a restructured OESE will incorporate cross-program and customer-oriented teams." These entities would be looked at from a "holistic and systemic perspective." And this would all be made possible because OESE would "model systemic reform."

As commendable as this perception of distinctive character is, the account of what took place in OESE reveals a gross lack of realism about its distinctive competence. For example, all programs could certainly not be incorporated in a unified effort. For one thing, very few people could work across programs, and it was necessary to send a dozen or more people into the field to cover the program bases on integrated reviews. Most of OESE's staff had no professional background in learning and teaching. Even fewer had any administrative experience in the nation's schools. It was rare to have a staff member give any reasonable technical assistance for holistic problem solving in a state or school district. Many of those who were experienced and knowledgeable educators reported that it was embarrassing to see some of OESE's staff attempt to discuss systemic reform with the professional educators in the field.

There were other reasons why the mission of OESE was not well conceived, but the competence of the staff to fulfill it was grossly inadequate. What shall we do? What shall we be? These are still very real questions for OESE, but they need to be reworded. The leadership of OESE should be asking themselves "What *can* we do? What *can* we become?" At the time of this writing, they still have not found a viable mission.

The Problem of Organizational Design. The design of the new OESE was the work of OESE senior staff, with no professional expertise in organizational design to assist them, or input from people actually doing the work. It was an administrative response to a political threat that led to a new mission, which, in turn, required a restructuring of the Office. It took on the characteristics of a reorganization. Consequently, the organizational design started by putting structure first.

With this internal decision made, the senior staff set in motion the mechanisms to implement a restructuring. They announced it at an All Hands staff meeting, followed a few days later with the packet of information that included the mission and vision statements, goals, guiding principles, a description of the structure, a statement about delayering, and the intention of establishing six teams of volunteer staff. The six teams reflected the senior staff's perception of what was needed to flesh out and implement the restructuring. The types of teams chartered revealed the limits of the senior staff's understanding.

Professional consultants in the field of organizational change would certainly have approached the task differently. They would have most likely recommended the establishment of a representative steering committee comprised of both internal and external members. Customers such as chief state school officers, and superintendents would have been included, as would national leaders in education from universities, research centers, and professional associations, staffs of congressional committees dealing with education, and staff from the Department of Education (top level leadership from the Department as well as persons from within OESE). In addition, an outside professional in organizational change would have insisted on including representatives of the American Federation of Government Employees.

Such a steering committee would have overseen the whole process of organizational change. They would have had OESE staff and consultants assisting and reporting to them. They would have set up needed committees, such as an organizational design committee, and they would have been the major decision-makers in the whole process.

The organizational design committee would most likely have started with an analysis of the OESE's entire external environment, not just those threatening its extinction. It would have looked at customer requirements in the light of OESE's core capabilities in order to form a strategy. Knowing the strategy would help them identify the components of OESE that must be *changed* and the *magnitude* of the change required. It would also help identify the gaps in OESE's performance and the size of those gaps. This would have been a safeguard against prescribing a mission that could not be realized.

Unfortunately, there was never any serious consideration of the specific outcomes of either the existing OESE or the desired OESE. The designers had a general conception of modeling systemic reform and providing cross-program technical assistance for the systemic reform of education in the states. It was an admirable vision of the future, but senior management never checked it out with their customers, stakeholders, or influential organizations. There was no systematic scan of what chief state school officers, superintendents, other educators, or the communities of the nation expected of the Department. There was no assessment of what the legislators on the hill wanted from the Department or what the states believed they could administer better. Nor was there any assessment of what it would take to deliver these outcomes or what OESE could realistically accomplish.

In addition to the external factors, senior management also did not consider what it would take to change the internal technical, decision-making, people, or reward systems. To their credit, they did formulate new mission and vision statements, guiding principles, goals and organizational structure, all essential parts of design considerations.

In addition, there was no consideration given to keeping the organizational design elements in alignment. Paul Gustavson has written this about alignment:

> Alignment is the way organizational elements fit together. For example, if an organization really values quality, it cannot focus merely on its methods of measuring quality, i.e., information systems. It must also give thought to what *guiding principles* must be shared about quality, what *strategies* will best drive quality, what *tasks* and *technologies* make quality achievable, what *structure* will be needed to implement those strategies, what *competencies* are needed to produce a quality product, and what *rewards* will best compensate behavior aimed at quality. This is the holistic view of organizations: change in one aspect will necessitate—and may unavoidably generate—change throughout the system (*Guidebook* 1994: 4).

My colleagues and I on the Reengineering Team brought Gustavson's OSD Model to the attention of the Janice Jackson (Deputy Assistant Secretary) and the Senior Leadership Team and argued for its consideration. We also engaged a consultant, Mark Rhodes, who had extensive experience in organizational design in both the public and private sectors, and asked him to bring a more holistic, systemic view to the restructuring. Janice saw the need for a more holistic approach to the design of OESE and the validity of the OSD Model for this purpose, but the train had left the station and the Senior Leadership Team was not interested in switching tracks.

The question of organizational design continues to be a live question for the Department of Education. Assuming that a viable mission has been conceived and an agency has the distinctive competence for its fulfillment, one must ask how the agency will redesign and realign its organization? Will it be done in-house after the pattern of a reorganization? Or will it be done with the help of outside professional expertise? One of the most important decisions that leadership must make in organizational change is whether there is any institutional logic to the design and the alignment.

The Problem of Strategic Direction. The Congress of the United States has mandated strategic planning. When the Government Performance and Results Act (GPRA) became law, it required all federal organizations to (1) develop a five-year strategic plan by September 30, 1997, (2) develop a performance plan, based upon the strategic plan, by setting annual performance goals, beginning with the federal fiscal year 1999, and (3) make performance reports annually, beginning March 31, 2000, on actual performance compared to goals established in the strategic and performance plans.

The Congress had grown tired of agency administrators talking about what wonderful things they were doing or about to do without any evidence of outcomes, and they were responding to the loss of confidence by the American people. GPRA was about three things: change, obtaining results, and performance measurement. The Congress wanted the federal agencies to *change* the way they were doing business. They also wanted *results* from a customer-driven mission. Finally, they wanted success or failure to be *measured* in terms of stated goals.

As the GAO reports of the Department of Education had indicated, the Department had no history of strategic planning. In response to GPRA, the Department made two attempts at strategic planning. In early 1994, they sent out a set of guidelines and directed each principal office to develop a strategic plan. OESE put a committee together and in a brief time had their strategic plan ready to send to the Reinvention Coordinating Council (RCC). But there was no way that the Department could bring together the separate plans of the principal offices into one integrated, coherent plan. The Department's first attempt was a failure.

The RCC then put a team together to develop a plan at the top, and directed each of the offices to flesh out a plan for themselves that was integrated with the Department's master plan. Each assistant secretary was responsible for a specific part of the plan that especially pertained to activities of his office, but also had responsibility for any part of the plan that related to their office. Again, the OESE plan was sent upward.

Deputy Secretary Kunin boasted to the House Committee on Labor—HHS—Education Appropriations that: "The Department's strategic plan has been highly praised and recognized as a model across the federal government." Amid the praise she lavished that day, she said: "For example, program staff for the $7 billion Title I program are currently using 28 specific performance indicators, grouped under five broad goals outlined for the program and our Strategic Plan." Unfortunately, at the time there were no such performance indicators in use in either the Department or the OESE plan.

In the end, a strategic plan for the Department was developed by a small staff of the Planning and Evaluation Service in the Office of the Under Secretary. Very little from the OESE plan, or the plans of other offices, could be used. This was to be expected. My experience on the team of volunteers that had worked on the OESE strategic plan led me to resign, and after being talked into withdrawing my resignation, resign a second and final time. This effort had turned out to be one of the poorest examples of leadership, team relationships, and outcomes I had ever experienced. Even the team leader later admitted that nothing would ever come from OESE's strategic plan.

In his definitive and revealing history of strategic planning, *The Rise and Fall of Strategic Planning* (1994), Henry Mintzberg unmasked this process that has mesmerized so many organizations. This iconoclastic former president of the Strategic Management Society states that strategy cannot be planned because planning is about analysis and strategy is about synthesis, and organizations have failed to bring these functions together creatively. That is why the process has failed so often and so dramatically. States Mintzberg:

> Analysis may precede and support synthesis, by defining the parts that can be combined into wholes. Analysis may follow and elaborate synthesis, by decomposing and formalizing its consequences. But analysis cannot substitute for synthesis. No amount of elaboration will ever enable formal procedures to forecast discontinuities, to inform managers who are detached from their discontinuities, to inform managers who are detached from their operations, to create novel strategies. Ultimately, the term "strategic planning" has proved to be an oxymoron (*ibid:* 321).

When writing about strategic thinking, Mintzberg is referring to the intuitive and creative synthesizing that takes place in the minds of leaders who come up with the visions that lead organizations into a not-too-precisely articulated new direction. Consider the political strategy making for the Department of Education. In 1990, the President and the governors of the 50 states agreed upon a set of six national goals that would guide the federal government, the states, and the local communities in the improvement of the educational system of the nation. In 1994, the Congress passed the *Goals 2000: Educate America Act* with bipartisan support. It committed the federal government to support eight ambitious national goals (the original six plus two new ones on teacher training and parental involvement). In February 1997, President Clinton issued a "Call to Action for American Education" with ten new goals. When the strategic plan was submitted to Congress on September 30, 1997, it had seven priorities and four goals.

Chuck Hansen's concept of the new OESE was a rare creative synthesis. It was an attempt to pull the disparate programs of OESE together into a synthesis to aid in the systemic reform of the nation's schools. It was not the product of a political consensus. However, every leader's new vision is not a winner. Leaders are also vulnerable to "extinction by instinct." (Kast and Rosenwig (1970: 390). Chuck's strategy didn't work, but he should be credited with taking the risk.

Planning has always been about analysis—about breaking down a goal or set of intentions into steps, formalizing those steps so that they can be implemented almost automatically, and articulating the anticipated consequences or results of each step. The essential role of planning is to get the relevant information to senior managers so they can be informed about the details in order to make strategic decisions. States Mintzberg: "Planners should make their greatest contribution *around* the strategy-making process rather than *inside* it" (*Harvard Business Review,* January/February 1994:108).

What the Strategic Planning Team in OESE was doing (in its second attempt) was strategic programming after the strategy had been prescribed. They were not establishing priorities or objectives. They were expanding on the strategies of the Departmental plan by developing specific strategies and performance indicators for OESE in harmony with those of the Department. In doing so, they were extending the plan beyond the plausible. As I stated in my resignation memo:

> At this rate, how many strategies and performance indicators must we have if we addressed all of the objectives that related to OESE in priorities 1 and 4? If we continue in this fashion, I suspect that we would have 150-200 strategies and even more performance indicators. Even if we drastically reduced the number of strategies and performance indicators, which we should do, it is difficult for me to believe that the commitment will ever be given to this task. Even more important, it is difficult for me to believe that the resources will be granted to follow up on such a plan. And without follow-up there is no purpose in even beginning!

But, the bottom line of all this energy is that little, if anything, could be measured and considered results that would satisfy the purpose of GPRA.

If anything is going to come from strategic planning to satisfy the intent of GPRA, the Department of Education and the other federal agencies must understand the distinction between the work of strategic thinking and the work of planning—synthesis and analysis—the roles and the contributions of each. In addition, they have to be responsive to the strategic gyrations of politicians. Strategic planning requires a coupling of intuition and analysis—the creative use of the right brain and the left brain—with leadership that is able to guide an organization between "extinction by instinct" and "paralysis by analysis." "The fundamental dilemma arises," says Mintzberg, "how to couple the skills, time and inclinations of the planner with the authority, information, and flexibility of the manager, to insure a strategy-making process that is informed, responsive, and integrative" (1994: 325). When I left the Department of Education it was a long way from mastering strategic planning.

The Problem of Rolling out the Plan. OESE began rolling out its restructuring plan with two strikes against it, and a pitcher that was about to throw an implementation pitch that was impossible to hit. First, the concept was not valid because nobody had assessed the plan's expected outcomes or core work processes. Second, the senior leadership launched a fundamental, radical, and rapid change in the way they would do business, but thought of it as a reorganization (restructuring) rather than the high risk reengineering task that it really was. They focused on *organizational* change rather than *institutional* change. Consequently, they did not appreciate the dimensions of the changes that would have to occur.

It is no surprise that OESE did not connect with the implementation pitch. They were rolling out a concept and a plan that was unexamined and misunderstood.

In hindsight, it is doubtful that anyone could have saved the OESE restructuring effort with these preconditions. But some of the staff involved believed that one last option was available—outside professional help! The Reengineering Team had brought in Mark Rhodes to guide it in its thinking. Mark is a professional consultant in organizational design and implementation who had worked with Fortune 500 companies both in the United States and abroad. The Deputy Assistant Secretary saw his value for OESE and asked him to propose an implementation plan. However, he was never asked to deliver these services, so the restructuring of OESE remained an internal job.

The leadership of OESE continued with the restructuring teams made up of volunteers, whose reports were never formally acknowledged and largely ignored. It was not until the succeeding Assistant Secretary was appointed—and discovered that the restructuring was not working— that the leadership brought in professional consultants to assess the situation.

One would suspect that there are not many executives in the federal government who know how to make fundamental changes in their agencies. Until recently they were not rewarded for changes. Even if they did know how to make changes, they would need help. Making major changes in organizations in not something done everyday.

Of course, it is not easy to select the type of help needed. According to Micklethwait and Wooldridge, there are over 100,000 management consultants and over 700 business schools in the United States teaming with academics who would like to make a name for themselves as management gurus (1996: 44-48). This is a $50 billion industry. Keep in mind that it does not take much to go into business as a management consultant. One does not need a license and one's education and experience need not be extensive. It is a wide-open profession without any professional monitoring. Nor will the employment of a large, expensive, big-name consulting firm assure good consulting. (See *Dangerous Company* by James O'Shea and Charles Madigan, 1997.)

To avoid the pitfalls takes time in selecting professional assistance. One must look carefully at the credentials and the experience of the assigned personnel, and check out the work of the firm with their former clients. The purchaser of consultant services should set clear goals for the consultants they employ, insist on being served by senior consultants, closely measure results and base their pay upon performance. One is buying intelligence and experience. Failure can cost much more than consultant services.

There is no road map to make a success of every reinvention of a federal agency. Each organizational change is different. What it takes is good, sound, professional assistance and LEADERSHIP!

The Problem of Performance. Although there were constant references to OESE becoming a "high-performance" organization, the nature of the needed performance was never defined by the leadership of OESE. As is often the case, the leadership of OESE responded to an external pressure with a spasmodic effort to restructure their organization around a new concept. Although the concept was a worthy idea, and it would certainly require restructuring, the appropriate questions were not asked at (1) the *upper-level*, (2) the *work-process level*, or (3) the *job/performance level*. At the upper-level they might have asked:

- What are the appropriate functional goals for OESE?

- How will we know if our performance is satisfactory?

- Do we have adequate resources to allocate?

- How are we going to manage the interface between the functional units?

Neither did anyone ask any process-level questions, such as the following:

- What will be our process sub-goals?

- Will our core processes support our functional goals?

- Do we have sufficient resources to allocate to each process?

- Can we manage the interfaces between processes?

Key questions at the job/performer level, such as the following were not asked either:

- Do we have job outputs and standards linked to the process and organizational level requirements?

- Do we have any job performance models that prescribe what our staff must be able to perform?

- Do the performers have the necessary knowledge/skill to achieve the job goals?

- How will the performers know if they are meeting the job goals?

One of OESE's restructuring guidelines was to "promote and model systemic reform through the delivery of integrated services." But the leadership of OESE failed to systematically consider performance improvement in becoming a "high performance" organization. One of the most widely claimed holistic views of performance is provided by Geary A. Rummler and Alan P. Brache in *Improving Performance: How to Manage the White Space on the Organizational Chart* (1990).

> In our opinion, most American managers have been unable to respond effectively to the challenges [of change] because they have failed to create an infrastructure for systemic and continuous improvement of performance. We believe that their shortcoming does not lie in the understanding of the problem, in the desire to address the problem, or in the

willingness to dedicate resources to the resolution of the problem. Rather, *the majority of the managers simply do not understand the variables that influence organization and individual performance* (1990: 2).

In fairness, it should be stated that the Reengineering Team was established at the very outset to make recommendations regarding work process reengineering. The Reengineering Team did make a report with recommendations to the Senior Leadership Team, which Janice Jackson supported. However, after several attempts to convince the Senior Leadership Team of specific efforts, such work was turned down. Eventually, a Travel Improvement Team was established to look at the travel allocation and reimbursement processes, one of the enabling (as distinguished from core) work processes. This latter team soon discovered that the Department had recently awarded a contract for that purpose.

When it was operational, the Federal Quality Institute provided a one-week training program for work process reengineering. A number of federal agencies, including some of the other offices within the Department of Education, reengineered their work processes. A few federal agencies have focused attention on the job/performer level, mainly for the improvement of training programs. And a few agencies have attempted to look at performance improvement from all three levels—organization level, process level, and job/performer level.

The Problem of Organizational Competence. OESE was now in the unenviable situation of having to undertake a mission that it could not perform because its staff did not have the competence to carry it out. OESE had committed itself to restructure its organization and to reassign its staff at significant cost to its organizational well-being. But it could not deliver the role that it purported to fulfill. One of the major reasons for this predicament was that the agency never realistically faced the limitations of its work force when the restructuring was conceived. In fact, the reassignment debacle made the situation even worse.

There are several reasons why the current work force could not perform adequately:

- The critical criteria for a high performance work force were withdrawn from the position descriptions, thereby allowing recruitment and promotions without the requisite competencies.

- A large labor pool of workers were readily available in the Washington, D.C. metropolitan area who desired public service jobs, and they were able to obtain them in OESE, due to the lowered requirements.

- Government regulations make it difficult for management to deal with marginal and unsatisfactory employees, which means that employees who lack the abilities needed in restructuring remain in the workplace.

- Generic position descriptions developed for the restructuring of OESE further eliminated essential criteria for adequate hiring and promotions.

- Lack of trust in management prompted the specification of reassignment criteria that eliminated the consideration of competence, and management went along with it.

- Racial unrest permeated the reassignment process, resulting in a contentious reassigning of employees that undermined the entire effort.

Clearly, an organization's distinctive competence must be able to support its distinctive character. The lesson learned is that if an organization does not have the competence, it cannot have the character.

There is an equally important lesson to be learned, and that is the distinction between *routine* and *critical* decisions. Over an extended period of time, a number of decisions were made to eliminate key criteria from position descriptions. When the decisions to eliminate these criteria in position descriptions were made, they were thought to be a means to an end that was not critical at the time. They may have been made unconsciously, without awareness of their larger significance. The effect of recruitment and promotion of staff based on the absence of these criteria significantly changed the character of OESE.

What were thought to be routine decisions, were, in fact, critical decisions. They constituted limits on what OESE could become.

Those who think that the problem of competence was solely a problem of OESE might be interested in the remarks of Diane Ravitch, Assistant Secretary of the Office of Educational Research and Improvement (OERI) in the previous administration. States Ravitch:

> Among the 500 or so employees in OERI, about 130 worked for the National Center for Educational Statistics [a section of OERI], which collects data and regularly issues reports on the condition of American Education: of the remainder, there were perhaps thirty who could be considered educational researchers . . . Consequently, the agency lacked the capacity either to conduct the kind of major research projects that one would expect from the federal government or even to monitor the quality of the research it funded. Most employees were civil servants . . . who had no particular qualifications to assess the quality of research or to design new educational programs. The agency badly needed competent researchers to evaluate the work of the labs and centers and other research activities (Ravitch: 1995).

The Problem of Performance Improvement. The Department of Education is still following a traditional approach to training in which training is seen as the ultimate solution for a wide variety of troubling problems throughout the agency. OESE saw it as the solution to their restructuring deficiencies. They apparently are not aware that their "sheep dipping" approach to training did not transfer the necessary skills to the job.

Furthermore, the responsibility for training was also an in-house effort with no assistance from outside professionals. Although a team of employees was charged with setting up a professional development plan, the plan was largely ignored. Instead, the senior leadership took over and established a "Leading through Change" series for team leaders, group leaders, and program directors. Later on, after a new assistant secretary, was appointed, a partnership with the Training and Development Center (TDC) of the Department was established to provide team training. The new Assistant Secretary, Gerald N. Tirozzi, also established a series of training sessions on systemic reform, since most of the OESE staff knew little about the reform of schooling. There was also a collection of other training programs offered by TDC for those who chose to enroll in them.

The major problem with the training designed to support the OESE restructuring effort was that it was never systematically linked to the strategic goals. Nor did it address the performance improvement skills of the employees needed to meet those goals. Replacing the traditional approach to training with a learning support system that identifies the critical performance results required to successfully accomplish strategic and tactical goals is long overdue. The OESE should have identified the specific knowledge and skills of current employees and assess them against the critical results that were required for a high performance organization. The leadership of OESE should have developed learning support systems that closed the gap between their current competencies of the staff and what could have been reasonably expected of them.

Sadly, the leadership of neither OESE nor of TDC had the professional knowledge to do this job themselves. Asking another team of OESE employees to work on this without outside help was not the answer. It was time to get help. Other agencies in the federal government have moved in this direction with the assistance of performance consultants. One would think that the Department of Education would have been a leader in learning support systems. But in this case, as in others, the Department of Education was one of the least informed about learning.

The Problem of Empowerment. A basic feature of the restructuring of OESE was the use of teams. There were regional service teams (RSTs), program service teams (PSTs), integrated review teams (IRTs), cross-cutting teams, and *ad hoc* teams as needed. The major problem for the RSTs was that they were caught in an organizational configuration that was not functional for self-directed teams. The program directors were accountable for their programs above all else, not the RSTs, so they exerted power, authority and control as needed to get their programs implemented. In addition, the dysfunctional assignment of staff made it much more difficult to assign competent staff to appropriate tasks. Consequently, program directors felt it necessary to intervene in the work of the RSTs. As a result, the RSTs could not become the empowered, self-directed teams they were conceived to be.

As we discussed earlier, the role of the team leader, including his or her relationship with group leaders and program directors, was ill-defined, unstable, and frustrating. The roles, functions, and interface of the roles were constantly discussed and debated, disputed and refuted, written and revised, and complained about over and over again. Regardless of what was put down on paper about the role of the team leaders and their relationships with others in authority, it was frequently ignored under the pressure to get the work done. Consequently, the intended theoretical descriptions of the team leader working with a self-directed team never materialized.

There were no clear charters for the RSTs, no boundaries for team efforts, no identification of what decisions were theirs to make, and no prescribed evolution of increased responsibilities over time. The RST's spent most of their time and energy doing things by trial and error.

The Program Service Team (PSTs) fared no better. According to Coopers & Lybrand, none of the PSEs actually functioned as a self-directed team. The personnel that ended up in the PSTs after the reassignment were largely the same people that had these jobs in the past. They were the people who made up the immediate staff of the program director and a program support branch. They continued to work as they had before, in mostly specialized jobs that were independent of each other. Program directors continued to work in their former management styles, which were part of the work culture with which the staff was familiar. Participatory activities were tolerated as long as they got the work done and did not challenge the traditional ways of doing business. Most new ventures received little or no support.

So there was little change for the personnel of the PSTs. They were the same people, with the same work, at the same desks, with the same culture, working under the same management with the same expectations. How could one expect self-directed teams to develop from this situation?

The lesson to be learned here is that if teams are to develop into empowered, self-directed working groups, they must be supported and protected by all the relevant elements of organizational design—structure, decision making, people, and reward systems. Most important of all, the leadership must model a participatory style of management and take the lead with it. The folly of trying to fix this situation with team training was a waste of time and money.

Those who designed the new OESE structure never understood what it would take to make OESE into a participatory organization with self-directing teams. The top leadership that implemented the design never understood the outcomes in relation to cause and effect. (For example, the leadership thought training would change it.) Neither did Coopers & Lybrand, the consultants.

The Problem of Trust. In a private conversation, Janice Jackson told me that she had never worked in an organization that had so little trust of other staff. She felt that this lack of trust made the restructuring of OESE more difficult. Janice was correct.

It is often said that in today's business world, "organizations must embrace change or die." (Some members of Congress asserted that this applied to federal agencies as well as the private sector.) OESE was making a sincere attempt to embrace change, but an appropriate level of trust was not on its side. Robert Shaw states that "trust is a form of "collaborative capital" that can be used to great advantage (1990:1). He defines trust as "belief that those on whom we depend will meet our expectations of them" (1997). This applies to both individual and group expectations. It increases the likelihood that people will abandon past practices in favor of new approaches, especially when those changes involve more empowerment and more collaboration.

There is a "trust threshold"—a point at which we withdraw our trust. Without such a threshold, we would expose ourselves to risks that would harm us as individuals or harm the groups to which we belong. In OESE, employees had withdrawn their trust, especially from management. This was seen most clearly in the degree of distrust of OESE management by African Americans.

States Shaw: "Research, as well as my experience as a management consultant, indicates that trust is founded on a few basic imperatives: achieving results, acting with integrity, and demonstrating concern" (1997: 29). About achieving results he writes:

> The first, and perhaps most important imperative in earn-
> ing trust . . . involves people's performance in fulfilling their
> obligations and commitments. The results are the key: even
> if people's motives are characterized by goodwill, they will
> not retain trust if they are incompetent or powerless to ful-
> fill the expectations we have of them. In such cases, we deem
> them unworthy of trust not because they are malicious but
> because they can't deliver.

The distrust that many program directors had in RST members to competently represent their programs in the field is one of many examples of trust based upon results.

Shaw's second imperative is integrity. By integrity, Shaw says: "we mean honesty in one's words and consistency in one's actions." This corresponds with the expressions "walk the talk" and "do what you say you will do." If, for example, we see inconsistency in another's language or actions, we may conclude that he is at odds with our interests or unable to fulfill his professional responsibilities. Even the perception of inconsistency, whether factual or not, can result in distrust. Although Tom Payzant professed his support for diversity, his appointment of two white females to program director positions was seen as an act of inconsistency.

Shaw's third imperative is demonstrating concern for others. This may be on a personal level, or it may extend beyond individuals to one's family, work group, racial group or the organization as a whole. On the personal level, we trust those whom we believe understand our concerns and will act in a way that meets—or at least does not conflict with—our needs. Extending concern for others beyond the individual is particularly important for leaders, as their concern or lack of it can have an impact not only on individuals but on larger groups as well. By not responding to the reports written by the restructuring teams and by not implementing many of the recommendations the reports made, the senior leadership was seen as not caring about the months of work by the teams.

Many individuals and groups in OESE had crossed the trust thresh-old. And once lost, trust is not easily regained. A culture of distrust develops. People take note of any behavior that is suspicious. Suspicions become self-perpetuating and highly resistant to change. The consequences can be disastrous, especially when an organization needs the "collaborative capital" to successfully manage change. Unfortunately, OESE did not have much capital to draw upon.

When distrust is as robust and pervasive as it was in OESE, isolated efforts generally will not overcome it. In extreme situations the fastest, and in some cases the only way to move beyond distrust, is to change the leadership. There is little doubt in my mind that the leaving of Tom Payzant and the appointment of an African American to a program director's position by the new Assistant Secretary helped dissipate much of the distrust by African Americans in OESE. The increased sensitivity to the race issue by the leadership and the appointment of black staff to career ladder and higher positions also helped. So did the opportunities to discuss the problems in open meetings by all staff.

But failure to change the organizational architecture still perpetuated distrust within OESE. For example, the tension between the regional teams and the program leadership continued to generate distrust. The inability to deliver services because of the discrepancy between expectations and staff competency levels continued to generate difficulties. Almost half (48.9 percent) of OESE staff are African Americans, many whom are discontented because of being in the lower grades and who are distrustful of management. This situation also continued to inhibit change.

The Problem of Racial Distrust. The large presence of African Americans in OESE is largely the result of a confluence of a socioeconomic phenomena and Departmental personnel policy and practice. A large labor pool of African Americans was available in the Washington metropolitan area, many of whom were displaced by the private sector due to technological change. Because Uncle Sam was one of the first employers to eliminate all racial criteria for employment, and OESE had been reducing employment criteria, large numbers of African Americans gravitated to federal public sector jobs. This is not to say that highly competent and well-educated blacks did not find employment in OESE. Nor does this assert that less competent and less educated whites did not find employment in OESE. It simply means that an unusually large number of African Americans with fewer skills and less education found employment in OESE, predominantly in the lower grade levels. One simply needs to look at the EEO data of the Department to confirm these phenomena.

The current personnel situation in OESE includes a predominantly white management and a predominantly African American staff. This situation is unstable and has been growing more unstable for a long time. White managers were operating with a system of distributive justice, in which they would apply the criteria and the work ethic of their culture to the employment and promotion of personnel and to the allocation of resources in their management of programs. Many of the African Americans in OESE brought with them a different cultural experience of aggressive self-help to the work place, and with a different set of criteria for the management of personnel and resources. When it came to personnel issues, there was a lack of common ground.

Unfortunately, few people attempted to deal with this situation. The TDC occasionally had a workshop on diversity, but few people attended. Nobody really dealt with the growing racial conflicts in OESE. Most of the staff knew that distrust and ill will was present in OESE, albeit under the surface. But the staff did not feel comfortable talking about it. A parade of politically appointed leaders passed through, but usually left in less than two years. Most of the leadership kept sweeping the racial issues under the rug, hoping they wouldn't stumble over it during their tenure.

This was the situation when Ricardo Sanchez asked Tom Payzant to explain why he had appointed two white women to program director positions, and Tom, apparently unprepared for the question, did stumble over the lump in the rug. From that time on, the race issue dominated just about every facet of the restructuring of OESE.

In OESE the race issue was felt on both the organizational level and the interpersonal level. The primary question for OESE is still the question of organizational character. "What shall we be?" "What shall we do?" If OESE continues to strive for a distinctive competence that provides cross-program technical assistance on systemic change to America's public schools, it will have to acquire a labor force much more sophisticated and experienced than the one it has. Many people in OESE would find that they do not have the distinctive competence for this type of mission. The African American staff are not alone in this, but they would bear much of the burden. Changing the distinctive competence of the OESE labor force will take a lot of "tough love."

Regardless of the type of mission OESE pursues, or even if it continued to muddle through, they will have to deal with the basic roots of the race problem. This means that the facts would have to be faced. Participants must know what the characteristics of OESE's labor force are, what the performance requirements are, and what the deficiencies are. They must also understand the characteristics of differing cultures and work out some sort of accommodation. They would have to work through the imperatives of trust, i.e., results, integrity and concern. This is going to take more than just sensitivity training. OESE would have to become a genuine learning community.

A Change of Leadership

The need for organizational change in government agencies and the need for leaders who know how to change organizations successfully are not temporary political phenomena. The need for change in government agencies is here to stay. Just as private enterprises have had to adjust to the demands of their customers and engage in rapid change to compete for a share of the market, federal agencies now have to compete for their right to serve the nation's citizens. Just as many of the nation's school leaders have made the transition from administration to leadership, so must the Department of Education. In fact, all governmental agencies must come to the realization that *there is more than one way to provide public services.* And it will take leadership—not more management—to make the transition. The public debate of how best to provide government services is much more visible than ever before. The public now demands high quality service for their taxes.

This calls for leaders with a "new logic" at the upper echelons of government agencies. It calls for leaders who (1) understand institutional change, (2) think creatively, and (3) act responsibly.

Institutional Leadership. The "change masters" of the twenty-first century in governmental agencies will have to transition from administrative managers to institutional leaders. They must get beyond reorganization and think systemically about changing the whole institution they lead. They must get beyond organizational forms and procedures, even beyond human engineering, to an awareness of all the elements of an institution that interact with each other. There must be an under-standing that when one part of an institution is changed, it affects the other parts as well. A change master must bring all elements of an organization into alignment to effect successful change.

A large part of a change master's knowledge is his or her comprehension of an organization as a social organization, that is, a human institution. People do not easily give up traditional procedures, em-bedded values, and established commitments, especially when they are long standing. These are the characteristics around which they have organized their behavior and for which they have been rewarded. Consequently, that is why the decisions to change organizational form and procedure are seldom neutral, routine decisions. When a leader's decisions impact upon people's values, commitments, and self-percep-tions, they are critical decisions with after-effects.

Philip Selznick writes: "As we ascend the echelons of administration, the analysis of decision making becomes increasingly difficult, not sim-ply because the decisions are more important or more complex, but because a new 'logic' emerges" (1957: 3). Governmental agencies need leaders with a new logic—they need a whole different understanding of organizational change. Reorganizations are not sufficient any more.

Creative Leadership. In Henry Mintzberg's article entitled "Planning on the Left Side and Managing on the Right" (*Harvard Business Review*, 1976, July/August: 49-58), he made the point that "there may be a fundamental difference between formal planning and informal managing, a difference akin to that between the two hemispheres of the brain." What Mintzberg hypothesized in 1976 has since been documented by considerable research in the intervening years. What we have learned is that people tend to think with the dominant por-tion of their brain because they access it more easily. Often the less accessible portion of the brain does not come into play, and if it does it may be difficult to respond to it. To use Mintzberg's analogy, most of the leadership in OESE were left-brain dominant. They were experts at analysis and planning, and in the details of their programs. But they were less likely to lead creatively and take risks.

In 1930, Harold Laski wrote about the "trained incapacity" of the expert in an effort to explain why experts can sometimes be so narrow-minded.

Here, perhaps we have a further insight: the experts know all of the details and they avoid the clearly delineated pitfalls while missing the more fundamental, less tangible, fallacies about which they are so engrossed. One of the things that Peter Drucker tells us is that "efficiency is doing the thing right, but effectiveness is doing the right thing." Someone has defined an expert as "someone who knows more and more about less and less until finally he knows everything about nothing." In OESE, there were leaders who mastered the details of their programs, but knew little about the context in which they existed.

In his article, *"Managers and Leaders: Are They Different?"* (1977), Abraham Zaleznik concluded unequivocally that managers and leaders are psychologically different types and that the conditions that foster their development are antithetical. More recently, in an article entitled *"Letting Leaders Replace Corporate Managers"* (1992), Zaleznik called for organizations to seek out leaders instead of perpetuating the practice of promoting managers. He asserted that managers tend to have a dedication to form—structures, processes, power, and indirect communication—at the expense of substance—ideas, people, emotions, and straight talk.

Whether the psychological differences observed by Zaleznik, the research on the physiology of the brain, or the observations of Henry Laski about the trained incapacity of the experts, provide the reasons for the lack of creativity in the leadership in OESE, there is substantial evidence that the current mind set does not generate the creativity or the institutional logic that is needed. What Chuck did not perceive was the institutional logic of his conception— it simply could not be implemented. It may sound inconsistent to say that they need more creative thinkers like Chuck Hansen, despite the fact that his conception of a different OESE was flawed. Chuck was one of the few persons thinking "outside the box" and this type of thinking should be encouraged. If OESE is to find a viable mission and role for the twenty-first century, it must have leadership that can generate a viable vision. Of course, the same is true for the entire Department of Education. It must find a mission and vision that will accommodate the political gyrations of the Congress and constantly changing administrations, and communicate realistic expectations of its interventions in the nation's schooling.

Strategic thinking, as distinct from strategic planning, is often intuitive. It is more simultaneous, holistic, and relational than it is linear, sequential, and orderly. In particular, strategies that are novel and compelling are usually the products of single creative brains, those capable of synthesizing a vision. Many of the great strategies are simply great visions, "big pictures." They do not come out of three-ring binders jammed full of data or financial reports. Formal planning is rarely the father of strategic thinking, but strategic thinking is essential to strategic planning. Strategic thinking comes first. Then, creativity can be exercised by strategic and tactical planning.

But even strategic thinking must have internal viability. The utopian vision of an OESE that could provide cross-program technical assistance on the systemic reform of the public schools was not viable. One can not give OESE a new distinctive character without the distinctive competence to make it so. Without such competence, there was no way that OESE could have uniquely adapted to this distinctive role so as to distinguish itself as a vital and essential entity, thereby assuring its survival as a federal agency.

In addition, creative leadership must be able to embody the definition of mission and role within the institution if it is to create a new distinctive character for itself. The purpose of the changed character must be embedded deep into the social structure of the organization. The people within the organization must be transformed, from whatever they have become through the historical evolution of the organization, into a committed body of people, expressing their new purpose in their daily experiences as living people. In other words, there should be no sharp division between the mission that the leadership has defined for them and what people do every day at work.

This did not happen in OESE. The union of mission and behavior never materialized. There was instability and confusion in the roles, responsibilities and functions of the leadership. Internal interest groups became divergent internal sources of energy, fracturing the purpose of the restructuring. There was recalcitrance in the participation of both leadership and staff. Essential beliefs in the mission were grossly lacking, and the leadership was not able to neutralize or disable contending beliefs. There was never an embodiment of purpose by the staff of

OESE. Yet, this is one of the essentials of creative leadership in organizational change.

Responsible leadership. Another necessary element of change called for in the leadership of federal agencies is the need for responsible leadership. As Philip Selznick writes: "From a policy standpoint . . . most of the characteristics of the responsible leader can be summarized under two headings: the avoidance of opportunism and the avoidance of utopianism" (1957:143). In explanation he adds:

> Responsible leadership steers a course between utopianism and opportunism. Its responsibility consists in accepting the obligation of giving direction instead of merely ministering to organizational equilibrium; in adapting aspiration to the character of the organization, bearing in mind that what the organization has been will affect what it can be and do; and in transcending bare organizational survival by seeing that specialized decisions do not weaken or confuse the distinctive identity of the enterprise (*ibid*: 149).

The responsibility of OESE, as well as the whole Department, was really tested during the decade of the mid-1990s. Push came to shove in the Department when Deputy Secretary Kunin, under pressure from the President's Management Council, insisted that there would be no dawdling when it came to change. It was not a matter of accepting the obligation of giving direction, it was a matter of survival. A case could be made that because OESE had to move fast, it lost its credibility because of opportunism and utopianism.

It must have been tempting to announce a utopian goal, and let the Congress know that a fundamental rethinking and radical departure had been established for the delivery of OESE services. But it was wishful thinking. OESE did not have the competence in leadership or staff, and the organizational change was much too radical to accomplish in a short period of time. In the words of Selznick, the leadership could not "adapt their aspiration to the character of the organization." They did not bear in mind "that what the organization has been will affect what it can be and do." In attempting to "transcend organizational survival," their decisions produced an attenuated and confused character for OESE.

In the process the leadership also fell back upon the easy opportunism of doing what they had always done when organizational change was necessary—reorganize. So in the name of "restructuring," they reorganized. Because they were not *institutional* leaders, they did not realize that the change to which they aspired required more than reorganization. Even when the option was given to obtain external help, they would not acknowledge that they needed it. Consequently, the mistakes of both utopianism and opportunism compounded the failure.

Another indication of responsible leadership is the level of trust in an organization, and the level of trust in OESE was well below an acceptable threshold. In many ways, the level of trust begins and ends with the actions of leaders. State Bennis and Nanus, trust is "the emotional glue that binds followers and leaders together. The accumulation of trust is a measure of the legitimacy of leadership. It cannot be mandated or purchased; it must be earned. Trust is the basic ingredient of all organizations, the lubrication that maintains the organization" (1985:153).

Developing a high level of trust is difficult in a federal agency when the average political appointee stays on the job for only slightly longer than two years. The low level of trust in OESE was not a recent development. Each change in leadership brought with it a different agenda for change, expecting the staff to become enthusiastic about it. After a short period of time each new leader moves on to "challenging new opportunities." But during their brief tenure, many persistent, pervasive problems that undermine change do not get attention. It is no wonder that staff became disillusioned and their attitudes jaded. It was largely an accumulation of incredibility about leadership in general that faced Tom Payzant when he became OESE's Assistant Secretary. Unfortunately, he did not address any of the residual, pervasive problems of distrust, e.g., racial discontent, before he attempted to restructure OESE. Neither was he able to establish his own credibility with many of OESE's staff. Consequently, the collaborative capital of trust upon which Tom could draw to change OESE was minimal.

Trust requires much more than just a senior person acting in a credible way. Trust begins with the senior leader, but it is always linked to the behavior of key leadership teams as well. Throughout the attempted restructuring, the Senior Leadership Team, and especially the program directors, were not accorded high levels of trust. Their *modus operandi* as managers was that of traditional managers, not one of shared decision making and empowerment. Consequently, OESE was not a workplace where staff felt that success depended upon shared collaboration to meet a common goal. It was more often seen as a place where people reported for work, did their job, went home to their family, and drew regular paychecks to pay the bills and enjoy life off the job.

The leadership of an organization is also responsible for building trust-sustaining mechanisms. Paradoxically, states Robert Shaw, this "results from doing many fundamental things right rather than from direct attempts to raise the level of trust within an organization . . . Those seeking to increase the level of trust are better served by going about it indirectly" (1997: 118). Working for success in an organizational goal by cultivating trust to accomplish it will generally build more trust than attempting to go about building it directly.

When people in leadership positions are responsible, they build trust. And they do so it by modeling trustworthy behavior, by building trustworthy leadership teams, and by developing trust-sustaining organizational practices. Trust is essential if organizations are to work well, and it is the responsibility of the leadership to build and sustain it.

Above all, responsible leaders are ethical about organizational change. They must clearly care about the outcome of an organization, especially when it renders a public service. And they must care about what happens to the people when an organization undergoes change. It is clear that organizational change will make people anxious and stressful. And not everyone can be a winner when organizations change—it may be critical that an organization downsize when those cutbacks are critical to survival. Because responsible leaders care about the outcomes of the organization and the welfare of its human resources, they know they must move with knowledge and understanding to effect change in a responsible way. Responsible leaders have an organizational change ethic.

OESE did not have a distinctive character for serving the nation's schools. It did not know what it could be and what it could do, because it did not know what it was. It did not identify its competence, so it did not know how it could perform for the public. Consequently, the public is not well served. This is not the product of responsible leadership.

261

I believe that anyone who's been pulled through the knothole of organizational change to emerge into a dysfunctional work environment, because their leaders were not capable of transforming an organization, has good reasons to complain. Anyone who has worked in a dysfunctional organization, illogically designed for the work it does, has a right to gripe. Anyone who works with competence and dedication at his job, while marginal employees fiddle away their time and receive rewards for outstanding service, has good reason to be disillusioned. Ending up with these sorts of problems is not the work of responsible leadership.

With today's pace and high degree of expectations, organizational change is inevitable in both the private and the public sectors. Leaders in the upper echelon of an organization are commonly expected to lead their organizations through change. It is understandable that many leaders do not have the expertise to perform this type of leadership. When this is the case, as it was in OESE, it is imperative that professional expertise be sought.

I believe it is wrong for leaders to make fundamental, radical changes without the expertise to do so, or the professional assistance to guide them. It is wrong for leaders to manipulate an organization's structure and its work processes, thereby throwing a functioning organization out of alignment, because they know nothing about organizational design. It is wrong to jeopardize vital public services simply because leaders do not know what they are doing. It is wrong to devastate and debilitate the human resources of an organization because a leader is working beyond his competence. Too much is at stake.

Max DePree, in his profound book entitled *"Leadership Jazz,"* has this to say about the ethics of leadership:

> One of the most sacred relationships among teams of people is that between leaders and followers. This relationship, so central and crucial, depends to an extraordinary degree on the clearly expressed and consistently demonstrated values of the leaders as seen through the special lens of followers. This is why leadership and ethics are inextricably woven together (1992:126).

The Politics of Federal Leadership

From the experience of this account of reinvention, I have identified ten major problems with which the leadership of the Department of Education could not deal. I have also identified the need for a different type of leadership. To meet the challenges of organizational change, agency executives must move beyond administrative management into institutional leadership. This type of leadership requires a new logic, a different perspective and different skills.

We also saw how politicians in the executive and legislative branches of the federal government used political initiatives to change the federal establishment. This is not to say that the political approach can not be successful. For example, the Congress can enact legislation such as GPRA to mandate strategic planning, start or eliminate programs, provide or eliminate funding, and establish or close down whole agencies. The President, with cooperation from agency executives, can implement policies that alter the mission and vision of an agency, restructure or downsize an agency, and further regulate or deregulate personnel and programs. These and many other types of actions have an impact upon federal agencies. But they are not sufficient to attain the outcomes currently desired by either the politicians or the public. Unfortunately, our political leaders cannot legislate or order much of what they want changed.

Furthermore, both the executive and legislative branches, both Democrats and Republicans, have created a leadership debacle that inhibits institutional change. Our executive and legislative branches have created a glut of upper level leadership that has been a barrier, not an instrument, of change. Paul C. Light, in his book *Thickening Government: Federal Hierarchy and the Diffusion of Accountability,* reports:

> The total number of senior executives and presidential appointees grew from 451 in 1960 to 2,393 in 1992, a 430 percent increase . . . However, it is not just the sheer number of leaders that matters. More important may be how those leaders sort into layer upon layer of management. The top of the federal government contains senior management layers that simply did not exist thirty years ago. In 1960, there were seventeen layers of management at the very top of the government, of which eight existed in at least half or

more of the departments. By 1992, there were thirty-two layers, of which seventeen existed in at least half of the departments (1991: 7).

Management guru Tom Peters has written: "We are being strangled by bloated staff, made up of carping experts and filling too many layers on the organizational chart. Today's structures were designed for controlling turn-of-the-century mass production operations under stable conditions with primitive technologies. They have become perverse, action-destroying devices, completely at odds with current competitive needs" (1991: 426). Peters asserts that five layers, the same number that the Roman Catholic Church uses to manage 800 million members, should be maximum for very complex organizations. All others can do with no more than three layers (*ibid*: 430).

Paul Light cites a number of reasons for the thickening of upper management; not the least of these was the interest presidents have in increasing their influence over the executive branch and, consequently, over the implementation of public policy. More recent presidents have increasingly justified thickening because they want tighter control of bureaucrats they do not trust. Ironically, Paul Light argues that controlling the bureaucrats has become increasingly less likely as upper management has become more bloated. States Light, "The true cost of thickening appears to be in the diffusion of accountability that comes in nearly infinite numbers of decision points throughout government. Almost by definition, thickening increases the number of actors in any decision, thereby raising the costs of both creating and implementing presidential policy" (1995: 64). Hence the subtitle of his book, *Federal Hierarchy and the Diffusion of Accountability.*

Another obstacle to finding and/or developing institutional leadership is what political scientist G. Calvin Mackenzie calls "epidemic" turnover rates. Notes Mackenzie:

> The average appointee now stays on the job for only slightly longer than 2 years; almost a third have a tenure shorter than 18 months. Given the political and substantive complexity of the jobs they hold, this high turnover among presidential appointees directly and deeply affects the quality of the leadership and management they provide to the

presidents they serve. Teams of administrators are constantly changing and readjusting to new members. Persistence in pursuit of policy objectives is increasingly rare as administrative agendas and priorities change almost constantly (1994:5).

The repeated decapitation of agencies leaves career employees without direction and without a leadership they know and trust. The sheer number of appointees, coupled with the high number of vacancies that accompany high leadership mobility, makes it almost impossible to build the connections central to positive working relationships between appointees and careerists. The more layers, the more time it takes to forge positive relationships.

In addition, there is a lack of continuity in leadership styles and approaches to organizational change. This leads the career work force to enormous uncertainty. The staff feel yanked around from one hyped-up administrative fad to the next. A cultural malaise permeates agencies, and many staff settle in to ride out one innovation after another. On the other hand, there are always a significant number of staff who have given the new appointees the benefit of the doubt, have become enthusiastic, and feel they could have done much more. States Light: "The thickening leads to a curious problem: appointees eventually come to see their civil servants as competent and responsive, but the realization may come too late to be of much value in promoting cooperation" (1995: 69).

The problem of the bloated top level leadership in federal agencies has not gone unnoticed. The Volker commission, the National Commission on the Public Service (1989), recommended that Congress should reduce the number of political appointments in the federal bureaucracy by one-third. But the Clinton administration opposed cutting when Congress attempted to do it. This administration left upper-level management basically as it was and targeted middle level managers and supervisors. The attitude was that the basic problem in government is at the middle or bottom, not the top. By not including even one political appointee in their proposed cut of 272,900 employees, this administration accepted the "orthodoxy" of thickening that sees more leaders as equal to stronger leadership.

Two of the major problems of moving from administrative management toward institutional leadership in federal agencies is the existence of the bloated upper level leadership and their short terms in government service. The creation of this upper-level administrative monstrosity has been a bipartisan political phenomenon. It will take bipartisan cooperation to correct it. The logic of political distrust of career employees and the need for control is the antithesis of the logic of trust and institutional leadership.

In their book, *Civil Service Reform: Building a Government that Works,* Kettl, Ingram, Sanders, and Horner leave us with some optimism about the future. They state:

> There can be little doubt that the nation is in the midst of another period of historic change for the federal bureaucracy. Nor can there be any doubt that this change will reshape the people who work in it. What values will undergird a reshaped civil service? What attitudes will the public and the times demand be elicited by its restructuring? To answer these questions, one must look at the character, scope, and magnitude of the change occurring in the federal political environment. It is also necessary to recognize the seriousness and intensity of the American discussion about government's shape and purposes that is being conducted in every civic venue. Large, not small, changes are clearly imminent. Moreover, for the civil service, the most salient issue is not its mere organization but its very legitimacy (1995: 88-89).

For the sake of America's citizens and all federal civil servants, I hope that this optimism is justified. In its ability to respond to the needs of the public it serves, the private sector is way ahead of the federal establishment. So are many leaders of the nation's schools. I believe it is time for the Department of Education to "get with it." But, how many more OESEs are there? The problems of this reinvention effort are not unique to the Department of Education. I know that administrative managers greatly outnumber institutional leaders in the federal establishment. We all know that the partisan politics of the past has controlled the selection of political appointees who manage and control our federal agencies. Is our past a prologue to the future? If "large, not small, changes are clearly imminent," where will the requisite institutional leadership come from? The challenge confronting the governance of our nation as we enter the twenty-first-century is monumental.

Appendix

The Restructuring Packet

(Note: The author made only minor editing changes in these selected components of The Restructuring Packet. It is printed here as distributed with all the blemishes and warts of a committee-drafted document.)

<u>OUR MISSION</u>

The mission of the Office of Elementary and Secondary Education (OESE) is to promote academic excellence, enhance educational opportunities and equity for all of America's children, youth, and families and to improve the quality of teaching and learning by providing leadership, technical assistance and financial support.

Recognizing the changing needs of children and families, OESE has established the following goals and objectives on which it will concentrate its resources and efforts:

<u>GOAL I</u>

Encourage and foster systemic educational reform to improve teaching and learning for all children.

OBJECTIVES

- Improve OESE services in support of systemic reform.

- Tailor support to States and local school districts consistent with their stages of reform.

- Develop policies, practices and procedures that facilitate systemic reform.

<u>GOAL II</u>

Assist States, communities and schools in developing plans and strategies to meet the National Education Goals.

OBJECTIVES

- Align OESE program and budget priorities with the Goals.

- Disseminate information to help States and local school districts attain the national Education Goals.

270

<u>GOAL III</u>

Provide leadership for the implementation of GOALS 2000 and the reauthorization of the ESEA.

OBJECTIVES

- Provide support for the enactment of the administration's GOALS 2000 and the reauthorization of ESEA.

- Through the ESEA reauthorization develop a plan for a unified approach to assisting States and local school districts to achieve the National Education Goals.

- Develop implementation plans for GOALS 2000 and the ESEA reauthorization.

<u>GOAL IV</u>

Improve the quality of OESE administration and human resource management.

OBJECTIVES

- Develop an OESE organization strategy for implementing GOALS 2000 and the new ESEA.

- Develop assessment strategies that demonstrate OESE accountability.

- Provide professional development for preparing OESE staff and managers to implement and model desired practices of systemic reform.

<u>OESE RESTRUCTURING PLAN</u>

The OESE senior leadership team, comprised of the program directors and the administrative staff of the front office, has designed a new structure for the Office of Elementary and Secondary Education (OESE). This new design is in response to the reauthorization of ESEA; the Department's strategic plan; the NPR mandate to streamline our processes and flatten the organization by achieving a supervisory ratio of 15 to 1; and suggestions from the OESE staff through the brown bag lunches, the employee survey, experiences with teams, and the OESE strategic planning process. In discussions, which began in early June, we explored issues and options on how best to achieve organizational restructuring to better serve the field while minimizing disruption. Better service to the field requires two key changes — a change in our structure (restructuring) and a change in our work processes (reengineering). In this memo are the five components of our plan: (1) the OESE vision statement, (2)the guiding principles and parameters which shaped our discussions, (3) the new structure, (4) ideas to move the process of delayering forward, and (5) a plan for employee involvement.

Vision Statement

The mission of the Office of Elementary and Secondary Education (OESE is to advance systemic education reform by providing educational program direction, technical assistance, and financial support to promote excellence, improve teaching and learning, and enhance educational opportunity and equity for America's children, youth, and families.

The **goal of restructuring** is to drive systemic reform by providing improved customer service to states and school districts to assist them in improving teaching and learning.

Students are our ultimate customers, however, we do not deliver direct services to them. Out work is accomplished through intermediaries such as SEA's, LEA's and schools.

GUIDING PRINCIPLES

1. Make systemic reform, GOALS 2000 and the ESEA reauthorization the cornerstones for the OESE restructuring.

2. Involve employees because they are an essential and critical component for successfully designing and implementing a restructured organization.

3. Promote and model systemic reform through the delivery of integrated services.

4. Use restructuring as a comprehensive strategy for holistic problem-solving and achieving organizational change.

5. Sustain and institutionalize systemic reform.

6. Improve customer service in order to support and enhance teaching and learning.

7. Continue our service to populations who require special attention based on our philosophical commitment, not simply statutory requirements.

In addition to the guiding principles, we have agreed on eight parameters for reinvention. These provide a basis for transforming our staff and culture toward the three "C's" of cooperation, collaboration and customer service. They include:

- Recruiting up to 15 outstanding scholars or Presidential Management Interns (PMIs).

- Reduce the number of GS-13/15s supervisory and management positions.

272

- Achieve an aggregate supervisory ratio of 15:1.

- Develop an orientation and rotational assignment system for training new employees.

- Developing strategies (such as details, lateral transfers, short term team and rotational assignments) for enriching and enhancing job satisfaction for career employees of all levels for whom promotional opportunities are limited.

- Meet program statutory requirements (e.g., OIE and OME).

- Achieve a more diverse staff particularly among senior level managers and supervisors.

- Implement changes without adversely impacting grades of OESE employees.

THE STRUCTURE

In our approach to restructuring OESE, our new organization should retain elements of the present structure while adopting several substantive modifications. We must emphasize changes in roles/relationships and behaviors rather than undertaking a fundamental reorganization. The modifications acknowledge that our basic work responsibilities require a continuation of a programmatic base that uses generic supervisors who coordinate program and team operations. We will reconfigure our program offices which will have three components: (1) a program base, (2) regions comprised of cross program teams, and (3) cross cutting teams to look at functional issues that arise.

OESE employees will be involved in the development of implementation plans and other activities related to restructuring. These changes will be implemented as quickly as possible.

Although there are many details to be worked out our configuration assumes at least three important kinds of expertise: (1) program expertise, (2) expertise about the regions being served, and (3) managerial expertise. The structure is described below:

1. **Program base:** The OESE components will retain the present program structure and responsibility, e.g., Migrant Education, Indian Education, Impact Aid, School Improvement, Compensatory Education . . . and the newly formed Safe and Drug-free Schools. Each program office will retain individuals who will be responsible for program policy and administration as well as professional development for the teams.

2. **Cross program teams:** Service to the field will be delivered through regional teams which will be assigned to an area office. The teams composed of staff from vrious

273

OESE programs will provide program services to the states and school districts in specific geographical regions . . . .

3. **Cross cutting teams:** At times there will be a need to organize teams around functional areas or issues, e.g., professional development, healthy children, technology, integrated services, and joint monitoring. . . .

Supervising/Delayering

The NPR mandates that each agency reduce the number of supervisors. Individuals on the cross program teams will continue to be "formally" supervised by a supervisor in the program office. This configuration will not require the present number of supervisors. Secretary Riley and Deputy Secretary Kunin have given their assurance that we will work with individuals who no longer have supervisory responsibilities to change their duties and ensure that grades are not reduced. . . .

FOLLOW-UP

OESE ALL HANDS MEETING

Our work re: substantive change in OESE has two arms: (1) a change in structure (restructuring) and (2), a change in behavior (reengineering). There are several important steps to take:

1. Follow up the meeting with a reminder about feedback. . . . Distribute the detailed packet on restructuring plans immediately. . . .

2. Senior staff would continue to work on the issues of delayering and supervision. . . .

3. Develop a large restructuring team. The large group would meet together once to hear the overall charge and then break into several smaller restructuring teams. There are several areas to be assigned to teams:

   - **The area offices (policy/administration and regional teams):** This team would make recommendations about regions (number of regions in each area office, the geographical areas served by a region, number and kind of program staff for the regions, selection criteria and process for assignment to the region, duties of team members, relationship to the area office program/administrative staff) and policy/administrative staff (duties of members, criteria and process for assignment to an area, relationship with the regions). This group would develop generic position descriptions where needed.

- **Internal Communication:** This team would develop a plan for two-way communication (internal and external) about OESE restructuring and reengineering as well as develop an internal and external system for communicating and sharing program information and data in the regions. This plan should consider the integration and location of data sources, training implications, and transitional steps necessary for implementation. This could also develop the recommendation that "brown bags" be held with managers/supervisors.

- **Professional Development:** This team would develop a professional development strategy to support restructuring and reengineering. The plan should look at the needs of 4 layers in the organization: staff, team leaders, group leaders/coaches, and senior leadership. The team could include such things as understanding the change process, chaos management, team leadership facilitation skills, team building and working in teams, conflict resolution, program/customer service, and methods of joint monitoring and evaluation.

- **Space:** This team which has already been constituted could add to its charge a transition plan for the co-location of staff in the restructuring of OESE. . . .

- **Reengineering:** This team will design a strategy to be used for changing the way we do our work. It should spell-out the steps to be taken by a program office or a cross cutting team to change core processes.

- **Dissemination (external communication):** This team will develop a plan to disseminate information about reauthorization and the restructuring OESE for persons not a part of OESE.

The workload of these groups will vary. Due dates for presenting the reports to the senior staff will vary. Senior leaders team should provide one week after the presentation for employees to comment on the recommendations. Teams should revise their reports and recommendations based on the feedback and present them to the senior leadership team for a decision.

Janice Jackson will chair a restructuring council to ensure coordination among the teams. The council will be comprised of a representative of each of the restructuring teams and other individuals who can provide needed expertise. The council members will serve in an advisory role.

Figure A-1

CURRENT ORGANIZATIONAL PROTOTYPE

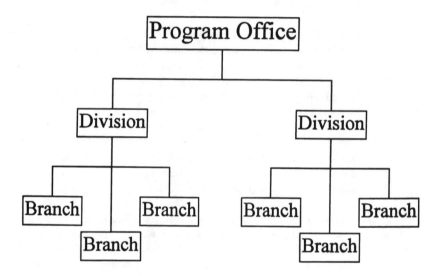

Figure A-2

NEW ORGANIZATIONAL PROTOTYPE

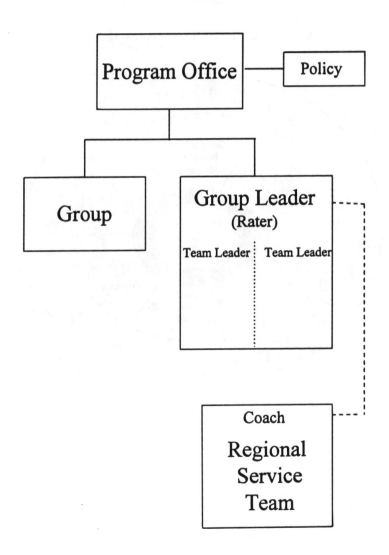

Figure A-3

OESE'S RESTRUCTURING MODEL

References

Baldwin, Timothy T. and Kevin K. Ford. 1988. Transfer of training: A review and directions for future research. *Personal Psychology*. 41.

Bennis, Warren and Burt Nanus. 1985. *Leaders: The Strategies for Taking Charge*. NewYork: Harper-Collins.

Blanchette, Cornelia M. 1998. *Information Needs are at the Core of Management Challenges Facing the Department*. House Subcommittee on Labor, Health and Human Services, Education and Related Agencies, Committee on Appropriations. Washington, D.C.: GAO.

Broad, Mary L. and John K. Newstrom. 1992. *Transfer of Training*. Reading, MA: Addison-Wesley.

Brown, Michael and Stephen Erie. 1981. Blacks and the legacy of the great society. *Public Policy*. 29 (summer).

Causey, Mike. Report on diversity. *Washington Post*. 15 June 1997: B2.

Champy, James. 1995. *Reengineering Management: The Mandate for New Leadership*. NewYork: Harper Business.

Coopers & Lybrand Consulting. 1996. *OESE Organizational Assessment: Draft Report*. Arlington, VA: Author. (August).

DePree, Max. 1989. *Leadership is an Art*. New York: Bantam Doubleday, Dell Publishing Group.

_____. 1992. *Leadership Jazz*. New York: Bantam Doubleday, Dell Publishing Group.

DiIulio, Jr., John J. ed. 1994. *Deregulating the Public Service: Can Government Be Improved?* Washington, D.C.: The Brookings Institution.

DiIulio, Jr., John J., Gerald Garvey, and Donald F. Kettl. 1993. *Improving Government Performance: An Owner's Manual.* Washington, D.C.: The Brookings Institution.

Dixon, George. 1988. *What Works at Work: Lessons from the Masters.* Minneapolis, MN: Lakewood.

Dubois, David D. 1993. *Competency-Based Performance Improvement: A Strategy for Organizational Change.* Amhurst, MA: HRD Press.

Fordham, Signithia. 1988. Racelessness as a factor in black students' school success. *Harvard Education Review.* (February).

Gilbert, Thomas F. 1996. *Human Competence: Engineering Worthy Performance.* Amhurst, MA: HRD Press, (Tribute edition).

Hall, G., J. Rosenthal, and J. Wade. 1993. How to make reengineering really work. *Harvard Business Review.* (November/December)

Hammer, Michael and James Champy. 1993. *Reengineering the Corporation: A Manifesto for Business Revolution.* New York: Harper Business.

Hammer, Michael and Steven A. Stanton. 1995. *The Reengineering Revolution: A Handbook.* New York: Harper Business.

Johnson, Haynes. 1994. *Divided We Fall: Gambling with History in the Nineties.* New York: W. W. Norton.

Herrmann, Ned. 1996. *The Whole Brain Business Book: Unlocking the Power of Whole Brain Thinking in Organizations and Individuals.* New York: McGraw-Hill.

Kast, Fremont E. and James E. Rosenweig. 1970. *Organization and Management: A Systems Approach.* New York: McGraw-Hill.

Kettl, Donald F. 1998. *Reinventing Government: A Fifth-Year Report Card.* Washington, D.C.: The Brookings Institution.

_____. 1994. *Reinventing Government? Appraising The National Performance Review*. Washington, D.C.: The Brookings Institution.

Kettl, Donald F. and John J. DiIulio, Jr. 1995. *Cutting Government: A Report of the Brookings Institution's Center for Public Management*. Washington, D.C.: The Brookings Institution.

Kettl, Donald F., et al. 1996. *Civil Service Reform: Building a Government that Works*. Washington, D.C.: The Brookings Institution.

Kettl, Donald F. and John J. DiIulio, Jr. eds. 1995. *Inside the Reinvention Machine: Appraising Governmental Reform*. Washington, D.C.: The Brookings Institution.

Kim, W. Chan and Renee Mauborgne. 1997. Fair process: Managing in the knowledge economy. *Harvard Business Review*. (July-August).

Kinni, Theodore B. 1994. A reengineering primer. *Quality Digest*. (January).

Kotter, John P. 1995. Leading change: Why transformation efforts fail. *Harvard Business Review*. (March-April).

_____. 1996. *Leading Change*. Boston, MA: Harvard Business.

Kunin, Madeleine M. 1996. *Management Improvements at the Department of Education*. House Subcommittee on Labor-HHS-Education Appropriations. (16 May).

Laski, H. J. 1930. The limitations of the expert. *Harper's Magazine*. (December).

Light, Paul C. 1995. *Thickening Government: Federal Hierarchy and the Diffusion of Accountability*. Washington, D.C.: The Brookings Institution.

Mackenzie, G. Calvin. 1994. *The Presidential Appointment Process: Historical Development, Contemporary Operations, Current Issues*.

Background paper for the Twentieth Century Fund Panel on Presidential Appointments. (1 March).

Metropolitan Washington Council of Governments. 1992. *Demographic Data about People, Households and Families by Jurisdiction in the Washington Metropolitan Area*, No. 92457. Washington, D.C.: Author.

Micklethwait, John and Adrian Wooldridge. 1996. *The Witch Doctors: Making Sense of the Management Gurus*. New York: Random House.

Mintzberg, Henry. 1976. Planning on the left side and managing on the right. *Harvard Business Review*. (July-August).

Mintzberg, Henry. 1994. The fall and rise of strategic planning. *Harvard Business Review*. (January-February).

_____. 1994. *The Rise and Fall of Strategic Planning: Reconceiving Roles for Planning, Plans, Planners*. New York: The Free Press.

Morin, Richard and Dan Balz. Reality check: The politics of mistrust. *The Washington Post*. 28 January 1996.

National Commission on Public Service. 1989. *Leadership for America: Rebuilding the* Public Service—The Report of the National Commission on Public Service and the *Task Force Reports of the National Commission on the Public Service*. Washington, D.C.: GPO.

National Performance Review. 1993. *Creating a Government that Works Better and Costs Less: Department of Education*. Washington, D.C.: GPO.

_____. 1993. *Creating a Government that Works Better and Costs Less: A Report of the National Performance Review*. Washington, D.C.: GPO.
Nonaka, Ikujiro and Hirotaka Takeuchi. 1995. *The Knowledge Creating Company: How Japanese Companies Create the Dynamics of Innovation*. New York: Oxford University Press.

Organization Planning & Design. 1994. *Organizational Systems Design Guidebook*. San Jose, CA: Author.

_____. 1994. *Organizational Systems Design Workbook*. San Jose, CA: Author.

Osborne, David and Ted Gaebler. 1992. *Reinventing Government: How the Entrepreneurial Spirit is Transforming the Public Sector*. Reading, MA: Addison-Wesley.

O'Shea, James and Charles Madigan. 1997. *Dangerous Company: The Consulting Powerhouses and the Businesses They Save and Ruin*. New York: Times Books.

Peters, Tom. 1991. *Thriving on Chaos: Handbook for a Management Revolution*. New York: Harper (Perennial edition).

_____. 1994. Attention strategy planners. *Monday*. (4 April): 3D.

Prahalad, C. K. and Gary Hamel. 1990. The core competence of the corporation. *Harvard Business Review*. (May-June).

Reinhart, Carlene. 1997. No more sheep dipping. *Training and Development*. (March).

Ravitch, Diane.1995. Adventures in wonderland. *The American Scholar*. (Autumn).

Rifkin, Jeremy. 1995. *The End of Work: The Decline of the Global Labor Force and the Dawn of the Post-Market Era*. New York: G. P. Putnam's Sons.

Robinson, Dana Gaines and James C. Robinson. 1995. *Performance Consulting: Moving Beyond Training*. San Francisco: Berrett-Koehler.

Rummler, Geary, A. 1989. Performance is the purpose. *Training*. Minneapolis, MN: Lakewood.

Rummler, Geary A. and Alan P. Brache. 1990. *Improving Performance: How to Manage the White Space on the Organization Chart*. San Francisco: Jossey-Bass.

Selznick, Philip. 1957. *Leadership in Administration.* White Plains, NY: Row, Peterson.

Senge, Peter. 1990. *The Fifth Discipline: The Art and Practice of the Learning Organization.* New York: Doubleday.

Senge, Peter, et al. 1994. *The Fifth Discipline Fieldbook: Strategies and Tools for Building a Learning Organization.* New York: Doubleday.

Shaw, Robert Bruce. 1997. *Trust in the Balance: Building Successful Organizations on Results, Integrity, and Concern.* San Francisco: Jossey-Bass.

Stewart, Thomas A. 1993. Reengineering: The hot new management tool. *Fortune.* (August).

Synectics for Management Decisions and Price Waterhouse. 1994. *1993 Employee* Survey of The United States Department of Education: Report on the Office of *Elementary & Secondary Education.* Authors. (March).

Tichy, Noel M. and Eli Cohen. 1997. *The Leadership Engine: How Winning Companies Build Leaders at Every Level.* New York: Harper Business.

United States Department of Education. 1996. *Affirmative Employment Program for* Minorities and Women: FY 1995 Report of Accomplishments and FY 1996 Plan Update.

United States General Accounting Office. 1998. *Education's FY 1999 Performance Plan,* B-279999. Washington, D.C.: Author.

_____. 1998. Managing for Results: *Agencies' Annual Performance Plans Can Help Address Strategic Planning Challenges,* B-278878. Washington, D.C.: Author.

_____. 1997. The Results Act: *Observations on the Department of Education's June 1997 Draft Strategic Plan.* Washington, D.C.: Author.

_____. 1993. Department of Education *General Management Review Report,* B-241690. Washington, D.C.: Author.

_____. 1995. Federal Reorganization: *Congressional Proposal to Merge Education, Labor and EEOC.* Washington, D.C.: Author.

United States Office of Personnel Management. 1982. *Education Program Specialist Classification Standard.* Washington, D.C.: Author

_____1996. *Annual Report to Congress: Federal Equal Opportunity Recruitment Program—October 1, 1995 — September 30.* Washington, D.C.: Author.

Washington Post, Kaiser Family Foundation, and Harvard University. 1996. *Why Don't Americans Trust the Government?* Menlo Park, CA: The Henry J. Kaiser Foundation.

Willhelm, Sidney M. and Reva H. Kobre. 1970. *Who Needs the Negro?* Cambridge, MA: Shenkman.

Zaleznik, Abraham. 1977. Managers and leaders: Are they different? *Harvard Business Review* (May-June).

_____ 1992. Letting leaders replace the corporate managers. *Washington Post.* 27 September: 1-5.